21st
Century
Logistics:

MAKING
SUPPLY CHAIN
INTEGRATION
A REALITY

ISBN 0-9658653-2-0

Council of Logistics Management
2805 Butterfield Road
Suite 200
Oak Brook, IL 60523-1170
www.clm1.org

Printed in the United States of America.

 **Printed on Recycled Paper**

21st Century Logistics:

MAKING SUPPLY CHAIN INTEGRATION A REALITY

DONALD J. BOWERSOX
The John H. McConnell University Professor of
Business Administration

DAVID J. CLOSS
Professor of Marketing and Logistics

THEODORE P. STANK
Assistant Professor of Logistics and Supply Chain
Management

MICHIGAN STATE
UNIVERSITY

COUNCIL OF LOGISTICS MANAGEMENT

TABLE OF CONTENTS

This book is dedicated to:

Mr. John H. McConnell
Chairman (Retired)
Worthington Industries

John's quiet confidence and generous support of meaningful academic research through establishing The John H. McConnell University Professor of Business Administration at Michigan State University remain an inspiration.

And To

The dedicated managers who committed valuable time to contribute to the research stream either as survey participants, reviewers or contributors. This book is for those managers who consistently seek a better understanding of the value of superior logistics performance.

21ST CENTURY LOGISTICS: MAKING SUPPLY CHAIN INTEGRATION A REALITY

*21*st *Century Logistics: Making Supply Chain Integration A Reality* is presented for managers who have embarked along the road to logistical and supply chain excellence but have yet to realize its full benefits. *21*st *Century Logistics* presents a framework to help recognize and overcome common obstacles that undermine both internal and external integration of value-added logistical operations. Such integration is essential for providing maximum value to end-customers. The book offers a narrative interpretation of empirical research that identifies critical areas of integration needed to boost supply chain effectiveness. A research-based methodology and diagnostic assessment software are presented. These aids provide a framework for facilitating improved integrative management among internal business unit and corporate operations, external material and service suppliers, and customers.

*21*st *Century Logistics* is the fourth in a series of research books written by faculty and doctoral students at Michigan State University spanning well over ten years. The first, *Leading Edge Logistics: Competitive Positioning for the 1990's*, identified and documented best practices of logistics management in North America. The next book, *Logistical Excellence: It's Not Business as Usual*, offered in narrative form a managerial interpretation of the research findings presented in *Leading Edge Logistics*. It integrated the generalized capabilities of leading edge performers into a relational model to help guide managers in the process of logistical renewal. Together these initial books synthesized academic research and business practice regarding logistical activities, established the importance of logistics to firm competitiveness and presented an understanding of the underlying processes that make logistics tick.

The research findings revealed in the third book, *World Class Logistics:*

The Challenge of Managing Continuous Change, built upon the knowledge established in the earlier publications. This research focused on four goals: first, to elaborate and better understand the fundamental aspects of superior logistics performance; second, to confirm the growing belief that the capabilities and supporting practices of world class logistics are fundamentally the same throughout industrially developed nations; third, to better understand how logistics managers accomplish high impact change; and fourth, to develop factual and circumstantial evidence to support the contention that being world class matters.

21ˢᵗ Century Logistics: Making Supply Chain Integration A Reality is for managers who face the challenge of developing corporate competitiveness in the coming decade through the power of supply chain management. Although the book is based on research, it is not a research report. Instead it follows in the path blazed by *The Goal* in 1984 which presented a narrative story of operational change based upon the author's broad experience and understanding of the field. Following this lead, *Logistical Excellence* was written in a style that utilized narrative prose to support presentation of logistical research findings. While the precedence for this type of book exists in other fields, this was the first such endeavor in logistics. The narrative premise has recently been used in *Precipice* (1997) and *Goose Chase* (1997). *21ˢᵗ Century Logistics*, however, is not a novel that seeks to promote understanding of the logistics process through story telling alone. Like *Logistical Excellence*, it is a research-based narrative that interprets research findings in a manner that provides managers with insight into how the discipline of logistics contributes to supply chain effectiveness.

The current publication focuses on a research update and extension completed during 1998 and 1999. At the outset the authors of this particular book wish to extend their gratitude to the following co-authors who participated in earlier publications related to the research stream, in particular: Dr. Roger J. Calantone, Dr. Steven R. Clinton, Dr. M. Bixby Cooper, Dr. Patricia J. Daugherty, Dr. Cornelia L. Dröge, Dr. Stanley E. Fawcett, Dr. Robert Frankel, Dr. David J. Frayer, Dr. Richard N. Germain, Dr. Edward A. Morash, Dr. Lloyd M. Rinehart, Dr. Dale S. Rogers, Dr. Judy M. Whipple and Dr. Daniel L Wardlow. Their contributions of the past represent the foundation of this book.

The authors are extremely grateful to numerous individuals and organizations who help support this particular initiative. The research was funded primarily from research grants from The John H. McConnell Endowment and the Council of Logistics Management. Additional financial support was provided by A.T. Kearney Management Consultants, Mercer Management Consultants, Michigan State University Collaborative Research Fund, and

United Parcel Service Foundation.

The team is deeply indebted to the 340 senior logistics managers who participated in this research. Their contribution to the understanding of supply chain competencies and capabilities will be valued by logisticians throughout the world. Particular thanks and gratitude are extended to members of the Council of Logistics Management appointed Advisory Board who lent their insight to the research. The board offered numerous examples to bring the story of Charlie Change to life and provided countless suggestions to increase management understanding and relevance. The time and effort expended by these board members were invaluable in framework and manuscript development: Joseph C. Andraski, Vice President Retail Development, AmeriCold Logistics and OMI International; Sandra L. Geiselman, Vice President Logistics, Pfaltzgraff Company; Robert T. Moore, Vice President Strategic Planning, Ryder Integrated Logistics, Inc.; Stanley P. Nelson, Supply Chain Technology Manager, Dow Chemical Company; Robert E. Sabath, Managing Director Supply Chain, Integrated Strategies; and Dr. Elaine M. Winter, Director Communication and Research, Council of Logistics Management.

Finally, the support of Michigan State University was essential to completing the book. Dean James B. Henry and Chairperson Robert W. Nason continue to provide an environment that permits research to be completed in a timely manner. Cheryl E. Lundeen, Catherine J. Guitar, and Nicholas W. Lycos completed assignments that were critical for timely completion of the manuscript. Elizabeth Johnston and Barbara A. Towner provided technical assistance in editing and presentation material development. Matthew S. Albin, Rebecca S. Flannery, Brian C. Kay, Jenine M. Ladiser, Katrina P. Savitskie, and Devin C. Shepard provided various types of support throughout the research. Matt, Jenine, Katrina, and Devin played key roles in the development and testing of the diagnostic assessment software.

With so much assistance, there is no excuse for whatever shortcomings the book may have. Nevertheless, the authors accept sole responsibility for any deficiency.

Donald J. Bowersox

David J. Closs

Theodore P. Stank

East Lansing, MI

August 1999

> Research is the process of once again examining something we already know a great deal about. The purpose of research is to confirm what we know and believe is, in fact, true and to develop a more knowledgeable understanding of its essence.

*P*rior to this research inquiry, a fairly clear understanding of the role of logistics in supply chain management existed. While no radically new or substantively contradictive insights are reported as a result of this research, the increased understanding of what constitutes best logistical practice in a supply chain context is significant. This research further confirms the structuring of logistics and the role it can contribute to making 21st century supply chain integration a reality. This research update:

- Reconfirms and extends into a more comprehensive structure the capabilities and competencies that engender superior logistics.

- Serves to further substantiate that leading logistical practice is generalizable across industries, along the supply chain, and across cultural boundaries.

- Provides more insight into the relationship between best logistical practice and superior financial achievement.

- Extends the assessment diagnostic and related benchmark to help managers implement continuous and meaningful improvement in both internal and across the supply chain integrative management.

It is important to clarify that this is not a book about the specifics of logistics work. Many excellent texts listed in the reference materials are available that adequately explore such specific knowledge. This research-based book focuses on *why* the work of logistics is fundamental to supply chain success. Its most important contribution is an updated and more comprehensive approach to achieving effective logistics change management.

To facilitate interest and ease of reading, *21ˢᵗ Century Logistics* uses a continuing dialogue of Charlie Change and Spartan Enterprises, his hypothetical firm, to help describe each area of supply chain integration. The case dialogue follows Charlie from chapter to chapter as he and an integrative change management team first identify performance improvement areas, created action plans, and then suggest strategies to more effectively achieve integrative management.

Presented in this manner, the Charlie Change dialogue allows us to share our understanding concerning how logistical performance, in most firms, can be significantly improved. Presentation in a non-technical manner delivers the message without the boredom of statistical analysis.

While many examples are provided to elaborate a specific point or practice, we have refrained from naming specific companies. This principle of anonymity serves to retain confidentiality and to avoid what might otherwise appear to be partiality. For most best practice examples a variety of different firms could have been specified. To facilitate practical application of the research, a compact disk is enclosed with this book that contains an assessment diagnostic and comparative benchmark data. The book provides complete instructions concerning use of the compact disk.

LOOKING BACK ACROSS THE 20ᵀᴴ CENTURY

Logistics is the process of moving and positioning inventory to meet customer requirements at the lowest possible total landed cost. Logistics typically includes functional responsibilities for forecasting, customer service, transportation, warehousing, and inventory management. The performance of these traditional functions is essential for day-to-day operation of supply chains in both business and not-for-profit organizations. On a global basis, logistical operations are continuously taking place 24 hours per day, 365 days a year.

To size the logistics challenge an estimate of global logistics cost, which in 1997 exceeded $5 trillion, is provided in Exhibit 1-1. Suffice it to illustrate that the business of logistics is truly big business. Appendix A provides details of the method used to derive these estimates. Because the typical commercial enterprise spends 10 – 25 percent of every sales dollar for logistics, it is a prime arena for cost reduction and containment. Of greater importance is the growing realization that competitively superior logistical performance attracts and helps maintain the patronage of preferred customers. For these reasons, managers in the 21ˢᵗ century need to understand what constitutes best practice logistics and the role logistics plays in supply chain integration.

EXHIBIT 1-1

	1997			1992		
Region	GDP	Logistics Expenditure	Percentage Logistics GDP	GDP	Logistics Expenditure	Percentage Logistics GDP
North America	9.436	1,035	11.0	7,149	837	11.7
Europe	7,982	884	11.1	7,086	876	12.3
Pacific Rim	10,063*	1,459	14.5	4,387	516	11.7
Other	11,263	1,717	15.2	5,120	662	12.9
Total	38,774	5,095	13.1	23,742	2,891	12.2

Comparative Global GDP And Logistics Expenditures
1997 And 1992, In Billions Of U.S. Dollars
(see Appendix A for details)

*1997 Pacific Rim data includes the People's Republic of China. These data are not available for 1992.

This book is based on more than three decades of research into logistical best practice. Logistics activities and priorities have changed rapidly throughout the 20th century and the pace is likely to continue in the new millennium. The Research Addendum following Chapter Twelve provides an overview that summarizes output of the research stream during the 15 years. Using this prior research as the base, this book incorporates recent results to offer a blueprint of operational and managerial behavior to achieve competitively superior logistics performance. The bulk of the statistical support for our findings is presented in spreadsheet files contained on the enclosed compact disk.

The essence of this book involves change management. Since example and anecdote demonstrate change management best, we will follow the progress of a fictional manager, Charlie Change, as he strives to reinvent the logistics operations of his firm. In a previous book, *Logistical Excellence: It's Not Business as Usual* (1992), we introduced Charlie and traced his initial trials and tribulations. Because the earlier scenario may be useful to the new reader, it is reproduced as Appendix B. Charlie now faces the challenge of leading his firm, which is still struggling to perform logistics well on a day-to-day basis, into the 21st century. He must reposition its strategic and operational focus in the context of supply chain management. In short, Charlie must *fix* a logistical competency that many managers would not consider broken.

To position what follows, this first chapter covers three topics. First, a brief overview of logistical development positions our current research. This kaleidoscopic view captures the ever-changing but interrelated aspects of the logistics discipline.

Second, the essential features of logistics process integration are discussed in the context of supply chain management. Logistics is an essential part of the supply chain. Integration of logistics is critical in achieving superior supply chain management, *but supply chain and logistics are not synonymous.* We view the former as a broader strategy challenge that requires exacting logistics performance.

Third, the fundamental importance of managing change is revisited. While the challenges of the change process are not unique to logistics, they lie at the heart of achieving superior performance in the logistical arena. The need to master change management is a central focus of our research. In the final analysis, success in implementing best practice logistics depends on the lead manager's ability to envision and implement a new order and priority to daily operations.

At the end of the chapter, we will find out what Charlie and his company face on the eve of the new century.

LOGISTICS KALEIDOSCOPE

A kaleidoscope uses a combination of mirrors, color, and light to create various patterns. The word also is used to describe something that is constantly changing but builds on past experience. The concept is appropriate for viewing change in the field of logistics.

The challenge of moving goods has confronted society since the beginning of civilization. For thousands of years managers have worried about how to achieve dependable and low-cost transportation. Only during the last half of the 20th century, however, has the modern discipline of integrated logistics emerged. Over those fifty years, the scope of logistics has expanded beyond transportation to encompass a broader and more integrated perspective about cost management and service provision. Logistics managers began to understand and capture cost tradeoffs between essential operating areas, such as transportation and inventory. In addition, it became increasingly clear that substantial competitive advantage could be gained by providing superior logistical service to selected customers. The logistical profession rapidly shifted attention to new and challenging frontiers. The explosion in logistical knowledge and capabilities was largely driven by ever-expanding, affordable information technology. The ongoing transition from the Industrial Age to the Digital Information Age will extend well into the next century. At the same time, what constitutes leading edge logistics will be continuously redefined. Fortunately, much can be learned from the recent past to help meet the emerging challenges.

In the 1950s, the great potential of integrated logistics was discovered, and total cost awareness became widespread. The notion of cost-to-cost tradeoffs was introduced. That is, the lowest total cost might not be achieved by pursuing the lowest achievable cost in each individual part of the logistics process. One solution was to spend a greater amount on one function, such as transportation, in order to reduce other costs, such as those related to inventory, in a manner that reduced total landed cost.

The concept was deceptively simple but the measurement and implementation of total cost integration was extremely difficult. Cost tradeoff often required management that cut across organizational units and involved divergent cost drivers. During centuries of business practice, the emphasis had been on minimizing each functional cost. Although many managers today accept the principles of total cost tradeoff, it remains difficult to implement. In fact, cross-functional activity-based costing is still not practiced by many organizations.

As the potential of cost-to-cost tradeoffs was being understood, leading practitioners began to explore an even more intriguing facet of tradeoff analysis. As the discipline of marketing matured, an increasing number of managers became aware of how superior service could positively impact sales. By the mid-1950s, the concept of what constitutes viable long-term strategic advantage was shifting from a production to a marketing orientation. Superior customer service through high-performance logistics came to be viewed as a strategy for generating revenues and achieving competitive advantage. In general, however the potential of managing cost-to-service tradeoffs was obscured by prevailing attitudes about functional best practice. A full appreciation of logistical performance as a way to sustain customer relationships, while introduced in the 1950's, was widely neglected until the mid-1980s.

By 1965, the idea of expanding logistical competency through outsourcing was gaining ground. The use of for-hire transportation and public warehousing had long been an accepted practice, but a new spirit of cooperation began to emerge. Cost and service tradeoff benefits could be obtained by firms integrating the multi-functional services. These firms came to be known as third-party service suppliers. The acknowledgement of core competencies and the economics of specialization justified such outsourcing. The pioneers of the outsourcing movement launched an integrated service industry that has become one of the fastest growing business segments and one that is likely to sustain double-digit growth well into the next century. Once more, the logistics discipline refocused on a new and meaningful resource base, namely, the integrated capabilities of third-party service specialists.

During the 1970s there was renewed interest in internal operational integration. The increasing availability of affordable information technology enabled logistics managers to focus on improving quality performance. It became clear to many executives that true logistical integration required a broad perspective of operations spanning from procurement of raw materials to delivery of products and services to end-customers. This perspective included the notion of reverse logistics. The widespread concern with quality and time sensitive operations led to reexamination of some long-standing ideas about customer service. For example, economic order quantity logic began to be replaced by just-in-time replenishment, that is, precise delivery of exact quantities when and where needed to meet each customers unique needs.

By the mid-1980s, another major shift occurred as leading-edge organizations began to embrace the concept of zero defect performance. This was driven by the total quality movement (TQM) and an increasingly competitive environment. Almost overnight, operational service expectations soared. Logistics managers began to measure and report operational performance in financial terms, such as revenue generation, asset utilization, cash-to-cash conversion and working capital reduction. The realization that substantial capital invested in logistics-related assets could be freed for alternative use led to emphasis on achieving free-cash spin. The capital freed up from revamped logistical operations was not really *free* in terms of capital funding, but previously capitalized resources could be redeployed to other areas of business development.

As recently as 1995, the definition of logistics again expanded. The concept of two older areas of customer and supplier integrative relationships gained renewed attention. Businesses in general began to develop extremely close relationships with selected clients, sometimes called strategic customers, and significantly more emphasis was placed on improving working arrangements with suppliers. The driver behind such collaboration was the desire to *extend* the effective control of the enterprise. This need was further evidenced by increased globalization of both markets and production. The needs and capabilities of material suppliers, service suppliers, and especially customers, were incorporated into strategic planning. Almost overnight, firms began to view operations in terms of supply chain engagements and strategies. Collaboration and cooperation began to replace adversarial attitudes that had long dominated business relationships. The growth of E-commerce and the Internet has further increased both the need for supply chain integration and the opportunities to achieve it. Managers identified operational tradeoffs with customers and suppliers in order to reduce supply chain duplication and eliminate nonvalue-adding work. Leading logistical practice shifted from a purely internal focus to extended enterprise integration across the full range of supply chain participants.

Exhibit 1-2 summarizes the history of change in logistical focus. Without question, a new and expanded perspective of what constitutes logistics is emerging.

EXHIBIT 1-2

Shifts In Logistical Focus

• Transportation Efficiency	3000 BC
• Total Cost Awareness	1950 AD
• Customer Service	1955
• Comprehensive Outsourcing	1965
• Operational Integration and Quality Performance	1970
• Finance Positioning and Operational Excellence	1985
• Customer Relationships and Enterprise Extension	1995

The following definitions are used throughout this text. The Council of Logistics Management defines logistics as follows: *Logistics is that part of the supply chain process that plans, implements, and controls the efficient, effective flow and storage of goods, services, and related information from the point of origin to the point of consumption in order to meet customers' requirements.*

The challenge for logistics managers is to integrate logistical performance across all operating facets of a business. This holistic concept has become known as Supply Chain Management (SCM). SCM can be defined as *a collaborative-based strategy to link interorganizational business operations to achieve a shared market opportunity.* The activities associated with logistics are included in the definition of SCM. SCM, however, is a broader concept concerned with activities to plan, implement, and control the efficient and effective *sourcing, manufacturing, and delivery processes* for products, services, and related information from the point of material origin to the point of ultimate consumption for the purpose of conforming to end-customer requirements.

THE PROCESS INTEGRATION CHALLENGE

The most demanding issues in logistics today remain all about integration processes. It is clear that the major obstacles to end-to-end functional integration, both internally and across the supply chain, will continue to preoccupy managers well into the new millennium. These obstacles include organizational structures, inventory responsibility, information sharing, and measurement systems.

In the simplest of terms, a *process* is best viewed as a *sequence of work that creates value*. When a firm successfully fulfills a customer's order and simultaneously meets all related expectations – performing on time, damage-free delivery of 100 percent of the exact items and quantities ordered, with error-free invoicing – then and only then has full value been created. However, simply meeting customer expectations may not maximize the potential value for the end-customer. Such value is created by the coordinated efforts of all firms involved in the entire supply chain logistics process. If the sequence of essential work is perfectly orchestrated, then maximum value will be achieved. To satisfy performance objectives, the logistical process must integrate all necessary work and avoid all non-necessary work. Internal work related to the firm's logistics must be coordinated, and operational integration also must be achieved across the supply chain.

One deliverable of this book is to help facilitate integrative management of internal and across the supply chain logistical processes. Managers who participated in this update reported growing concern with both facets of integration. Managers continue to confront many and varied obstacles to a seamless flow of inventory from sourcing to manufacturing to distribution to end-customer. Most managers strive to integrate internal processes in an effort to increase value by reducing waste, excessive work delays, and redundancy. Such efforts can maximize value by achieving the lowest total landed cost without sacrificing superior service. The Supply Chain Council data indicates that superior supply chain performance can actually lower cost by 3-7 percent and enhance cash flow by more than 30 percent (*Integrated Supply Chain Benchmarking Study*, Weston, MA: PRTM Consulting, 1997). However, despite significant refinements in costing techniques, advances in technology, as well as sweeping revisions in integrative performance metrics, process integration still eludes many firms.

It is noteworthy that a great number of firms involved in the research reported that they have achieved more meaningful integration with suppliers and/or customers than within their own operations. The inability to fully integrate across the entire scope of internal logistics work – something we refer to as the "great operational divide" – remains one of management's greatest problems. There is increasing evidence that failure to achieve internal integration is a leading cause of why strategic alliances do not work. A failure of firms to operate on an integrated basis prevents them from making good on promises to supply chain partners.

This book and its supported research introduce an expanded framework that blends together the integrative capabilities of leading-edge performers. This new framework is referred to as Supply Chain 2000. No specific firm involved in the research excelled in all aspects of the framework, although some have achieved significantly more than others. An index was used to develop a comparative measure between responding firms concerning relative integrative achievement. Firms significantly advanced in comparison to others merit the label high index achievers. Even such comparatively high achievers have room for substantial improvement. For the average firm, improvement opportunities are more abundant.

In Chapter Two, the Supply Chain 2000 expanded framework is introduced and is then elaborated over the next 6 chapters. This framework extends the World Class Logistics Model introduced in previous research to embrace the challenges of simultaneously achieving both internal and across the supply chain integrative management. The Supply Chain 2000 framework identifies six competencies essential to internal and supply chain wide integration. The framework embodies twenty-five capabilities that fulfill the six interrelated competencies.

Three general observations can be made about how the Supply Chain 2000 framework stacks up in comparison to the Logistics 95 framework. *First*, selected attributes that differentiated firms as recently as five years ago no longer are sufficient to drive competitive advantage. In 1995, the capability to provide superior service, operating efficiency, inventory sensitivity, and technological sophistication were key differentiators. Today, these are best viewed as prerequisites or business qualifiers. A high level of performance in all these categories is essential if a firm hopes to be a meaningful competitor.

Second, the new differentiators in gaining competitive superiority reflect the current and growing emphasis on integrated relationships and enterprise extension. Future competitiveness will hinge on responsiveness, flexibility, speed, dependability, and continued sensitivity to cost. These attributes represent an increasing focus on operating agility and continued efficiency as key to satisfying end-customers.

Third, the evidence continues to mount that superior logistical performance makes a difference in terms of financial achievement. A long-standing objective of our research is to create a cause and effect link of logistics to superior financial achievement. Widespread variability in activity based costing, different accounting practices, and the lack of access to confidential financial information make it difficult to develop even a circumstantial case using measured performances data. Nonetheless, when managers were asked to compare their firm's perceived logistical capabilities to those of competitors with respect to 13 operating features, manager's of high index achieving firms perceived their performance to be significantly superior to competitors in every one. Managers of lower achieving firms reported a far lesser degree of perceived performance. The varied perception is even more significant in that firms ranked as high achievers also were identified as most likely to benchmark competitive performance. It logically follows that those who regularly benchmark are likely to have a better fix concerning their relative operational performance. The results of this analysis are reported in Chapter Nine.

CHANGE MANAGEMENT

Our earlier research emphasized the need for skills related to complex process change management. This need remains critical. At an operating level it is important for logistics managers to identify and close performance gaps. An even more far-reaching facet of change management involves the arduous task of reinventing logistical processes that currently work – but not at superior performance levels. This need for substantial modification in both logistics practice and operating structure continues to be important. Logistics cross-functional responsibility makes this need and task even more daunting

In 1995, analysis of managerial behavior in world class firms revealed an ability to determine when fundamental change was appropriate, create a meaningful vision of the future, and then move their organization toward its achievement. Based on the Supply Chain 2000 framework, a new and more robust Change Process Model is introduced in Chapter Ten, and the expanded methodology and diagnostic spreadsheet to help assess relative index achievement is presented in Chapter Eleven.

The final chapter offers our perspective concerning logistics in the future. Mega-trends currently emerging on the competitive landscape are identified and reviewed in terms of their impact on best practice logistics. It is safe to assume that changes will continue to occur in the 21st century, and what constitutes superior logistics will again need to be redefined.

UPDATING CHARLIE CHANGE

The last we heard of Charlie Change was in 1992, when the CEO of Spartan Enterprises approved Charlie's plan for implementing integrated logistics within the company (Appendix B). The successful reorganization at Spartan resulted in dramatic improvements. Charlie's initiatives led to operating efficiencies and effectiveness that not only cut costs but also helped Spartan compete through better customer service. Under Charlie's leadership however, providing customers with perfect orders – 100 percent filled, on time, every time – became the goal that the organization strived for.

Charlie's understanding of marketplace needs and his ability to manage change

helped Spartan's transition as it acquired first one and then another competitor. Charlie was promoted to the newly created position of Vice President of Integrated Operations just before a new CEO was appointed. Under the tutelage of Warren Thompson, Charlie's stature at Spartan continued to grow. He was increasingly recognized both nationally and internationally for his organizational innovations. Requests to speak at professional meetings, such as the Council of Logistics Management, and at universities were common. Managers from a wide variety of industries acknowledged Spartan's "leading edge" reputation and sought to benchmark Charlie's process.

Things were not as rosy as they appeared, however. Many of the operational managers, particularly the old hands who had begun their careers during the days of transportation regulation, had scoffed at the goal of delivering the right product at the right time in the right place 100 percent of the time. Spartan had never tried to be the best in class. It had always been too complex hence too expensive to achieve. Charlie had attempted to implement a new philosophy that enabled Spartan to offer different service levels to different customers based upon their requirements rather than offer an average service level to all customers. Some of the management team could never adjust to the operational rigor brought on by this concept. Many of them eventually resigned their positions or were asked to leave. The majority, however, eventually accepted the challenge. At least that's what they said publicly.

Evidence to the contrary crossed Charlie's desk on a daily basis. At times it seemed that the operational modifications required to effect behavioral change were too complex to ever accomplish. One recent problem that had been called to his attention, for example, involved an attempt to change the way on-time delivery was measured. Until recently, delivery windows for most customers were established by a dynamic routing and scheduling system operated at each distribution center. The system provided delivery windows that approximated the lowest cost alternative within given service constraints. On-time delivery was measured as plus or minus ten minutes of the scheduled delivery. This worked well as long as the delivery window scheduled by the system matched up with a time that was expedient to the customer. When it didn't – which occurred often – problems resulted.

Charlie had pushed the DC general managers to expand the complexity of the scheduling system to allow top customers to express preferred delivery times as well as to identify non-acceptable windows. It had been over one year since the DC managers agreed to institute the change. The latest report, however, showed that only five of the twelve distribution centers were actually incorporating customer preferences into their scheduling. The others were trying, but obstacles ranging from incompatible information systems and preoccupation with Y2K compliance to high employee turnover hampered progress.

Another tremendous problem that Charlie had had to confront, thusfar unsuccessfully, was what the MSU research team referred to as the "great divide."

Charlie's new integrated operations organization included procurement and manufacturing as well as the traditional distribution-oriented activities of warehousing, transportation, and customer service. He quickly discovered that neither side of the "divide" was willing to part with the apparatus that they used to generate planning forecasts. This resulted in procurement and manufacturing schedules based on one forecast, while marketing and distribution worked off of another. Under this scenario, synchronization of the two arms of his department was nearly impossible to achieve.

Gradually – and painfully – some benefits of Charlie's efforts began to surface. Top customers were happier with the service levels Spartan provided, and some other customers began to turn a profit. Departmental costs began to drop, although more than once a manager had stormed out of Charlie's office furious over a decision that Charlie believed would ultimately decrease system cost at the expense of functional cost increases. Unfortunately, the rate of internal change was not keeping up with the rate of external change.

Despite the marginal improvements, Charlie was concerned. Warren – and the board of directors – had come to expect greater annual cost savings and service performance improvements from the operations department. During the last year in particular the pace of change had declined. Some blamed the world market situation, but Charlie wasn't the sort to lay blame elsewhere. He worried about what Warren's reaction would be when the low-hanging fruit of logistical benefits, such as systemwide inventory reduction and transportation consolidation, were harvested and improvement continued to slow.

Charlie was increasingly frustrated by his inability to affect change in areas that seemed outside his control but had a critical effect on logistics and overall company performance. Despite his best efforts, the promotional activities that stimulated forward promotional buying of inventory continued in many markets. Some operating facilities and managers had not yet embraced the concepts of manufacturing and distribution postponement/responsiveness, and a number of purchasing agents continued to buy in large volume to gain maximum unit discounts. In addition, the purchasing agents seemed to spend an excessive amount of time completing clerical tasks. Furthermore, customers who had witnessed some improvement in service had increased their expectations but continued to treat Spartan's sales representatives as they always had – at arm's length. And suppliers who had promised a great deal in the way of service and cost improvements too often delivered much less. The sales force had always been able to push the product before but customers seemed to be looking for something else.

The board of directors planned to meet in six months to approve Spartan's financial and operating plan for 2000. Warren viewed this meeting as an opportunity to introduce dramatic change that would make Spartan competitive well into the new millennium. He asked the vice presidents to present their ideas about how *the firm should look and act at the beginning of the 21st century. Charlie was named coordinator of the management team's efforts. Not entirely pleased with the new assignment, Charlie walked back to his office lost in thought. How am I going to tell them, he wondered, that after all the effort, time, and money we have poured into developing operational excellence – often at my request – I'm not sure that any functional area, as currently defined, will exist much longer.*

SUPPLY CHAIN 2000

*C*harlie saw the "Millennium Meeting," as some managers had begun to call it, as an opportunity to present his ideas for change for Spartan in the 21ˢᵗ century. Some of the ideas he was contemplating made him nervous and he expressed his concerns to Amy Thornton, the Director of Order Fulfillment.

"Well," Amy said, "that's what Warren asked you to do. Why are you so worried about how the directors will take it?" His response surprised even Amy, who had worked with Charlie since his days as GM of European Operations and was accustomed to his penchant for "thinking outside the box."

"What bothers me," said Charlie "is how Warren and the board, not to mention the other VPs, will react when I tell them our entire operational structure, including our relationships with customers and suppliers, is still broken after all our efforts to fix it over the past 6 years. And I'm afraid that Javi Suarez (VP of Manufacturing), Gwynne Miller (VP of Marketing), and Lawrence Ingram (VP of Administration and Finance) will think I'm after their jobs when I go into the details of how I think we should look and act."

Amy knew Charlie was frustrated by Spartan's apparent inability to satisfy top customers. In fact, she had championed an effort to coordinate key customer purchasing systems with her order management system to shorten lead times and improve perfect order percentage. To some degree this had worked, but problems with new products as well as heavily promoted products continued to give her nightmares, not to mention frequent calls from disgruntled customers. She also knew of Charlie's struggles with various departments as he tried to integrate product and information flow so Spartan could serve customers better at lower total cost. Each time a battle occurred, there was agreement about the need to coordinate marketing, procurement, manufacturing, and distribution processes. Then nothing happened, since no manager was eager to concede turf in order to facilitate seamless operations.

They had not been able to devise a strategy that would solve the operational problems without creating World War III.

Charlie invited Amy to his office and showed her the results of an assessment of internal logistics operations he had conducted using the 1995 Michigan State University World Class Logistics framework (Logistics 95). The assessment revealed continued improvement in many activities since the baseline was established in 1995. A number of logistics initiatives had clearly taken hold. Spartan's mission and objectives were pointed in the right direction. Routine operating processes had been standardized and simplified such that work efficiency and effectiveness were improved. These steps had freed time and capital to focus on emergent situations. However, the firm was facing more pressure in three key areas; 1) meeting unique customer requests; 2) enhancing shareholder value; and 3) smoothing the interfaces with key supply chain partners. These also happened to be the areas in which Charlie, and everyone working for him, he reasoned, spent 95 percent of their time.

The logistics assessment clearly showed continued trouble with integrating the planning and movement of goods and information both internally and between Spartan and its supply chain partners. Charlie told Amy that if they could find a way to get all the players involved in creating value for end-users–including customers, suppliers, and internal operating areas–they could reap more benefits from logistical integration. Their job was merely to decide how to do that and get the support of the other top managers in less than six months!

When Charlie set out to evaluate Spartan's integrated supply chain performance, the challenge was to find a credible way to assess the broad range of processes under his control. It was particularly important to include some comparison with other industries to measure how well Spartan was using its expertise and capabilities. He needed a tool that would provide a snapshot of supply chain integration at the business and process level as well as permit more detailed analysis of each. The Logistics 95 framework and accompanying diagnostic spreadsheet had been a fair basis for previous comparison, but Charlie wasn't sure it was sufficiently broad to meet his current needs. He was also concerned that the original benchmark data were no longer timely.

Charlie felt that many elements of the Logistics 95 framework pointed the way to successful supply chain integration. After all, logistics required coordinating materials and information flows from conception to consumption. Charlie mused that of all the people in the company, logisticians were the ones who really understood integration. To survive, they had to know the activities with which they interfaced almost as well as they knew their own. Most other people in the supply chain were expert at their job, but once they sent the product downstream they had very little idea of what happened to it. He believed that if Spartan needed a blueprint for supply chain integration, it could be found in the logistics area.

Charlie contacted the faculty at Michigan State and asked about recent research on integrated supply chain management. He was told that the 1995 framework was being updated and expanded with data from a large number of North American firms. A new framework focusing on the supply chain would be available shortly and would provide a diagnostic and benchmarks for assessing internal and external integration capabilities, both currently and relative to past performance. The new framework was called Supply Chain 2000.

When Charlie received Supply Chain 2000, he and a few key directors completed the diagnostic and were disappointed by the results. As expected, Spartan scored relatively well on capabilities related to internal functions, such as responsiveness to changing customer needs, standardization and simplification of work routines, and functional measurement. In a few areas, Charlie found that Spartan's capability level exceeded the world class benchmark–placing them in the top 15 percent of firms. In other areas, however, Spartan rated average or significantly below average. These related to integration capabilities, such as unification of horizontal processes, integrated deployment of physical assets, development of a vision at the supply chain level of value creation, and management of supplier relationships.

Some managers might be satisfied by an average rating on many of these capabilities, but Charlie knew that Spartan would have to do better if it wanted to be competitive over the long term. Top performance would require overall excellence throughout Spartan's supply chain. With that objective in mind, Charlie began devising a plan that used Supply Chain 2000 as the basis for identifying and prioritizing internal and external change.

Charlie decided to ask the other VPs to let their operating managers and directors participate in a task force. Such a cross-functional approach should pinpoint areas in which Spartan was having trouble integrating operations among departments and with external customers and suppliers. Identifying these breakdowns or "gaps" would help the task force focus on weak spots and suggest improvements. While he knew that the implementation would be the real difficult part, even problem definition and prioritization would not be trivial.

The other VPs agreed to Charlie's plan. Each openly recognized the need for better operational coordination. Of course, Charlie had heard that song before. Javi Suarez said half-jokingly that he would agree to anything that allowed him to stay out of the process as long as he still had a job after all was said and done. Charlie gave him a half-grin in response and could tell that Javi wasn't very comfortable with that!

Charlie announced that Amy would head the task force. Other participants were the directors of Purchasing, Production, Sales, Marketing, Logistics Operations, Financial Operations and Information Systems. The group would also seek active involvement from representatives of Spartan's top customers and material and service suppliers. Charlie would meet with the group weekly for an update on progress and to discuss future directions.

The first task force meeting began shortly after 9 a.m. the following Monday. Along with Amy, the Director of Order Fulfillment, the Spartan executives in attendance represented the activities that spanned the internal supply chain: from sourcing and purchasing of inbound materials, to manufacturing, to marketing and sales, which design programs to create demand, through to delivery of finished goods to end-customers.

In 1995 the Michigan State University Logistics Research team introduced a framework and process to assess logistical achievement. The World Class Framework (Logistics 95) was widely used to assess achievement level and identify continuous improvement opportunities. As management interest expanded to a comprehensive supply chain orientation, the assessment scope of Logistics 95 was not sufficient to integrate the full range of managerial concerns. Thus, research was completed to extend the framework to cover the broader range of supply chain capabilities. This chapter reviews the research effort that developed and supports Supply Chain 2000.

THE GROWTH OF SUPPLY CHAIN MANAGEMENT

The historical framework for conducting business was a simple supplier-to-manufacturer-to-wholesaler/distributor-to-retailer distribution channel. This channel model dominated the way most goods moved to market until the post-World War II business era. From 1945 forward, the spawning of new ways to get materials in and get products to end-customers has been almost a daily occurrence. Contemporary business operations reflect a complex maze of relationships in which many different distributive arrangements may be simultaneously used to satisfy unique end-customer requirements. These complex business arrangements are increasingly referred to as *supply chains*. When a firm's management makes a unique effort to strategically position and align distributive capabilities to gain and maintain competitive advantage, the process is referred to as *supply chain management*.

Supply chain management employs comprehensive arrangements that span from source of raw material to end-customer delivery and includes activities ranging from new product introduction through the end of the product life cycle. End-customers of a supply chain are individuals or organizations who *use* a physical product or service either in personal consumption or as a component in creation of other products. For example, when a family eats breakfast cereal, they are end-customers. Likewise, when farmers purchase farm equipment they are end-customers. Such consumption typically eliminates the possibility of reconstituting the original product.

While the supply chain must ultimately focus on the needs of these end-customers, effective strategy must recognize that there are intermediate customers as well. These include distributors and retailers. While they buy the product only for resale, their requirements must also be considered when designing supply chain strategy.

Not all products and materials moved through supply chains are consumed. For a variety of reasons, a specific product may not be timely to an end-customer's needs or expectations. In addition, a wide variety of packaging material may be distributed with products creating a need for reclamation. Thus, a major supply chain mission is to accommodate reclamation or reverse logistics movements.

Every firm, by nature of the free enterprise market system, is in some way or another involved in supply chain relationships. No firm can be self sufficient in a complex business environment that is based on specialization. The selection of suppliers, combined with a firm's customers, create the nucleus of the firm's supply chain. The notion of managing a supply chain simply acknowledges that relationship formulation and implementation need not be left to chance and may become a primary determinate of the ultimate success of an enterprise. It is becoming increasingly clear to senior managers that such fundamental strategic commitments must be carefully planned. Substantial opportunity exists to gain competitive advantage by selecting and developing competitively superior supply chain alignments. Such alignment is unique to the firms who enable or agree to participate in the relationship. Unlike their predecessors, today's managers have technology available to facilitate integration with customers as well as material and service suppliers.

Modern information technology and communication capabilities such as the Internet can be deployed to facilitate unprecedented integration across the supply chain. The potential exists to forge supply chain relationships that yield resource synergies between participating firms. Collaborative efforts can achieve superior end-customer satisfaction while simultaneously eliminating operational duplication and potential resource waste. Such arrangements can also create value through post sales support, such as product servicing, supply service, product reclamation, and improved environmental sustainability.

The scope of what is involved in a supply chain is clearly broader than logistics. As the first chapter began—logistics is *the process of moving and positioning inventory to meet customer requirements at the lowest possible total landed cost*. Logistical performance is fundamental and essential to making supply chains work. It follows that the success of any supply chain arrangement is directly related to the effectiveness and efficiency of its logistical component. The firms who have used unique supply chain capabilities to develop a specific competitive niche range across all industries. Without quality logistics, the notion of a competitively superior supply chain is, at best, a figment of imagination.

EXPANDING THE FRAMEWORK

It is necessary to continuously redefine what behavior constitutes best logistics practice, given the rapidly changing business structure within which logistics services are performed. This required a review of the range of capabilities associated with best logistical practice by the research team and, as appropriate, expansion to accommodate challenges related to supply chain management. Essentially, the same challenge is faced by logistics executives as they expanded their operational reach to exploit emerging supply chain opportunities. This logistical content modification was achieved by the research team through three initiatives: (1) a review of the constructs that are fundamental to logistical integration; (2) case study development and validation; and (3) research survey generalization. Each is discussed below.

Framework Constructs

Expanding the Logistics 95 framework to encompass the broader range of capabilities and competencies reflective of supply chain integration was a significant challenge. The goal was the development of an assessment process capable of identifying areas having potential for integrative improvement. A meaningful assessment requires a scoping framework that structures the interrelationship of specific practices. To move from the framework to specific improvement action plans requires an assessment process that includes diagnostic software and benchmarks. The assessment process, detailed in Chapters Ten, Eleven, and the compact disk (CD), provides this diagnostic.

The key to effective assessment is the scoping framework. To establish a framework that integrates logistics into the broader context of supply chain management required a logical review of the interrelationship of work, functions, capabilities, and competencies.

A job or *work*, such as order picking or truck driving, is the most visible part of the logistics process. Jobs may be industry or firm specific, but they usually are grouped into organizational units to facilitate control. For example, all the jobs related to warehousing are often grouped. Another common grouping is to organize all jobs related to transport into a transportation department or *function*. These functional groupings are significant because they are highly visible elements of an organization. Departments have traditionally been the focal point for financial budgeting, performance measurement, and operational control. Functional work arrangements constitute the drivers of logistical best practice. It is the functions or drivers that combine to create value.

The ease and simplicity of measurement associated with discrete functional groupings, however, can be a major obstacle to process integration. Historically, functions have been the focus of enterprise management. There is no question that they are important, but only in the context of how they add value to the specific process they facilitate. Functional management falls short when processes cut across functional boundaries. The most fundamental shift in logistics thinking is to view functional excellence in terms of performance that enhances *overall* supply chain integration.

To generalize this integrative process, functional value is expressed in terms of universal capabilities. A *capability* is the knowledge and achievement essential to developing logistical competency. A capability relates to *why work is being performed* as contrasted to *how it is performed*. The capability reflects the value of the work's performance. Inherent in a capability is the application of integrative principles that allow multiple processes to be synchronized. Whereas jobs and functions may be highly relevant to specific industries and work situations, capabilities are universal. Capabilities span the supply chain and are equally applicable to suppliers, manufacturers, wholesalers/distributors, and across the full range of retail formats. Capabilities also transcend industries, nations, and even cultural boundaries. Furthermore, they are *observable* and most importantly *measurable* among firms of all sizes. Previous research reviewed in the Research Addendum following Chapter Twelve, firmly established that capabilities reflecting best logistics practice are, to some degree, observable in all firms that constitute a supply chain structure. Specific capabilities are, at times, more visible or prominent in selected situations because economic, social, cultural, or competitive situations differ. It is the imbalance in capability achievement that creates logistical improvement gaps. A key conclusion of this research is that select firms have a higher overall level of capability achievement than their less accomplished competitors. Examples of such capabilities include: 1) the ability to identify and accommodate the logistics needs of specific customers; 2) the ability to work with supply chain partners to achieve an integrated process; 3) the ability to effectively share operating and planning information between supply chain partners; 4) the ability to measure and understand overall supply chain performance; and, (5) the ability to share benefits and risks.

The fusing of capabilities results in highly visible competencies. The contextual framework of supply chain integration contains six universal competencies. These competencies are discussed later in this chapter. A *competency* reflects the synthesis of selected logistical capabilities into a logically coherent and manageable state of affairs sufficient to gain and maintain supply chain collaborations. The most important of these collaborators are end-customers. Firms that achieve a high level of integration across the six competencies are positioned to exploit logistics to gain and maintain competitive advantage. The blending of these capabilities by a firm across the supply chain forms logistical competency. Three points are significant concerning logistical competency.

First, when the overall process of performing logistics becomes one of a firm's most admired and differentiating proficiencies, it has the potential to become the firm's strategic cornerstone. Logistical core competency is quite easily identified in today's competitive environment.

Second, from an academic viewpoint, the abstraction of logistics from function to competency forms the constructs of a viable theoretical structure. The identification of capabilities offers the first level of generalization. The fusing of capabilities into universal competencies serves to blend the specific discipline of logistics into the sum of the business. The positioning of logistics as a core competency expands this holistic integration.

Third, logistics is the operationally-based process in a firm that must be truly integrative. Such integration is required to work extensively with other functions of the firm to provide overall customer value. Since there is not much precedent regarding such intensive integration, pioneering supply chains is both critical and challenging.

Case Study Expansion

Following publication of *World Class Logistics: The Challenges of Managing Continuous Change* in 1995, by the Council of Logistics Management (CLM), there was considerable opportunity to apply the Logistics 95 framework working with specific firms. In a rewarding sense, the framework and assessment process proved to be a powerful tool to assist managers in developing action plans for improving logistical performance. Such action plans resulted in meaningful change management initiatives for those managers who sought to dramatically improve their logistics performance. In fact, in a variety of applications, the logistics integrated framework and implementation guidelines provided stimulus for reinventing and changing long-standing functional practices. In short, application of the assessment process and diagnostic of Logistics 95 provided a way and means to help change currently working or non-broken logistical processes into significantly superior initiatives.

During the post research period, it became increasingly clear that the full range of practical integrative issues involved in supply chain management were broader than those dimensioned in Logistics 95. To explore the expanding supply chain horizon, case study research was completed with twenty firms. All of these firms had participated in the world class research and each became involved in post research implementation. The firms, as a group, consisted of twelve manufacturers, three wholesalers and five retailers. In addition to this base group, assessments were completed with six firms not previously involved in the research. These additional firms were equally divided between manufacturers and distributors. As a collective group, the case study firms were engaged in automotive, chemical, consumer durable, food manufacturing and wholesaling, health care, mass merchant, food and general retailing, and paper.

Based on the case studies, a supply chain framework began to emerge. This framework ultimately consisted of twenty-five capabilities that served to engender six interrelated competencies. During the case study process, an expanded set of assessment questions was developed and tested. These questions served to identify the presence and measure the intensity of the expanded capabilities. The combination of Logistics 95 and the expanded capabilities/competencies from the case studies became the context of Supply Chain 2000. The twenty-five capabilities and six competencies were structured into a normative framework symbolizing logistics integration in a supply chain context.

Research Generalization

In late 1998, the normative supply chain framework was subjected to broad-based validation. A survey population was selected exclusively from the CLM membership. Given the strategic focus of the expanded supply chain framework, it was decided to selectively present the research questionnaire to the senior logistics or supply chain executive in manufacturing, wholesale/distributing, and retail firms. Thus, each firm or strategic business unit of a firm who had a senior manager listed as a CLM member received *one* questionnaire. The total sample was 2,680 managers and the response was 306 fully validated responses.

While this 11.5 percent response rate was somewhat disappointing, it is understandable in terms of the length and comprehensive nature of the workbook. To some undetermined degree, the response rate was also impacted by the extensive confidential information being requested. While anonymity was guaranteed, some executives are suspicious of such claims. Finally, the response rate was, to some degree, suppressed by the decision to only seek response from the most senior executive in the firm. In addition to having the least amount of time, senior executives are typically bombarded by questionnaires.

The good news is that the 306 usable responses provided sufficient data to confirm the generality of the expanded framework. As in previous research, the respondents reported a wide range of integrative practices that substantiated the relevance of the framework in the context of supply chain integration. The data was sufficient to substantiate best practice across nine industry groups and to confirm the universal nature of the associated capabilities and competencies.

As in previous research, analysis revealed that a small subset of respondent firms have achieved far greater levels of integrated performance than typical within their industry. These accomplished firms tend to have similar attributes to those who are leaders in other industries. Additionally, no significant difference exists in achievement in terms of primary position in the channel of distribution. That is to say, leading retailers, distributors/wholesalers, and manufacturers have more in common with superior counterparts in other industries than they do with their less accomplished direct industry competitors. It is also worth emphasizing that no firm among our sample has achieved superior implementation across the full range of integrative capabilities and competencies. Even among the best of the best, considerable room exists for meaningful improvement.

The expanded supply chain framework is based on North America. All case study participants and survey respondents were North American firms. The earlier research conclusions that being world class was independent of geographic area of operations were not specifically tested in this update. In addition to the base sample the questionnaire was mailed to senior executives from foreign countries who are CLM members. Analysis of 34 responses revealed general compatibility with the primary respondent sample and no significant difference in reported achievement. Thus, given the noted constraints, the framework and generality of the research is valid.

THE SUPPLY CHAIN 2000 FRAMEWORK

The Supply Chain 2000 framework encompasses the range and continuity required to link raw material/resource suppliers to end-customers. It blends into one framework the capabilities essential to integrating supply chain logistics. The creation of value related to supply chain integration is achieved by simultaneous orchestration of four critical flows. Exhibit 2-1 illustrates critical supply chain flows.

EXHIBIT 2-1

RESOURCE BASE	← PRODUCT-SERVICE VALUE FLOW → ← MARKET ACCOMMODATION FLOW → ← INFORMATION FLOW → ← CASH FLOW →	**END CUSTOMERS**

The product-service value flow represents the value-added movement of products and services from the raw material provider to the end-customers. Product value is increased through physical modification, packaging, market proximity, customization, service support, or other activities that enhance the desirability of the product from the viewpoint of the end-customers.

While the product-service flow generally moves from the resource base to end-customers, supply chains must increasingly accommodate reverse flows such as product recalls and recycling. The market accommodation flow provides a structure to achieve all post sales-service administration, including reclamation. Market accommodation also involves information concerning sales and product usage to facilitate supply chain planning. Examples are product customization requirements, point-of-sale (POS) data, end-customer consumption, and warehouse releases. This flow provides supply chain members with channel visibility concerning the timing and location of product consumption. Planning and operations can be better synchronized when all participants have a common understanding of demand and consumption patterns.

The information flow is the bi-directional exchange of transactional data and inventory status between or among supply chain partners. Typical examples are forecasts, promotional plans, purchase orders, order acknowledgements, shipping and inventory information, invoices, payments, and replenishment requirements. Information exchange initiates, controls, and records the product-service value flow. Historically paper-based, an increasing amount of the information flow is now being conducted electronically.

Cash flow generally flows in the reverse direction of value-added activities. However, in situations involving promotions and rebates, cash flows in the same direction as products and services. Cash flow velocity and asset utilization are primary to superior logistics performance.

Naturally, these four flows occur between channel participants, even when the supply chain is not integrated. However, failure in coordination and integration among supply chain partners has historically resulted in delay, redundancy and inefficiency. To facilitate effective and efficient supply chain flow, competencies related to operations, planning and control, and behavioral management must be integrated. Exhibit 2-2 illustrates the Supply Chain 2000 Integration Framework. The operational context includes traditional processes related to procurement, production, and logistics. The planning and control context incorporates information technology and planning systems, as well as measurement competency. The behavior context relates to how a firm manages internal and external relationships among supply chain entities. Each is discussed in the following sections.

EXHIBIT 2-2

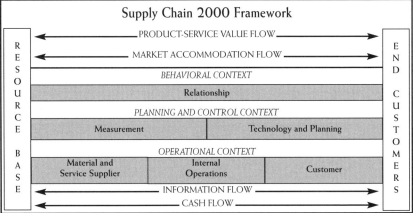

The Operational Context

Operations involve the processes that facilitate order fulfillment and replenishment across the supply chain. Effective order fulfillment requires coordination both within a firm and between supply chain partners. In the operational context, integration is essential internally as well as with customers and suppliers.

End-customer integration builds on the philosophies and activities that develop customer intimacy. The primary focus of any firm must be end-customers who consume products. End-customer integration is the competency that builds lasting competitive advantage. Firms have always paid attention to the needs of customers but have only recently begun to identify and consider their differences in terms of logistics requirements. Any firm seeking supply chain integration must demonstrate strong commitment to the customization required for effective customer integration.

Internal integration focuses on the joint activities and processes within a firm that coordinate functions related to procurement, manufacturer, and customer distribution. Many firms have attempted to integrate internal functionality for a substantial period of time, but anecdotal and quantitative evidence strongly indicates there are significant gaps. Logistics managers often report more success in coordinating with customers than with their own purchasing and manufacturing operations. In turn, buyers frequently perceive they have better integration with suppliers than with their own manufacturing, logistical and marketing operations. The existence of such operational separation is sufficiently common to highlight the importance of closing what we have come to refer to as the *Great Operating Divide*. There may be many potential reasons for the great operating divide. Two major causes are traditional organizational structure and the measurement emphasis placed on the performance of functional work. In most firms, there has been a lack of a balanced score card that reflects the performance of the integrated functions. Internal integration is the competency that links in-house work into a seamless process capable of supporting end-customer requirements. It is not clear just how much closure a firm must achieve with respect to internal integration in order to make extended enterprise goals a reality.

Supplier integration also focuses on activities that create close ties with material and service providing supply chain partners. While the end-customer is the overriding focal point or supply chain driver, overall success also will depend on coordinated performance with suppliers. Competency in this area links externally performed activities into a seamless flow with internal work processes. Firms that desire to excel must blend their operating processes into those of supply partners in order to meet increasingly broad and demanding end-customer expectations.

To achieve leading performance in an operational context, firms must be end-customer focused, must excel in functional and process performance, and must achieve interorganizational coordination.

The Planning And Control Context

Across the supply chain, information technology and measurement systems must facilitate planning and control of integrated operations. Operation excellence must be supplemented and supported by integrated planning and measurement capabilities. This involves joining technology to monitor, control, and facilitate overall supply chain performance.

Planning and control integration refers to the design, application, and coordination of information to enhance purchasing, manufacturing, customer order fulfillment, and resource planning. This competency includes access to databases that enable sharing of appropriate information among supply chain participants. It also addresses transaction systems required to initiate and process replenishment and customer orders. In addition, leading firms typically apply information-based decision support systems to assist facility, equipment, and inventory utilization.

Measurement integration is the ability to monitor and benchmark functional and process performance, both within the firm and throughout the supply chain. Because each firm is unique, each must define, operationalize, and monitor standard or common measures.

The Behavioral Context

Effective relationship management is essential in supply chain engagements. In final analysis, successful implementation of supply chain strategy will rest on the quality of the basic business relationship between partners. In general, managers are far better at the practice of competition than they are at the art of cooperation. Many long-standing barriers exist to thwart successful implementation of collaborative relationships. One major barrier is existing incentive systems. While many firms are looking to enhance overall supply chain performance, most firm incentive systems still are focused on firm or even functional performance.

Whereas guidelines exist for the development of meaningful and distinctive supply chain relationships, no two situations are identical. No shortcuts or substitutes exist for the detailed commitment necessary to build and develop successful long-term relationships. In dealing with customers, suppliers, and service providers, firms must specify roles, define guideline, share information, risk and gains, resolve conflict and, when necessary, be able to dissolve an unproductive arrangement. The managerial skill sets required for successful supply chain integration requires development of a unique inter-organizational culture. This is particularly true since the dynamic environment in which firms compete requires regular review of assumptions, processes, and measures to assure that relationships remain relevant.

THE ASSESSMENT DIAGNOSTIC

To help managers determine improvement opportunities, an assessment diagnostic is provided on the accompanying compact disk. The value of the assessment process is to allow firms to compare perceptions of their integrative achievement with perceptions reported by other managers within specific industries and across a range of combined industries. Two frameworks are presented: (1) Supply Chain Integration (Supply Chain 2000) and; (2) Logistics Integration (Logistics 99). Since Supply Chain 2000 is the most comprehensive of the two frameworks, it is discussed first.

Supply Chain 2000

The Supply Chain 2000 framework and related assessment process focus on measuring achievement across the six integrative competencies that characterize leading supply chain performance. They embody twenty-five capabilities identified and confirmed in the research as critical to success. Thus, the assessment process serves to operationalize the framework presented in Exhibit 2-2. This book is focused on the more-inclusive Supply Chain 2000 framework. Appendix C presents detailed results by individual question of the 1999 Supply Chain 2000 research survey. The data is also included as a file in the compact disk.

Logistics 99

Logistics 99 is a *subset* of capabilities contained within the more comprehensive Supply Chain 2000 Framework. The purpose of the Logistics 99 framework and assessment process is to examine the specific challenges related to a firm's internal logistics integration. The Logistics 99 benchmark data is structured and presented identical to the Logistics 95 framework. Thus, while the benchmark data is fresh, the framework replicates the original competency structure of Logistics 95. Logistics 99 is provided for managers who used the 1995 model and wish to compare their previous positioning to today's level of achievement. A statistical comparison and reconciliation of data shifts from Logistics 95 to Logistics 99 are presented in Appendix D.

SUMMARY

The Supply Chain 2000 framework introduced in Chapter Two provides a comprehensive view of logistical integration across an operating spectrum spanning from raw material source to end-customers. The framework focuses on integrative behavior required to achieve superior supply change management. Attention in the next six chapters is directed to a more in-depth examination of each of the identified competencies and their supporting capabilities. Keep in mind that capabilities constitute behavior that can be learned, implemented, and measured. They, and the competencies they engender, are the focus of meaningful change management.

CUSTOMER
INTEGRATION

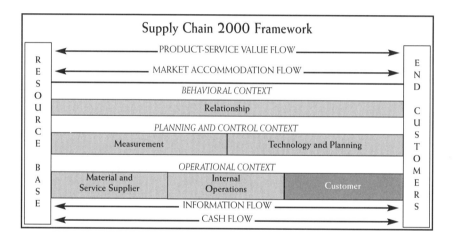

Supply Chain 2000 Framework

PRODUCT-SERVICE VALUE FLOW

MARKET ACCOMMODATION FLOW

BEHAVIORAL CONTEXT

Relationship

PLANNING AND CONTROL CONTEXT

| Measurement | Technology and Planning |

OPERATIONAL CONTEXT

| Material and Service Supplier | Internal Operations | Customer |

INFORMATION FLOW

CASH FLOW

RESOURCE BASE

END CUSTOMERS

*T*he Supply Chain 2000 framework and assessment process suggests that the best place to start the search for integration gaps is to review how a firm coordinates with customers. At the first meeting of the Spartan Enterprises task force, Amy Thornton opened the discussion by describing her phone conversation at 8:15 that morning with Winfred Adams, Director of Procurement at Super, Inc., one of Spartan's largest customers. The Super account was a success story linked to Spartan's improved logistical service but, the relationship was not secure and had become downright adversarial of late. The service levels established when Spartan was selected as the category leader more than 6 years before were no longer suitable. Super's tighter delivery windows, increased performance requirements, requests for special packaging and labeling, and demands for immediate reimbursement for unsold product had strained Spartan's operational capabilities and the relationship. Super also wanted Spartan to take responsibility for palletizing, and labeling orders for specific stores, which meant higher handling costs plus the added expense of applying barcodes and labels on product. Furthermore, Super was reviewing its suppliers, and one condition for preferential status was to pledge a 5 percent annual reduction in cost of delivered product to Super.

"It was not a good way to start the week," Amy said, and she went on to describe Winfred's complaint about the latest service breakdown. One of Super's distribution centers had turned away a delivery that was part of a direct-store cross-dock because it arrived six hours earlier than scheduled. Amy had pointed out that Spartan's transportation department was simply trying to follow the guidelines for savings by consolidating multiple shipments on one delivery truck. Roughly $2 million had been invested in routing and scheduling software to help them reach their goals. Winfred had said she understood the desire to reduce costs, but Super would not accept shipments outside the assigned delivery window, even if it meant that Spartan's high-tech routing and scheduling plan was inconvenienced!

This specific instance followed the reporting of some depressing performance measures over the last week. It was becoming more and more difficult to keep the firm's perfect order performance on a positive trend due to increasing new product introductions and expanded marketing activities. In addition, Spartan had seen its inventory turns slip by 20 percent over the last year.

Amy and the group reflected on the telephone call. This, they thought, was exactly what the benchmarking report meant by a customer integration gap. Bill Wingate, Director of Logistics Operations, stated it best: "We spend all our time working with new customers or trying to fix breakdowns in operations with old customers. We hardly ever take the time to meet with our top customers to discuss how they are planning to change their business and how we can figure in those plans. And, we view all customers the same – we set average service levels for an average group of service offerings for everyone. Since we still don't understand the differing cost/service mixes for different customers, we can't develop the capability to provide differentiated service."

At the weekly task force update, Charlie agreed with the group's conclusions. "The situation with Super is not unique," he said. "Most of our top customers are pressuring suppliers to tailor operations to improve service and reduce cost. But those same customers can't or won't provide the operating information necessary to help us do the job. Usually, they make operating decisions and resource allocations based on their marketing-based sales forecasts, but the estimates are wrong about as often as they're right. It's tough to predict product sales when your customer won't tell you when they're planning to promote. And still they want us to give them better service at lower prices. Something has got to change in the way we deal with our cus-

tomers – and in the way we expect them to deal with us. Some of our clients are exploring the possibilities of Internet-based communications. Could this be the way to bridge the gap with suppliers? Or is it just another passing fad?"

Consistent success ultimately depends on a firm's ability to create value for end-customers by providing products and services at prices that cover total cost and provide a profit. There is nothing new or revolutionary about this challenge. What is new, however, is the way some companies are implementing it. They start by understanding how end-customers define value. That can be very difficult, particularly when each customer may have a different perspective.

In general, value has long been thought of in two ways. The first is economic value, which involves operational economies of scale and scope to generate efficiency. For the past 50 years, cost trade-off analyses have supported volume procurement, consolidated transportation, economy of scale manufacturing, and inventory buffers. To help achieve economic value, managers have used such concepts as economic lot sizing, activity-based costing and lowest total landed cost. For customers, economic value means low price underpinned with an acceptable degree of service.

The second notion is market value, which involves supply chain effectiveness. Firms satisfy customer needs by performing tasks or services better than any competitor. For example, total quality management, time-based competition, and benchmarking initiatives frequently are used to reduce waste from operations and ensure customer satisfaction. Success is measured by how well service performance goals and operating standards are met, such as on-time delivery, shrinkage levels, and number of customer complaints. For customers, market value means product service positioning, such as quality, assortment, availability, timeliness, and accessibility of delivery.

Both economic and market value are important to customers and historically have driven business success. Over the last decade, however, leading firms have increasingly recognized that success also hinges on intimacy with the customer, that is, end-customer integration. The focus is on doing those things that will make a real difference in the competitiveness of the customer. Customer integration involves identifying the long-term requirements, expectations, and preferences of current and/or potential customers and markets. It also involves positioning for sustainable performance. A company that wants a lasting competitive edge must be proactive with its customers, anticipate their expectations, and measure the extent to which it helps customers succeed. This will ensure a focus on doing the things that create value. The customer benefit is business success. In the next millennium, value that facilitates customer success will increasingly take precedence over economic and market value.

In the extreme, customer integration means generating *unique and profitable* product/service offerings. This, of course, is in direct contrast to principles of mass marketing, and it is certainly cost prohibitive to all but the most narrowly defined market niche firms. A more realistic goal for most firms is to build lasting and distinctive relationships with *customers or business segments of choice* rather than all customers or segments. This can be accomplished by tailoring product/service offerings to meet the exact needs and desires of specific customers, not the average needs of the average customer. Such focused customer relevancy requires the total integration of business processes.

Managers must assess their firm's resources relative to the needs and desires of select individual customers. Then the firm can deploy its resources and capabilities to perform customer-valued activities and services that competitors cannot match at all or at a reasonable cost. Since few firms can satisfy every potential customer or market segment, each must decide when and when *not* to compete based on the fit between its strengths and customer needs. Therefore, customer integration depends upon thorough knowledge of the firm's and its supply chain partner's capabilities as well as customer requirements and expectations.

When competition is intense, product/service quality, features, and pricing converge to a single industry standard that defines basic service expectations. In other words, customers simply expect that level of operational effectiveness from everyone. It does not distinguish one company from another. Doing things that a customer really values, however, provides an important differential. A firm that establishes close relationships with customers can provide heightened value by understanding and excelling in the areas that customers consider important.

Four customer integration capabilities are integral to the Supply Chain 2000 framework. These are segmental focus, relevancy, responsiveness, and flexibility. Each is discussed below.

SEGMENTAL FOCUS

The segmental focus capability is critical to high achievement logistics and supply chain management. Firms demonstrating a segmental focus develop customer specific programs designed to generate maximum customer success. In effect, segmental focus implies that firms should develop customized supply chains for major customers. One manager stated it this way: "I manage 24 different supply systems – 23 for my best 23 customers and the 24th for everybody else."

Four indicators characterize the segmental focus capability. They are end-customer value identification, logistics as a basis for customer segmentation, unique logistics strategies, and integration of customer requirements across business units. A discussion of each indicator follows.

The first indicator is the existence of initiatives to identify the end-customer value-added that can be provided by logistics. To succeed in mature markets, firms must take the idea of customer focus to new levels. In order for a firm to become the preferred supplier for its top clients, managers of a firm must find ways to help clients become the top choice of *their* customers. Service providers can ensure growth if they identify and provide logistical services that are important to and add value for their customers' customers. Differentiation will result from *understanding* the specific service bundles required for the success of key customers.

Competitive advantage is facilitated if important customers are among the average firms but such is rarely the case. Top customers typically operate within significantly different classes of trade. If customers deemed most important to strategic success have needs that differ from average capabilities, then some competitor will eventually find a way to serve them better. High index achieving firms increasingly understand that the key to sustainable competitive service edge comes from uniquely meeting the needs and desires of the *important* customers. In general, important customers are the small percent of the customer base that account for a high percent of revenues or who have the potential to become part of this select group. By creating unique value-added services that exceed the industry level of basic service, a firm can protect important customers from competitive inroads.

The second indicator is the ability to use logistical requirements to *segment* the customer base. This indicator of segmental focus concerns a firm's support of the philosophy that a customer's logistical needs as well as marketing characteristics can be used as a basis of segmentation. The philosophy implies that the firm rejects the traditional mentality that implies all customers share the same type and level of logistical need and accepts the notion that logistical need is a key variant of customer demand. The traditional service approach is based on the averaged needs of all customers. By definition, any customers with service or cost requirements that fall outside the average range will not be satisfied. Customers with needs that differ from the average either do not get what they want or must pay for what they do not need. Four-day delivery, for example, may be too slow for many customers who would be willing to pay more for faster service and too fast for other customers who would be satisfied with slower service at less cost.

The third indicator of segmental focus capability is the actual *application* of different and unique logistics strategies for different customers. Once the service expectations of top customers are identified, providers must find a unique way to accommodate them. In establishing the categories of customer need, firms should consider both the service mix that customers need or desire as well as what level of those services will satisfy them. One manufacturer has redesigned significant components of its standard service package based on information generated by customers. Another has redefined product classifications according to customer-driven service expectations for fast and slow moving products. In both situations, the definition of planned service is based on customer specifications. These unique specifications have led to operational adjustments that serve each important customer and/or customer segment better.

One of the major food manufacturers has refined its supply chain to serve major customers directly while using wholesale distributors to service others. Despite the added operational complexity and higher costs associated with managing multiple logistics supply chains, it is clear that customization is required to gain and maintain top customers. Specialized assortment packaging, unitizing, relabeling, pricing, and barcoding represent areas that can be tailored to meet specific customer needs. Another major grocery manufacturer divides customers into key accounts and regular accounts. The latter are managed as a single group, following standard operating procedures. Key accounts are managed by dedicated cross-functional teams that focus on identifying and accommodating customer requirements to ensure high-level value-added service.

The fourth segmental focus indicator is combining logistical services across customer business units. High index achieving firms extend the idea of customer success horizontally across strategic business units. These special customers are commonly referred to as *Enterprise Customers*. Sharing information about customer requirements across divisions and coordinating logistical operations facilitates unique solutions. In addition to leveraging operational economy of scale such coordination can also reduce administrative complexity.

One electronics manufacturer consolidates finished goods inventory for three different divisions that sell to the same retail customers. Complexity and costs are reduced through shared facility costs, lower inventory levels, and transportation consolidation.

An emerging concept being tested or implemented by several leading firms is to offer customers varying levels of service at various prices. A customer may select delivered pricing, customer pick-up, palletized delivery, and mixed pallets as examples of service offerings. The trade name for such a practice is *menu pricing*. Each option has an associated price. Clients can select the service level and cost that most closely meet their needs.

High index achieving firms are strongly differentiated from average achievers on the capability of segmental focus. High index firms achieved substantially greater scores than average firms on all four of the primary indicators. These firms identify their strategically important customers, understand their needs and desires, and know how to utilize their resources to serve them better than their competitors.

RELEVANCY

High index achieving firms understand that customer success is not a static proposition. These firms have developed the capability of relevancy to ensure that they maintain customer focus by continuously modifying services they offer to match changing customer needs. Achievement of relevancy is indicated by logistics operations that focus on key customer success, use of formal visioning processes, pursuit of business relationships with customers, and review of current service offerings to determine future commitment. It is also necessary to maintain relevancy with suppliers so the firm's influence can be maintained.

The first relevancy indicator assesses the degree to which a firm's logistical operations are focused on facilitating key customer success. The success strategies of high index achieving firms stress commitment to key customers. These firms continuously refine their focus so that they can constantly meet the customer's changing expectations. The things they do remain relevant to their most important customers. Formal visioning processes, the second indicator of relevancy, identify future customer logistics requirements and provide a primary means for high achievers to ensure relevance. These processes provide a view of the future and enable management to plan for potential requirements rather than reacting to change in a crisis mode. It is not by accident that many industry leaders seem always to be one step ahead of the pack, introducing new products and services that raise the competitive bar just as other firms are finally able to equal the previous performance.

The third indicator of relevancy requires firms to actively pursue business relationships and programs that solicit involvement with customers at levels that exceed those associated with traditional sales transactions. Establishing joint business development teams, for example, involves customers in long-term plans to identify future logistics needs and demonstrate a commitment to retain relevancy. One firm cited the establishment of logistics development teams to sell the benefits of improved supply chain integration using a spreadsheet-based cost model. These customer teams regularly review specific service offerings, keeping track of opportunities for possible additions or deletions. One manager put the issue of customer relevancy quite succinctly. *"In mature markets the only sure way to grow is to share in the success of our customers. If we are the preferred supplier and they are the end-customer's choice, we can jointly identify breakthrough opportunities. Working together we can outperform the competition."*

High index achieving firms push relevancy even farther. They anticipate and protect selected customers from all types of threatening change. These firms are so close to vital operations of key customers that interlocking programs and activities become the norm. This process, which we earlier referred to as *customer cocooning*, locks in desired business by making it hard to switch suppliers. Cocooning is difficult and costly because it involves different structures to enable different mixes and levels of service offerings. This kind of relevancy requires a business relationship built on genuine concern, cooperation in resolving problems, and joint identification of breakthrough opportunities. High index achieving firms cite customer cocooning as a key way to help customers adapt to change. It enables them to become so valuable to the customer that the cost of switching suppliers becomes too great.

Supply chain management requires firms to focus on emerging needs and wants of selected customers. The fourth indicator of relevancy reflects the degree to which firms review current service offerings with an eye toward potential expansion or discontinuance. This relevancy indicator depends on joint research and information sharing. While the cooperative link between supplier research and development and customer new product commercialization is well documented, the extension of the joint process to include logistical synchronization offers a new dimension of customer relevancy. Most businesses really do not make money selling. The market determines price. High achieving firms attain profitability by buying right and then not losing margin through poor performance.

High index achieving firms were differentiated from average achievers on all four relevancy indicators. The key differentiator between high and average achieving firms for the relevancy capability, however, was the degree to which high achievers use formal visioning processes. High achievers employ this technique extensively compared to average firms.

RESPONSIVENESS

Most businesses spend considerable time and effort on planning and forecasting future logistical requirements in the hope that they can efficiently allocate resources to meet customer requests. It is very unlikely that plans will materialize as expected. Plans are best viewed as a reasonable starting point rather than an accurate prediction of the future. Responsiveness reflects the extent to which firms are capable of accommodating unique and/or unplanned customer requests. High index achieving firms respond more easily and quickly than competitors to unforeseen requests, which means that they capitalize on uncertainty to enhance customer integration. Responsiveness indicators assess firms' ability to authorize special customer requests, synchronize operations with customers and suppliers, automatically accommodate stockouts, and implement preplanned solutions.

In most firms, manufacturing and logistics operations are completed far in advance of the actual sale date to guarantee inventory availability. The problem is that many factors affect sales and are difficult or impossible to predict. Sales patterns are often erratic, with an abrupt beginning and end. The first responsiveness indicator assesses firms' operational capability to authorize and accommodate special requests from select customers without delays. High index achieving firms develop such responsiveness by providing decision-makers with information and authority to rapidly reconfigure operations with suppliers and customers. Full and timely information disclosure reduces dependence on forecasts, and enables authorized managers to rapidly deploy production and/or delivery resources to support the sale. Shared expectations make the vast majority of operations routine. This allows free time and resources to deal with unexpected situations that arise.

The second relevancy indicator assesses a firm's ability to synchronize logistical operations with customer and supplier operations. Here the focus is not necessarily on speed but on timing. Synchronization is the process whereby multiple firms or locations work out the effective sequencing of product and information flows. Many failures of just-in-time arrangements are due more to poor synchronization than to the inability to respond rapidly. A single firm can achieve speed. Synchronization requires two or more firms to share information and coordinate operations. Many continuous replenishment programs, for example, shift the product sorting responsibility from distribution warehouses to retail stores. Synchronizing delivery with labor availability ensures seamless and efficient receipt at the retail destination.

A firm's ability to respond to unforeseen customer requests is limited by the degree to which the relationship is based on preferred terms of sale and designated ship-to locations that introduce operational rigidity. High index achieving firms have operational capabilities that enable them to accommodate special requests and take advantage of unique opportunities by altering logistical operations to fit the circumstances. For example, product may be shipped directly to a retail store in one instance and may move through a distribution warehouse the next time, depending upon stock availability. As appropriate, the product may be configured for a flow-through or cross-dock assortment process. In other situations, a third-party consolidator may satisfy a customer's needs.

The third responsiveness indicator tracks cross-shipment, which allows firms to assign customers to primary and secondary stockpoints so that stockouts are automatically accommodated. Some firms have a procedure whereby orders that contain more than 50 percent merchandise manufactured at a single factory are identified during order processing. When possible, a partial order is originated at the source factory, and the balance of the order is merged enroute, either at a warehouse or at a transportation carrier's terminal facility. This eliminates the need for warehouse handling on part of the order. The customer gets the product rapidly, and the supplier avoids traditional handling and storage cost.

Pre-transaction planning by supply chain members, the fourth indicator of responsiveness makes special arrangements work. Pre-transaction planning enables high achieving firms to accommodate a wide range of unique customer requirements by implementing preplanned solutions. Instead of following rigid guidelines, high achieving firms scan the range of delivery alternatives and establish appropriate trigger points for each in advance of actual operations. Identifying which customer requests will trigger which type of alternative aligns the order-to-delivery options. Linkages with logistical service suppliers to support the options are established in advance.

Although average index achieving firms scored lower than high achievers on each of the responsiveness indicators, this capability did not notably differentiate the two groups. Such lack of differentiation suggest that the capabilities related to responsiveness are becoming ingrained as expected service attributes. The most significant area in which high achievers were differentiated from average firms was in implementation of preplanned solutions. These results indicate that responsiveness is a requirement for current logistical operations but responsiveness alone does not mark a firm as a high achiever.

FLEXIBILITY

The complexity of logistics can overwhelm the ability to react to anything out of the ordinary. Countless details, such as dock height, pallet size, and delivery presentation, are involved in daily operations. It is not unusual for one shipment to contain varied quantities of hundreds of different stockkeeping units. Value-added services, unique requests, and multinational movements magnify the complexity. Continued research at MSU has shown that routinization of fundamental work minimizes individual problems that need resolution as well as the demands placed on managerial or supervisory time. As a result, talent typically expended on day-to-day details is available to deal with unexpected events. Though it may appear to be inconsistent, such routinization is a prerequisite for flexibility

Firms that know how to avoid the pitfalls of forecast-driven logistics have more flexibility when adapting to unexpected operational circumstances. Flexibility improves responsiveness by enabling a firm to deliver the need identified through responsiveness. Primary flexibility indicators include increased operational supply chain collaboration, increase in responsive or pull-based logistical capability, development of information linkages with supply chain partners, and use of time and form postponement.

The first indicator of flexibility focuses on the benefits of supply chain collaboration. Flexibility is improved when organizations cooperate. Each member of a supply chain may have limited versatility, but the combined leverage within the chain can be substantial. High achieving firms with strong ties to supply chain partners can re-deploy assets from areas of under-utilization to areas of critical need in a timely fashion to defuse crises. This requires information linkages that enable accurate, cross-organizational information to be accessed in real-time.

Developing responsive or pull logistical capability as compared to pre-determined or push capability is the second indicator of flexibility. Flexibility centers on the ability to avoid premature commitment to an irreversible course of action. Most logistical actions can be reversed, but doing so is costly. Rigid operations are often characterized by production based on forecasts, followed by allocation (push) of inventory to warehouse and retail locations in anticipation of future sales. Inaccurate forecasts, however, often create inventory imbalances and result in price reductions to move merchandise. Nevertheless, anticipatory logistics facilitates economies of scale in transportation and warehousing, and relieves manufacturing of the need to hold finished goods inventory for long periods. Several manufacturers of personal computers exemplify how flexibility and make-to-order can change supply chain service and inventory dynamics. The direct to end-customer model responds to actual demand, sourcing and shipping only after a customized order is in received.

Information technology now facilitates the forward movement of inventory to be postponed until such time as exact specifications can be finalized. The third indicator of flexibility involves development of information linkages with customers. High index achieving firms' combat inaccurate forecasts by exchanging real-time information with customers to permit considerable last-minute accommodation without loss of planned efficiencies. The market or a specific customer *pulls* exact quantities and assortments of products as needed. The shift from anticipatory logistics and push procedures to postponement logistics and pull practices may be the most important paradigm shift of the 21ˢᵗ Century.

The idea of waiting until exact customer requirements are known before finalizing product configuration has a fundamental appeal. Pull practices based on meeting actual requirements reduce the risk and error associated with anticipatory logistics. As opposed to doing what may turn out to be the wrong thing in a very efficient manner, the goal is to do what is right as efficiently as possible. The final flexibility indicator assesses the development of methods that enable firms to postpone final product manufacturing, packaging, labeling, or assembly until customer requirements become more certain. Postponement logistics was not possible when information technology was inadequate to orchestrate the pull cues. Today, such technology is both available and affordable. The result is increasing adoption of two types of postponement, time and form.

Time postponement delays forward inventory movement as late in the operating cycle as possible. Flexibility in meeting customer assortment and volume requirements is greater and inventories are smaller when product is held in fewer but larger stockpiles. Form postponement delays finalizing the product until exact customer requirements are known. An extreme example is manufacturing make-to-order, although in most situations time does not allow this alternative. The challenge is to create the flexibility typical of make-to-order manufacturing while retaining economies of scale.

One example of what manufacturing firms are considering to foster flexibility and responsiveness to their customers is a move toward cellular or lean manufacturing. This requires a major cultural shift away from a strict make-to-forecast/make-to-stock environment toward a focus on responding exactly to what the customer wants, when they want it. Although implementation requires a significant shift in measurements, compensation, and planning and scheduling protocol, most firms are positive regarding the outcome.

Form postponement has obvious implications for manufacturing practice, but its effects are not limited to the production floor. Work that serves to differentiate products may be performed at logistical or retail facilities and can be separated from basic production activities. For example, it may be desirable to postpone labeling, coloring, accessorizing, assembling, and assortment packaging until specific customer preferences are known. When these product customization tasks are done separately from basic production, manufacturing can focus on large economical runs of standard, basic, or common parts and products.

Flexibility, like responsiveness, was not a capability on which high achieving firms differentiated themselves significantly from average achievers. High achieving firms scored higher than average firms did on each of the four indicators, although average firms achieved levels that demonstrated proficiency comparable to high achievers. The lone exception to this statement is the degree to which high achievers have developed responsive or pull logistical capabilities.

SUMMARY

Customer integration is a competency that enables firms to build lasting distinctiveness with customers of choice. It requires firms to assess their own strengths and weaknesses in service capability in terms of the needs and desires of top customers. Since few firms can fully satisfy every customer or market segment, leading firms are increasingly using such assessment to select where and where not to compete. Top firms recognize the differences among economic, market, and customer value and design offerings according to the relative importance of each value proposition to their major customers. If a customer requires services or service performance in which the firm is not strong, then these special requests are increasingly being outsourced to third-party providers.

Four capabilities drive customer integration. A *segmental focus* reflects the belief that all customers do not have the same service expectations and do not necessarily want or deserve the same overall level of service. It flows from the idea that firms should identify core customers best suited to be their business clients and then meet or exceed expectations by providing unique value-added services. These services may include assignment of specific focus teams to identify, design, implement, and refine specialized and synchronized offerings. *Relevancy*, the second driver of customer integration, requires firms to satisfy not only existing needs but also those that may emerge. By continuously matching service capabilities with changing customer expectations, providers can stay ahead of competition.

Responsiveness and flexibility, the other two drivers of customer integration, depend on operating systems that quickly react to change rather than forward deployment of inventory in anticipation of requirements. *Responsiveness* is the efficient and effective accommodation of unique customer requests. *Flexibility* is the capability to adapt to unexpected operational circumstances. Gathering and exchanging information throughout the supply chain as contrasted to guessing what may happen facilitates both capabilities. Exhibit 3-1 summarizes the competency customer integration and its four capabilities.

EXHIBIT 3-1

CUSTOMER INTEGRATION

The competency of building lasting distinctiveness with customers of choice.

Segmental Focus: Development of customer specific programs designed to generate maximum customer success.

Relevancy: Maintenance and modification of customer focus to continuously match changing expectations.

Responsiveness: Accommodation of unique and/or unplanned customer requirements.

Flexibility: Adaptation to unexpected operational circumstances.

INTERNAL INTEGRATION

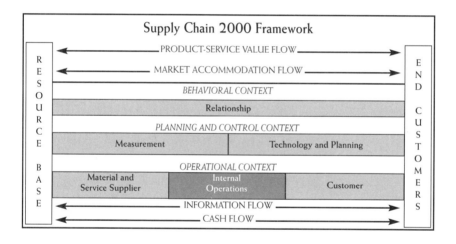

Supply Chain 2000 Framework

*C*harlie knew that benchmarking assessments often serve the same purpose as consultants – they confirm the suspicions of the manager most closely linked to the process. Charlie made such an assessment using the Supply Chain 2000 framework and it revealed that the integration of internal operations at Spartan Enterprises was seriously deficient. Problems with customer service gave Charlie headaches, but the challenges he faced in coordinating operating departments gave him ulcers. The cross-functional task force would have to address internal integration.

Charlie and Amy agreed that before any serious changes could be made in dealing with customers, they first had to coordinate logistical activities with marketing, purchasing, and production. "Do you remember that time I dragged you to the symphony in Chicago?" Amy asked. "You mean the night I had to miss the Cubs game so that I could prove I had culture? How could I forget?" Charlie replied. "Well," Amy continued, "if Spartan were an orchestra, we would make a noise that sounded more like rush hour in Manhattan than Beethoven's Fifth. At best we each perform our own separate piece of the music, with one finishing before the next can start. Think how long it would have taken the orchestra if it had played that way." Charlie smiled. "So you're saying that's how long our customers have to wait for an order?" "Right," Amy said, "and a process like that makes it hard to respond to any changes that come up in the meantime."

At the first task force meeting, Amy asked the group to list the internal operations that affected Spartan's ability to provide the kind of service that customers were increasingly demanding. It was agreed that operations consisted of four distinct processes. First, marketing had to create demand based on Spartan's competitive advantages. Then, once a demand estimate was made, sufficient raw materials and subcomponents to satisfy it had to be located and purchased. Next, these had to be moved to a facility where they could be transformed into products. Finally, the proper mix of finished goods had to be selected, merged, and delivered to customers. Of course, all this had to be done at a cost that did not exceed the value to end-customers, with a little left over for profit. Historically this was accomplished by planning, sourcing, making, and delivering product in large volumes to take advantage of economies of scale.

It all sounded pretty straightforward. Sixty years before, when Spartan was created, it probably was. The market at that time extended roughly 500 miles from headquarters, where the only plant was located, and all suppliers were within that radius as well. As a result, market desires were well known or readily influenced to accept Spartan's offerings. As Spartan expanded, however, the operating environment became more complex. Work rules and routines and performance measures were established to deal with the complexity. These reflected the goals and objectives of each department based on what seemed to be the critical performance criteria. The criteria rarely changed even as conditions and needs changed. It was not surprising that the various internal departments operated in ways that often conflicted with others as well as overall Spartan and supply chain goals to the degree that they were stated.

Marketing, for example, dealt with customers and booked orders. Product managers and sales representatives were evaluated on their ability to obtain orders and not exceed their budgets in doing so. This involved forecasting demand and promoting product to ensure that the forecasts were met or exceeded. Whether the rest of the firm was aware of the spikes and valleys in demand that resulted from such promotions was another matter. This often meant that popular products were out of stock in regions where promotions were held and/or greater transportation costs were incurred to ship orders from distant distribution centers to prevent order deletions.

Managers throughout the food industry, for example, joked that consumers only ate during the last week of the month because that's when they shipped 80 percent of their product. Of course, that's also when marketing offered strong promotions to ensure monthly goals were achieved. Furthermore, the high failure rate of new products created lots of dead stock. Regional distribution centers often had too much slow-moving product and not enough fast movers because forecasts were inaccurate.

Meanwhile, in another part of the company, purchasing sought to locate a source of stable supply and secure the lowest unit cost. This often was accomplished by purchasing in large quantities to gain lowest unit prices. The fact that this practice resulted in higher material inventory levels and warehousing costs was of little concern to purchasing managers, since they were measured by pure purchase cost. Bill Wingate could remember several times when he quickly had to arrange for additional public warehousing because the volume purchased on a deal exceeded available storage capacity. To complicate matters, purchasing also controlled inbound transportation. It was usually included in the purchase price for delivered product, and information regarding the costs of inbound freight couldn't even be passed to the transportation planners for potential backhauls or consolidation with outbound freight.

Production grew under different conditions. After World War II Spartan had all it could do to meet the pent up demand of domestic consumers. New innovations in technology enabled production to reach previously unthinkable volume levels, but the equipment was expensive, and its cost had to be spread over extended production runs to justify the fixed investment. As a result, production planners were encouraged to schedule economical manufacturing runs based on demand forecasts for periods of a year or longer. This mentality had begun to change in the last several years, but planners still resist short production runs and frequent changeovers as they struggle to achieve utilization goals set for operating equipment and personnel. Some efficient producers could even force their products on consumers who readily accepted performance mediocrity. Again, the cost of storing the inventory from these long runs fell to logistics.

After the latest meeting, Charlie mused that somehow everyone had to read from the same page with respect to the goals and objectives of operational activity and have their compensation tied to achieving these goals and objectives. If we could only comprehend and share the demand cues we receive and then respond to them, we could integrate planning and operations and get this orchestra playing together, Charlie thought. But when we forecast case volumes based on history at the same time production is coming up with its own volume-friendly forecasts, and then marketing chimes in with numbers that reflect what they hope future demand will be, how can we help but sound like a traffic jam?

In order to refocus an entire firm toward integrated performance, management must use the same sheet music regardless of functional responsibility. Such refocusing to achieve integrated management requires extensive behavioral change. The most fundamental challenge driving such change is the need to integrate marketing and sales, procurement, manufacturing and assembly, and finished goods distribution. Internal process integration requires a fundamental commitment to process excellence throughout an enterprise in a coordinated effort to achieve a high level of basic service at the lowest total cost. Process excellence is achieved by linking operations into a seamless, synchronized operational flow to satisfy customer requirements. Process integration unleashes a synergistic effect that enhances overall performance.

Current thought regarding integrated logistics in supply chain management is based on the total cost concept. The concept proposes that logistics should be viewed as an interconnected competency that performs best when managed holistically. Total system cost may be reduced when expenditures in one or more functional areas are increased. For example, the higher cost of using airfreight to move finished goods to market may be more than offset by lower inventory and warehousing costs and a decrease in unsalables. Top firms reengineer traditional functions to achieve better process interconnectivity.

Some of the most intriguing examples of using logistics to stimulate effective cost trade-offs have occurred in the mass merchant segment of the retail industry, which has made significant advances in integrating internal functions. Firms often sacrifice lowest cost logistics in order to achieve total cost efficiency. In the computer industry, one components manufacturer, transfers products by premium airfreight all over the world during the assembly process. This approach is complex and expensive, but there are substantial savings in labor, duties, and value-added taxes. The integrated strategy results in quick-to-market capabilities for new product innovations at the lowest total cost for procurement, manufacturing, and logistics. Similarly, a department store chain air ships finished goods from Pacific Rim clothing suppliers to North American distribution hubs. Transportation costs far exceed those of sea freight, but the reduced cycle times allow drastic reductions in inventory, quick response to changing fashion tastes, and fewer markdowns.

The capabilities that link internal activities into a seamless efficient process are cross-functional unification, standardization, simplification, compliance, and structural adaptation. Each is discussed in the following sections.

CROSS-FUNCTIONAL UNIFICATION

Successful internal integration centers on the ability to merge multiple operational activities into one synchronized, synergistic process. Aligning the processes through which human assets are managed and motivated with overall strategy is a major requirement. The primary indicators of cross-functional unification are reduced formal organizational structure, focus on managing processes instead of functions, middle manager empowerment, and use of cross-functional work teams.

Far too often, organizational and compensation structures motivate personnel to pull in directions that make sense for departmental goals but conflict with strategic goals. This has become increasingly difficult, as corporate goals are refined to include Economic Value Added (EVA), return on capital, growth, customer retention, and productivity. This is particularly true in a labor-intensive process such as logistics. Most logistics work requires hands-on effort. Workers frequently need to be self-motivated and self-disciplined. The logistics process is continuous, occurring every hour of every day throughout the year. The supervisory challenge is considerable, since more than 95 percent of the work occurs outside the direct vision of supervisory managers.

The first indicator of cross-functional unification is reduction of formal organizational structure to more fully integrate operations. For decades, managers sought to direct logistics activities by creating formal organizational structures. In order to facilitate integration, the prevailing belief was that as many logistics functions as possible should be assembled within the command and control structure. The emphasis was on communication up and down the organization, not horizontally across activities. It was common practice to assess the relevance of logistical organizations by measuring the scope of direct functional authority and responsibility. The assumption was that a greater functional span of control meant better integration. This approach may have facilitated coordination of activities within individual functional area, but it minimized interaction between areas.

There is increasing recognition among firms that achieve high scores on the Supply Chain 2000 index that grouping functional areas into vertically structured departments under a single manager does not ensure or facilitate integration. A more powerful organizing concept is to share information across functional areas in order to satisfy customer requirements at the lowest total cost. Under this free flow and exchange of information, middle managers no longer are information gatekeepers. Managers become enablers of informed employees who have the authority to do whatever is necessary to respond to customers while managing total costs. This shift in orientation from managing functions to managing processes represents the second indicator of cross-functional unification.

No single organizational structure will represent best practice in the 21st Century. Instead, organizational structures will reflect the unique culture of each enterprise. Certain general attributes of cross-functional integration, however, will be common in all organizations. One such commonality, empowerment, is the third indicator of cross-functional unification. High achieving firms encourage front-line managers and employees to use their own discretion within policy guidelines to make timely decisions. Empowered employees have the authority and information necessary to do a job and they are trusted to perform work without intense over-the-shoulder supervision. This is especially appealing in logistics, since most work occurs outside the purview of direct supervision. For example, a route delivery driver may be empowered to reorder a damaged product for a customer immediately upon discovery, rather than have the customer make a claim through channels. The result is faster and more customer-relevant performance.

Another general attribute closely associated with empowerment is the use of cross-functional work teams to manage day-to-day operations, the final indicator of cross-functional unification. Teams can focus collective talents on autonomous work challenges. One example is a team assigned to a customer account to facilitate all activities required to help that customer achieve success. The customer has a single point of contact for ordering, status reporting, and problem resolution. Such teams also work closely with customers to develop tailored responses to unique opportunities and typically have representation from sales, marketing, logistics, production, and accounting. The team has authority to make tactical decisions and is held accountable for its performance.

A common practice of functionally integrated organizations is training and education. Programs based on individual experience and expertise are designed to help transfer knowledge to others in the organization. This requires finding trained and trainable individuals who are capable of applying essential technologies and have the skills required for empowered management. Continued education is needed to avoid obsolescence. As personnel switch jobs both within and between companies at an accelerating rate, it becomes even more critical to capture the experience and knowledge of key workers. Such knowledge transfer serves to help newly hired personnel avoid inefficiencies of repetitive mistakes and rapidly learn about the best ways to do a job.

High index achieving firms are differentiated from average achievers on cross-functional unification capability. High index firms achieved superior scores compared to average firms on each of the four indicators of cross-functional unification, particularly on the degree to which they utilize cross-functional work teams. While the means for average firms indicated that they are implementing these concepts, they are not doing so at the levels of the high achievers.

STANDARDIZATION

Firms must discover how to deal with the logistical complexity of customer-focused operations and the need to provide unique value-added services that result from a segmental customer focus. Such accommodation is necessary to remain competitive, but it leads to a proliferation of services and activities that can vary by market area and customer. Moreover, desirable human resource capabilities such as empowerment and cross-functional teams contribute to the variation in work practices. All these complexities limit the effectiveness of system-wide improvements and increase the difficulty of transferring personnel between locations.

One proven way to deal with variation in work practices and the workforce is to establish standard policies, procedures, and practices to facilitate synchronous operations. Standardization serves to accommodate logistical detail and complexity while reserving scarce resources to achieve responsiveness and flexibility. Rigorous standardization is often what affords the creative logistics manager the ability to be flexible. This relationship, more fully explained in the research addendum, is opposite of the more general social science belief that standardization of behavior results in rigidity. In the case of logistics, the ability to handle countless detail through standardization frees up critical managerial talent to flexibly deal with emerging problems. The primary indicators of standardization capability are the existence of common logistical policies and procedures, standardized operations, implementation of best practices, and active standardization initiatives.

The first two indicators of standardization address the degree to which firms have established common logistical policies and procedures to uniform operations and whether operations are, in fact, performed in a standardized manner. High index achieving firms make the effort to coordinate work policies and procedures across activities to ensure that all personnel understand appropriate responses. Existence of standard policies and procedures, however, is only part of the solution. High achievers also ensure that work performance corresponds with those standards.

The third indicator of standardization is active encouragement of best practice implementation. High index achievers identify best practices and implement them uniformly throughout the logistical system. The first step is to determine areas that most need improvement and hence would benefit most from consistent performance. Obvious targets are activities for which benefits can be clearly defined. For example, a firm may want to standardize methods for handling unique customer requests to ensure that all service personnel have the knowledge, training, and assets necessary to provide rapid and effective response at the lowest total cost.

The final standardization indicator reflects the degree to which firms use best practice information to initiate standard supply chain practices and procedures. This step involves mapping internal work processes and comparing these with alternative practices across companies, industries, and channel positions. Process mapping in combination with benchmarking provides an opportunity to evaluate both external and internal best practices and also enhances organizational learning. For example, one distribution center may employ a particular practice that is worth studying for possible use at other facilities. The merits of various practices can be debated in workshops or roundtable sessions, and the approaches identified are candidates for system-wide implementation. Since some of the practices under review may represent significant and important work, aggressive standardization programs ensure that all opinions are considered. Once general agreement is reached, however, dissenters must support the change. Chapters Ten and Eleven describe the process for managing such change. It is important that the process allow for reconsideration after sufficient time passes or when changes occur in the operating environment. This may be particularly necessary as companies seek to dovetail operations with those of supply chain partners or if industry-wide standards are altered.

Based on current best practice it seems likely that firms will increasingly adopt industry standards for information formats, such as EDI, barcodes, and Universal Container Code (UCC), and operational configurations, such as pallet size and containerization. Standardization in these areas will lower total industry costs, will facilitate supply chain unification, and may provide the platform for logistical operating solutions, such as cross-docking and continuous replenishment. Beyond these forms of industry standardization, leading firms are pursuing aggressive programs to realize the benefits of doing their own key work in the most efficient way throughout their operations.

Means for the four standardization indicators for average index achieving firms show that they emphasize this capability. High achievers, however, scored considerably higher on each of the indicators. High index achievers report particularly high levels of best practice implementation and active involvement in initiatives to standardize supply chain practices and operations.

SIMPLIFICATION

Logistics involves a massive amount of detail. Major organizations deal with thousands of products, customers, suppliers, and orders. They operate numerous facilities, each of which may interface to varying degrees with customers and suppliers. Managers can become so immersed in the detail of everyday work that they have limited time to think about improved efficiency and effectiveness. Logistics processes are further complicated by mergers, which have become frequent in recent decades. When one firm merges with another, integration of the two logistics systems is difficult to achieve, and redundancies often take years to sort out and eliminate. Logistics complexity is also introduced through new distribution channels, product packaging introductions, legal requirements, increased smaller orders, and reduced lead times.

To excel, firms must create operational order from the confusion inherent in complexity. High index achieving firms seek to streamline logistical operations in order to eliminate waste and redundancy and to improve the cost, time, and quality of service. Simplification stems from identifying, adopting, implementing, and continually improving best practices. Four indicators of simplification capability are redesigning work routines and processes, reducing marketing complexity, reducing facility and operational complexity, and developing channel-specific operations.

The first indicator of simplification is extensive redesign of work routines and processes. High achieving firms redesign their logistics work practices to increase value to customers. One firm, for example, found a significant time delay due to requirements for customer credit verification. Orders often were held as long as three days, although very few were actually rejected. The system was simplified to allow simultaneous picking and staging of orders while the credit verification was being completed. The result was a significant reduction in order cycle time plus a reduction in operating cost. Other examples of simplification through redesign are the use of flexible filling equipment on the same line or modular packaging.

Because the logistics process continually interfaces with multiple supply chain partners, reengineering must be coordinated both with customers and suppliers as well as within the enterprise. Many firms, for example, do a quality inspection of processed orders immediately before loading them for shipment to major customers. Upon receipt, the customer often completes a similar quality inspection. Time can be saved and costs reduced if the two developed a joint process to eliminate the redundancy.

The second simplification indicator relates to reductions in product/promotion oriented marketing complexity. Managers for high achieving firms counter this proliferation with continual pressure to reduce the number of products handled. That does not signify opposition to product innovation and market share growth. Rather, effort is made to create awareness of the logistical implications of product managers' decisions. One approach requires that all new product proposals be accompanied by an analysis of existing SKUs in the same category with identification of candidates for potential deletion. In one high achieving firm no product line addition is considered unless concurrent product deletions are suggested. Other firms require the use of full activity-based costing of new products (and for products that might be cannibalized as a result of the introduction). This encourages product managers to consider the total cost/service and the logistics *supportability* implications of new products and to make decisions that add to competitive differentiation.

A major cause of increased logistics complexity in recent years is the proliferation of brands, sizes, colors, flavors, labels, special packages, and other product features. The growth is driven primarily by the desire to meet the precise needs of as many customer segments as possible in order to increase market share. This has created an operational nightmare for logisticians: higher cost, higher inventory levels, more stockouts, and less forecast accuracy. Any market advantage gained by broadened product lines may be offset by costs generated by these negative logistical consequences. Leading firms consider all factors when implementing product line extensions.

Another cause of logistical complexity stems from the perception that local stock is always necessary to meet customer requirements. Although deliveries often can be made in a short time from most distant regional distribution centers, many firms still cling to local facilities. One company had twelve warehouses in one state to ensure next-day service to customers. Improvements in information technology and transportation infrastructure have made such local presence costly. Often, however, there are still emergency stashes of local inventories in sales' offices or unreported warehouse space. Firms with consolidated networks frequently can meet or exceed traditional service at dramatically lower cost, some of which may be shared with customers. Many firms are demonstrating that they can effectively serve the entire United States from one or two sites using creative transportation arrangements. Nevertheless, many managers still want inventory in local markets just in case. The third simplification indicator relates to reduction of facility and operational complexity. High achieving firms break down the artificial barriers to network rationalization and consolidation.

In purchasing, the traditional concept centered on having an assortment of materials and service suppliers with whom to deal in order to foster competition. This practice typically resulted in more purchase orders, more processing complexity in material inventory, fragmentation of product flows, and loss of leverage with suppliers. Price was the one and only motivator of supply base proliferation. Managers believed that transaction prices could be reduced by continually positioning one supplier against another. Since they were difficult to measure, the operational efficiencies that could be gained by using a few core suppliers and the leverage derived from consolidated purchasing were overlooked.

Although it may not be advisable to sole source strategically critical materials, many firms are successfully reducing the number of suppliers with whom they conduct business. A major automotive company, for example, decreased its material supply base from 50,000 to 3,000 firms worldwide. A firm in the steel industry discovered that it had used more than 800 trucking companies in one year in its outbound lanes alone. After extensive evaluation and negotiations, the number was reduced to 50 core carriers. Another strategy is to sole source logistics by facility, that is, rather than rely on a single carrier for the entire country, use a single carrier for each facility. This provides simplification and economies of scale without exposing the manufacturer to the risk of using one national carrier. While there are risks associated with reducing the number of suppliers and carriers, the results generally indicate that total costs decline following the initiative.

The final indicator of simplification capability is reducing operating complexity by developing separate operations focused on individual channels. High achieving firms substantially reduce operating complexity by developing standardized service programs for important customers. While logistical segmentation initially increases operational complexity, in the long run it reduces the demand for special accommodations or exceptions to the standard service package. To maximize value and minimize logistical complexity, leading firms identify services that are valued by all customers and offer as options those services that only benefit selected customers. A portfolio of service capabilities provides flexibility but reduces complexity by avoiding services for customers who do not value them. Extensive examination of customer requirements is necessary to ensure that appropriate packages and options are created.

Simplification was not a significant differentiator of high index achievement. Both average and high firms achieved lower scores on three of the four simplification indicators than they achieved on indicators for other capabilities. The exception was the degree of redesign of work routines and practices. High firms achieved significantly higher scores on redesign although scores for average firms were also above midpoint. Interestingly, both average and high achieving firms scored poorly on reduction of marketing complexity related to product and promotions. Logistics managers must continue to battle for processes that reflect the total operating costs of marketing decisions. Exhibit 4-1 reports scores for high and average achieving firms in 1995 and 1999 on select areas of simplification. Exhibit 4-1 illustrates that high achieving firms continue to place a stronger emphasis on simplification efforts than their average counterparts.

EXHIBIT 4-1

	SIMPLIFICATION PRIORITY			
	HIGH ACHIEVERS		AVERAGE ACHIEVERS	
REDUCTION OF:	1995	1999	1995	1999
Logistics facilities	3.12	3.93	3.39	3.15
Product/material suppliers	3.75	3.90	3.65	3.45
Logistics service suppliers	3.75	3.86	3.88	3.44
Marginal customers	3.10	3.38	2.43	2.86
Products of UPCs	2.29	3.26	2.61	2.68
Overall complexity	3.41	3.88	3.72	3.43

Scores indicate managers' response to statements regarding existence of firm efforts to simplify operations, with 1 = strongly disagree and 5 = strongly agree

COMPLIANCE

Adhering to standardized logistics policies and procedures can be especially difficult because of the inherent complexity of logistical activities and because circumstances or special requests from key customers require unique responses. Without solid, disciplined execution, it is very easy to become operationally overwhelmed. Following the guidelines for routine tasks, however, frees up resources to handle the exceptions. Thus, in final analysis compliance similar to standardization increases flexibility and the potential for innovation. The primary indicators of compliance capability are enforcement of standardized work performance, development and implementation of compensation, incentives and rewards to encourage adherence to standard policies and procedures, and regular achievement of stated performance goals.

Policies and procedures that standardize and simplify operations are not much use if they are ignored. High index achieving firms are aware of the need to actively enforce standardized logistical performance, the first indicator of compliance. Since so much logistical work is done without direct supervision, high achieving firms understand that they must find innovative ways to encourage compliance.

The second and third indicators of compliance are associated with the means used to ensure compliance. High achieving firms accomplish compliance by developing performance incentives to encourage process improvement, indicator two, and through compensation and reward systems that encourage adherence to stated policies and procedures, indicator three. Rewards that are based on functional objectives may not be appropriate in terms of total process results. Changes that emphasize inventory reductions can mean great savings for warehousing but may add additional costs for order processing and transportation. Managers must be motivated to achieve integrated logistics performance goals rather than narrowly defined departmental goals. The same generalization is equally important in supply chain arrangements. True supply chain partnerships focus on sharing burden and benefit, not on shifting the responsibility to one partner or the other. Some firms are implementing systems that reward suppliers and share benefits of increases in end-customer sales. Others are willing to share cost savings with supply chain members when collaboration and compliance results in greater operational efficiency.

The final compliance indicator assesses the degree to which firms successfully achieve stated logistical performance goals. When logistical performance goals are consistently met, a firm can give more attention to supply chain issues and synchronization that have the potential to achieve competitive advantage.

Although average index achieving firms reported scores that reflected adequate levels of compliance capability, high achievers scored significantly better on each of the four indicators, particularly on the overall assessment of active programs to enforce standardized logistical performance. High achievers also reported notably superior levels of attainment of stated performance goals.

STRUCTURAL ADAPTATION

The internal integration techniques discussed thus far involve human resource deployment and work routines, equally important are the physical assets needed to service customers. Structural adaptation refers to the modifications in network design and deployment of physical assets to facilitate integration. Four important indicators of structural adaptation are use of time-based logistics solutions, reduction of order-to-delivery (OTD) cycle, increase in inventory turn, and employment of innovative logistics networks to reduce handling complexity.

The traditional design of logistics networks considered the number of distribution facilities needed for a market area, the inventory level each should stock, and which customers would be served from each location to achieve a specified level of service. The typical solution was a network of regional full-service warehouses that met average customer demand for product assortment from stock. Changes in the operating environment, however, have dramatically altered the way leading firms view their operating networks. Logistics networks of high index achieving firms look very different than the traditional model.

Technology and regulations related to transportation have made it possible to move products longer distances, less expensively. Computerization has enabled the implementation of time-based competitive strategies. Materials handling technology has transformed distribution centers from storage facilities to on-the-move mixing and assembly centers capable of efficiently cross-docking products on their way to retail or manufacturing destinations. Perhaps most significant is the growing international scope of logistics operations, which means that the diverse legal, social, and physical infrastructures of host nations will profoundly affect the design of logistics networks in the future.

This dynamic environment mandates continuous planning and redesign. Firms must be prepared to keep pace with global political, economic, and technological change. The political restructuring of Europe, economic turbulence in the Pacific Rim, and the emergence of Internet based e-commerce are just a few challenges firms are currently facing. Specific networks may have a life expectancy of one year or less. Some firms may have to reconfigure network linkages almost daily, depending on market, competitive, and supplier actions.

Logistical networks frequently are defined by customer demand for delivery service. More and more customers are requiring speed and precise delivery timing. One of the most pronounced changes taking place throughout industries is the shift to pull or response-based logistics, the first indicator of structural adaptation capability. Response-based networks reduce advanced positioning of inventory to an absolute minimum. Rather than allocate and distribute inventory according to forecasts, the strategy is to retain products at manufacturing or distribution locations until demand is known. Goods are then modified and transported rapidly in precise quantities to locations where they are required.

The shift to pull systems is especially prevalent in consumer goods and retailing, but firms in other industries, including such bulk commodities as chemicals and paper, are increasingly exploring ways to adapt response-based principles. Regardless of industry, frequent network modification is common. In order to make timely deliveries, firms must be highly responsive. The key is to find the appropriate balance of inventory staging locations, order transmittal and processing technology, order selection, handling technology, and transportation capability. The order fulfillment metrics that support pull logistics must be engineered in terms of total cost. Firms that seek to exploit time-based capabilities are fanatical about control, including the application of activity-based costing and total cost measurement.

The second indicator of structural adaptation capability is reduction in OTD cycle time. All logistical networks are linked by a series of OTD cycles, that structure the work that must be completed between receipt of an order and its delivery. Historically, OTD cycles were long and highly uncertain and required large safety stocks to buffer operations. Because rapid and dependable delivery was viewed as expensive, anticipatory inventory was positioned in multiple facilities close to customers. Traditional OTD cycles of several days are being replaced by much faster performance. High achieving firms are able to accept customer orders late on one day and complete delivery before noon the next. A world-wide delivery commitment of 48 hours from purchase order receipt is increasingly possible.

Shorter OTD cycles reduce the amount of inventory maintained in the pipeline. The reduction of inventory reserves, however, leaves little room for error. This increases the need for synchronized operations. An OTD cycle of 48 hours, for example, requires no more than 48 hours (plus safety stock) of inventory. Logistics networks characterized by fast OTD cycles are typically supported by a reduced number of distribution warehouses in centralized locations. Tradeoff analysis is necessary to support network reengineering efforts since electronic data transmission and modification in transportation practice all affect cycle duration, consistency, and functional cost. High index achieving firms are reducing the length of time required to perform basic work such as order entry, credit verification, inventory allocation, order selection, and shipment consolidation.

Many of the forces shaping the configuration of logistics networks are related to technology that enables essential work to be done faster and with increasing accuracy. Dwell time, also called inventory velocity, is a measure of the ratio of days inventory sits idle in the system compared to the days it is productively being used. Ideally, products will move after they are manufactured, rapidly and continuously going immediately and directly to where they are required. Once the goods begin to move, they should remain in motion without interruption until they arrive at their final destination. Under those conditions dwell time would be zero.

A similar notion is inventory turn, or how many days it takes inventory in the system to change. Increased inventory turn is the third indicator of structural adaptation capability. The faster the turn, the greater are earnings, since revenue is realized each time an item moves through the system. Faster turns also mean lower inventory-related cost. Logistics network configuration is closely related to inventory turn achievement. Rapidly transferring product through fewer logistical facilities can favorably impact dwell time and inventory turn and reduce facility cost. Such flow management is difficult to accomplish in traditional facilities, where merchandise typically is received in large volume shipments and transferred to a storage area. As required, product is moved to an order selection area, where it is selected, assembled, and staged for shipment. As transportation vehicles arrive, shipments are loaded for customer delivery. In a traditional distribution warehouse products are handled and moved a minimum of four to six times between their arrival and departure.

Innovative techniques to reduce handling complexity are a feature of emerging logistical networks. The final structural adaptation indicator assesses the level to which firms employ logistics networks that combine distribution facilities, cross-docks, and specialty delivery operations to accommodate unique customer requirements. Cross-dock distribution facilities capable of receiving products ordered by a specific customer, merge it with other products bound for the same customer, and ship out the consolidated merchandise without storage, are becoming common. When cross-docking is not applicable, customer order staging can reduce product handling. The typical approach coordinates procurement/buying practices so that discrete quantities are purchased for specific stores or customers. These are often received in customer-specific unit loads, and are positioned in a staging area, where they become part of a growing accumulation of merchandise destined for that customer. Outbound delivery is initiated on schedule or when sufficient merchandise has accumulated.

Given the continued challenges of new product proliferation and growing reverse logistics needs, warehouse capacity is a critical concern. One way to do more with less capacity is through selective stocking. Facilities may be designated to support the logistical requirements of specified slow-moving products for the total enterprise. Specific orders are then assigned to different logistical facilities based on order composition. If products from different locations are required, then the order is split and transmitted to each facility. Split orders filled by two or more supply locations are merged during delivery to the customer. The fact that multiple facilities were used to fill the order can be transparent to customers.

Cross-docking, customer order staging, and selective stocking reduce handling and dwell time. The increase in inventory velocity allows firms to get more logistical productivity from their existing inventory and facility network. These and other innovative methods are enabling high index achieving firms to reduce the overall number of distribution facilities, inventory investment, and exposure to risk.

All firms in the database scored above the mid-range on the achievement index. High index achieving firms differentiated themselves on their successful utilization of time-based logistics solutions with customers and suppliers as well as on their use of logistics networks that combine multiple facilities and techniques to accommodate unique customer requirements.

SUMMARY

Internal integration involves cross-functional planning, sourcing, manufacturing and delivery to achieve excellence throughout the enterprise. The goal is high-level basic service at the lowest total cost. Linking internally performed work into a seamless, synchronized process supports customer requirements and yields superior performance. Internal integration creates a synergistic effect that enhances the firm's competitiveness.

Internal integration is driven by five capabilities: cross-functional unification, standardization, simplification, compliance, and structural adaptation. *Cross-functional unification* centers on the extent to which potentially synergistic internal activities are merged into manageable operational processes. Managers of cross-functional work teams use information from multiple sources and are empowered to make immediate decisions. *Standardization* establishes common policies, procedures, and practices to reduce the uncertainty associated with routine logistical operations. It forces resources to focus on emergent situations and exceptions to the norm. *Simplification* streamlines operations and work routines and reduces the complexity associated with product proliferation and marketing promotions. *Compliance* relates to enforcement of and adherence to established operational and administrative standards across facilities. *Structural adaptation* refers to the modification of logistics and supply chain networks and the deployment of physical assets to facilitate integration. Exhibit 4-2 summarizes these concepts.

EXHIBIT 4-2

INTERNAL INTEGRATION	
The competency of linking internally performed work into a seamless process to support customer requirements.	
Cross-Functional Unification:	Operationalization of potentially synergistic activities into manageable operational processes.
Standardization:	Establishment of cross-functional policies and procedures to facilitate synchronous operations.
Simplification:	Identification, adoption, implementation, and continuous improvement of best practice.
Compliance:	Adherence to established operational and administrative policies and procedures.
Structural Adaptation:	Extent to which the network structure and deployment of physical assets has been modified to facilitate integration.

MATERIAL AND SERVICE SUPPLIER INTEGRATION

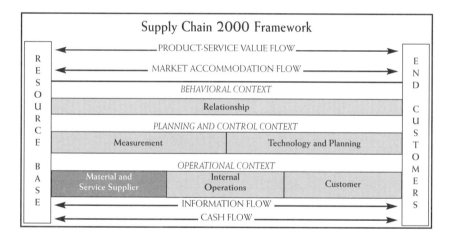

Supply Chain 2000 Framework

ay back at the first task force meeting, Amy had said: "If we can per-suade our top customers to work with us in developing an accurate plan for meeting their requirements, and then get those numbers to each operating area in a way that is meaningful to the decisions we make, we should have this thing licked – on paper anyway!"

As long as our goods and service suppliers play along," added Melissa Brighton, Director of Purchasing. "But that's a big assumption."

The task force members were more than aware of the changing relationship between Spartan and its suppliers. Increasingly, managers were realizing they could not meet the multiple service and cost standards being demanded by top customers without the help of suppliers. It was one thing to be asked to do better at activities in which they had a core expertise, but some customer requests were for services that exceeded Spartan's capabilities. Suppliers could be the solution, but sometimes they were the problem. For example, suppliers chosen for their ability to engineer subcomponents to the exact specifications of production often could not deliver the goods in a way consistent with the outbound flow to customers. In those cases, Spartan was forced to buy in large lots and store the balance, to be sure that orders could be shipped within days of receipt.

Even when Spartan spent months selecting supply partners, the results were often disappointing. For whatever reasons, cost and service levels did not live up to expectations. Melissa described one relationship that was going sour. Whether because of inaccurate baseline cost or service numbers, failure to provide accurate tracking information, or plain inability on the part of the supplier to deliver what was promised, the situation had gradually deteriorated. Now managers from both companies were slinging accusations back and forth.

Part of the problem was that most of the mid-level managers at Spartan had little experience with external suppliers. They were accustomed to direct control of activities within their area of responsibility. Someone in the task force pointed out that outsourcing from direct management of capital and human assets, along with the associated planners and dispatchers, to external management of activities provided by another firm required a very different mindset. Ensuring operational, financial, and relational linkages that gave the supplier both the ability and the motivation to do things "our way" had been extremely challenging.

Charlie suggested that the group focus on ways to improve operational linkages with suppliers. Unfortunately, it seemed that in this area the only teacher was experience, a teacher with a very high price tag.

Our 1995 research concluded that successful external supply chain integration was to a significant degree related to internal process integration. A primary objective of supplier integration is joint operations that reduce duplication, waste, and redundancy. Such boundary-spanning efficiency can only be achieved if coordination benefits all participants. In essence, supply chain integration applies the concepts of systems integration and trade-off management on a more comprehensive or cross-enterprise basis.

Supply chains tailored to the individual value perspectives of major customers have become common business practice. As noted earlier, industry is shifting from push methods driven by anticipated sales to pull methods that focus on delivering value to end-customers through rapid response to demand. To do this profitably, firms must strip redundancy and duplication of materials and effort from supply chain operations. The task is all the more challenging because it is not limited to internal activities. It requires linking internal work processes with those of material and service providers.

The divergent goals of external supply chain organizations often prevent operational integration. Historically, firms have tried to reduce supply chain conflict by owning consecutive levels in the business process. Henry Ford's original business strategy is a legendary attempt at using ownership to achieve vertical integration of the supply chain. Ford's dream was full ownership and management of the entire value creation process in order to reduce waste and increase relevancy. Among other operations he owned rubber plantations, ships, and foundries. Ford could convert raw iron ore to a finished car in seven days, a speed that many industries envy today.

The problem with ownership based vertical integration is that a tremendous capital investment and an incredibly complex organizational structure are required. Even then, there are still insufficient economies of scale. Therefore, firms increasingly need to harness the expertise and synergy of external supply chain partners to achieve success. Collaboration is a relatively low cost alternative to vertical ownership as a way to reduce operational waste and redundancies while improving service quality and relevancy. This relatively new idea is being realized through transformation of supply chain structures and practices.

Structural modification can serve to integrate the core competencies and capabilities of all supply chain participants to jointly achieve world class performance status. Specialization previously performed internally is now being done by supply chain members to avoid operational and resource duplication. The aggregate result is resource efficiency. This kind of transformation requires a whole new way of thinking about business operations. Decisions are no longer simple buy-sell transactions but include joint operational planning, shared assets and technology, and, most importantly, a willingness to share information and risk.

An important integration decision is how many material and service suppliers to include in synchronized operations. Streamlining the number is critical, partly because of the leverage that results from large-volume purchases. The integration process also requires extraordinary commitment of time and administrative resources, and it may entail significant capital investment for a shared information system and compatible operating equipment. It makes sense to work closely with relatively few suppliers.

This chapter discusses the operational capabilities that support material and service supplier integration: strategic alignment, operational fusion, financial linkage, and supplier relationship management.

STRATEGIC ALIGNMENT

Firms that achieve high scores on the Supply Chain 2000 index reflect strong commitment to develop a common vision of the total value creation process and share such insight and related responsibility with supply chain partners. The capability to strategically align the value creation process with supply chain partners is indicated by consideration of the strategic role of suppliers to firm success, basing selection decisions on supplier logistical capabilities, developing interlocking programs and activities with suppliers, and reducing the overall number of suppliers.

The first indicator of strategic alignment capability is the degree to which a firm believes that consideration of the strategic direction, role, and performance of suppliers is critical to its own success. A single enterprise rarely has all capabilities for satisfying customers. Each firm involved in delivering value to the end-customer must commit to perform unique roles that contribute best to overall value creation. If a firm can find a supplier that can more effectively or efficiently make a part or perform a service, then that activity should be a candidate for outsourcing. Exceptions should be limited to core incentives where success or failure is fundamental to a firm's overall performance. In the short run, there also may be limitations to out-sourcing due to such factors as labor agreements and community relations. Specialization enables the overall supply chain to leverage each participant's core competencies in a coordinated effort to reduce duplication and waste. By delineating specific supplier responsibilities, expectations and tasks, firms are able to eliminate delay and increase productivity. Possibilities include inventory management, transportation planning, facility operations, and document preparation.

The decision about which partners to select is difficult. The most basic requirement is a shared or common vision of the total value-creation process. Beliefs and understanding regarding service, internal process integration, and segmental logistics must be compatible. Corporate culture, integrity, commitment to information and communications systems, and views about incentives and innovation all must be aligned to facilitate a successful arrangement. Without such agreement, it is not possible to gain maximum benefit from joint synergistic operations. For example, a firm committed to reducing dwell time through the use of time-phased operations probably would not be well served by a material supplier wedded to the traditional principles of functional efficiency generated through economies of scale, and vice versa. It is critical, therefore, that the evaluation and selection process considers the strategic direction and operating philosophy of potential part-ners. It is particularly important that the firm have a developed and accepted strategy to guide their partnership decisions.

To assure true integration, the goals and objectives of partners must be complementary and focused on joint achievement. In other words, the parties need a strong sense of the benefits each brings to the relationship. One important aspect of this is that firms consider logistical capabilities as a basis for supplier selection, the second indicator of strategic alignment. For example, one manufacturer engaged a trucking company for dedicated runs several times a day between production facilities in Iowa and Texas. The transportation supplier provided cross-dock and terminal operations at either end, brokering outbound freight to other core carriers. These were critical logistics capabilities that the manufacturer could not achieve without significant capital investment. The manufacturer also was able to improve delivery service at lower cost by simplifying its transportation network, which simultaneously reduced transit times as well as administrative and shipping costs. This demonstrates how the selection process must consider supplier performance on the critical capabilities being sought in the relationship.

Many of the problems that emerge when integration is implemented can be traced to insufficient joint commitment to overall supply chain goals and objectives or the lack of an effective logistics strategy. Potential partners may talk the talk during negotiations. However, ingrained business practices that focus on short-term financial advantage at the expense of longer term performance eventually may limit what can be accomplished. One food wholesaler found that a major retail chain with which operations were integrated used the wholesaler only at certain times for selected products. In effect, the retailer cherry-picked the wholesaler's products and promotions to such an extent that it was unprofitable for the wholesaler to provide the high levels of service required by the arrangement. Numerous efforts were made to resolve the situation, but the retailer was unwilling to change its purchase behavior. Some managers still espouse the philosophy of leveraging economies of scale to coerce suppliers into doing exactly what needs to be done.

The third strategic alignment indicator assesses the degree to which firms integrate operations with suppliers by developing interlocking programs and activities. Integration with suppliers demands significant commitment to developing the organization and resource infrastructure that will ensure that joint operations achieve customer performance goals. Rules and work arrangements as well as innovative performance measurement and reward systems must be devised. Owing to the effort and dedication required, it is easy to understand why many have not made significant progress in establishing integrated supplier arrangements.

The final indicator of strategic alignment focuses on reduction of the overall number of suppliers to foster improved operational integration. It is not uncommon for a traditional manufacturer to engage dozens of transportation carriers to avoid dependence on a single provider. Of course, the commitment of each carrier to the manufacturer's success is equally minimized. A firm that pursues operational integration with suppliers takes a different approach. The complexity of guidance and control systems necessary to establish interlocking operations and provide joint customer solutions requires significant resource commitment with a relatively few supply chain partners. Rather than deal with multiple suppliers to decrease dependence, it streamlines the number of suppliers to facilitate operational integration. These partners then become critical to the value creation process and are no longer viewed as interchangeable parts that can be exchanged on the basis of who offers the lowest transaction price.

Development of interlocking programs and activities to accomplish operational integration was the strategic alignment indicator that most significantly differentiated high index achieving firms from average firms, although high index firms reported higher scores than average firms on all four indicators. Interestingly, firms from both achievement groups reported high levels of supplier reduction.

OPERATIONAL FUSION

After outsourcing activities are identified and appropriate suppliers are chosen, the actual work of integration begins. Many firms are in favor of the idea, but strategies and practices for accomplishing integration are undeveloped and misunderstood. High index achieving firms have discovered that operational synchronization requires linkage of systems and operational interfaces to reduce duplication, redundancy, and dwell. The primary indicators of operational fusion capability are improved performance from integrated operations, sharing technical resources with suppliers, sharing responsibility for new product and service development with suppliers, and creating innovative ways to facilitate coordination with suppliers.

A major criticism of outsourcing among manufacturing and retail customers is that suppliers over promise and under deliver. This may occur for several reasons. In the competitive pursuit of new business opportunities, potential suppliers may make promises they cannot fulfill. Perhaps more critical, however, are the difficulties brought on by insufficient communication and inadequate performance measurement. Firms that engage external suppliers often feel their job is done once they make the operational handoff. Lack of follow through and monitoring coupled with incorrect or insufficient information regarding products or expectations may result in false assumptions by the supplier about performance elements and standards.

Supplier and service provider scorecards are becoming common as a means to facilitate this communication.

The first operational fusion indicator assesses the degree to which firms' experience improved performance as a result of operational integration with suppliers. To attain this improvement, high index achieving firms find that they must increase their involvement with suppliers, particularly in the early life of the relationship. For example, customer preferences known to a firm's employees as a result of years of experience are not necessarily obvious to an external provider and must be specifically communicated. One food manufacturer who outsourced distribution saw a troubling rise in costs and customer complaints. Managers sent to the field to investigate discovered that customer preferences for the order in which product was off-loaded at the distribution center were not being communicated to the load planners for the third party logistics provider (3PL). The customer often had to off-load several pallets and stage them on the receiving dock in order to reach the products scheduled for immediate cross-docking. The solution was an additional information link, which not only alleviated the problem but also enabled the supplier to improve load utilization.

The practices and processes that improve performance most often develop from shared innovations. Firms must be willing to share technical resources with key suppliers, the second indicator of operational fusion. This may be accomplished by increasing the amount and depth of communications through enhanced information systems, frequent multilevel managerial meetings, or even locating employees with key suppliers to facilitate coordination. In the food industry, better forecasting and planning gained from collaboration is enabling suppliers to replenish customers based upon actual demand information. Costs are down due to lower inventories and unsalables, and sales are up because of improved product availability and more effective promotions. High achieving firms and their key suppliers are pioneering collaborative supply chain designs that link personnel around the world through a real time computer network that continuously updates plans.

The third indicator of operational fusion assesses a firm's commitment to share responsibility with suppliers in new product and service development and commercialization. Integration of operational responsibility with suppliers provides flexibility that enables better management of inventory. Improved replenishment times and in-stock availability of products from centralized inventory managed by a vendor or 3PL, for example, allows managers to rapidly react to actual demand. Minimizing inventory deployment during new product introduction lowers start-up costs and reduces the sales threshold required to attain profitability. A new product may achieve financial success because lower sales volumes may recoup startup costs. In the case of an outright product failure, lean launch results in lessened inventory exposure.

The final indicator of operational fusion assesses the degree of coordination between firms and their supplier partners. One important aspect of coordination is performance monitoring. Measures and systems established for internal employees and resources are typically not appropriate for external suppliers. As in the case of communication, monitoring often must be increased to achieve successful integrative supply relationships. Techniques include meetings of operational personnel to review performance, discuss upcoming operations and investigate how both partners can foster improvement. For example, monthly or quarterly strategy meetings to review past performance, establish performance levels, and discuss strategies for the next period. High index achieving firms also use innovative techniques such as placing employees at the business facilities of key suppliers to facilitate coordination.

The emphasis on coordination should not be to establish guilt or blame but to solve problems and ensure continuing improvement. Specific, objective benchmarks help facilitate the process. Many successful arrangements use joint scorecards to monitor performance over time and ensure consistent progress toward goals. Such goal monitoring led one manufacturer to discover that suppliers were often ignorant of service breakdowns due to high turnover in operating personnel. Scorecards ensure that everyone understands what is being measured, how it is defined and measured, past performance levels, and future targets.

High index achieving firms reported significantly higher scores than average firms on all four indicators of operational fusion. In particular, high firms differentiated themselves by their commitment to shared responsibility with suppliers in new product and service development and commercialization as well as placement of employees at supplier business facilities.

FINANCIAL LINKAGE

As the potential for interorganizational tradeoff increases, firms must be willing to go beyond operational linkages to derive long-term competitive advantage from material and service supplier integration. Leading firms are beginning to structure joint financial ventures with suppliers to support and drive goal attainment. Critical indicators of financial linkage include helping goods and service suppliers finance capital equipment, sharing research and development costs and results, and entering into long-term agreements with suppliers.

The first two indicators of financial linkage assess firms' willingness to help suppliers and service suppliers finance capital expenditures. Mechanisms that provide resources for joint endeavors can be explored as operations become more integrated and supply chain partners are included in strategic plans. Capital equipment needed by a specialized supplier in an exclusive relationship is one of the most resource-intensive examples. When the relationship dynamics are appropriate, a firm should consider helping partners finance capital requirements, especially when it is the major or sole beneficiary of the investment. While this may seem unreasonable in a traditional sense, joint investment helps ensure longevity. Information technology needed to support a specific relationship is another opportunity for joint investment. An equipment parts supplier, for example, developed and offered an information system to its dealers to establish common information structures and to unify management practices and measures. In such instances increased operational efficiency and effectiveness often offset costs.

The third indicator of financial linkage relates to sharing research and development costs with primary suppliers. Joint endeavors are often characterized by the need for highly customized product offerings that require significant research and development costs to create new products for unique specifications. One automotive seat supplier, for example, has customized its products such that seating units unique to the automobile make and style are delivered fully assembled to the manufacturer for direct installation. High index achieving firms recognize the long-term benefits of such innovation and are willing to support supplier research and development that leads to these benefits.

Another way firms encourage suppliers to develop assets specific to their needs is to guarantee sales volume through long-term agreements, the final indicator of financial linkage. Suppliers are usually much more willing to make a specific investment if they can be sure it will generate revenues. A glass manufacturer realized that using a unique trailer design would reduce handling costs and damage. The design was so unique, however, that the trailer had limited capability to transport other products. Because of no backhaul, the carrier would have to charge higher rates to cover the cost of an empty inbound or outbound run. This would offset any potential gains from lowering handling and damage costs. The problem was solved by developing a special trailer configured to carry glass that could be easily be reconfigured to a standard flatbed to accommodate other freight. The carrier agreed to purchase a large number of the specialized trailers based on the glass manufacturer's guarantee of significant freight volumes over ten years to protect the investment.

Financial linkage capability was not a strong differentiator of high and average index achieving firms. High achievers scored higher than average achievers on all four indicators. Neither group, however, reported high levels of helping goods and service suppliers finance capital equipment or research and development. Both groups reported high levels of willingness to enter into long-term agreements with suppliers.

SUPPLIER MANAGEMENT

Supplier integration requires relationship management that extends beyond suppliers to include suppliers' suppliers. Supplier relationship management must consider not only suppliers but also their suppliers, much as customer integration requires helping customers succeed with end-customers. The primary indicators of supplier relationship management include development of active programs to positively impact suppliers' suppliers, specific actions taken to develop extended supply networks, willingness to consider investment in supplier development, and allowing suppliers to participate in strategic decision making.

The first indicator of supplier relationship management capability assesses the extent to which a firm commits to developing active programs that influence suppliers' suppliers. The second indicator relates to the specific actions that a firm has undertaken to create such extended supply networks. High index achieving firms develop a strong network of primary and secondary suppliers. This supply chain is designed to ensure success for different major customers or customer segments. The focus is on innovation rather than control, and traditional thinking about internal and external work functions is replaced by practices that create supply network superiority. Organizations that achieve this level of sophisticated integration are industry leaders.

The third indicator of supplier relationship management relates to a firm's willingness to consider investment in supplier development. To achieve high index achievement status, each link in the supply chain must perform at best practice standards. In reality, this may mean strategic investment in raw material or supply process development, or even the creation of new companies to perform an activity that cannot be procured from existing suppliers. This may be particularly necessary in developing countries. By promising sole-source status, for example, an electronics firm operating in Mexico persuaded local partners to launch a plastic molding facility to make housings and cabinets. The firm benefited from local supply as well as a new partner whose focus was the success of its primary customer.

A critical factor in supply network success is active participation by suppliers in strategic planning and decision making, the final indicator of supplier relationship management. As they perform increasingly vital and irreplaceable roles in providing value, suppliers' views on resource needs and constraints, threats, opportunities, and weaknesses must be considered when setting goals, objectives, and action plans. Material and service suppliers that represent a firm's extended family will contribute as much to the success or failure of the supply chain as any internal department. Managers who interface with these firms must learn how to manage assets and activities that they do not directly control and cannot directly see, but whose performance they can and must monitor to ensure success.

Most logistics and supply chain executives begin their management career as functional managers with direct responsibility over equipment and personnel. On visits to the warehouse, they become accustomed to drinking coffee with the forklift drivers or chatting with truckers as they lean against the fender of trucks. Many have a hard time relinquishing primary control over operational assets in favor of a management style that uses information and delegation. They are not always comfortable in an environment in which the only equipment is a computer, and the personnel are clerical and administrative, performing information-related tasks and not front-line operations. Increasingly in the future, effective managers must be able to stimulate innovative behavior on the part of key suppliers through the use of both technology and relationship management. The need to create strong and synchronized supply chain relationships reinforces the need for simplification focused on reducing the number of suppliers and third parties.

Supplier relationship management was a capability on which high index achieving firms were able to clearly differentiate themselves from average achievers. High firms recorded recorded strong scores on each of the four indicators while average firms failed to score above the scale mean (3.0) on any of the indicators.

SUMMARY

Acknowledging that each major customer will require a business plan tailored to its individual needs is quite a challenge. Managers of top firms clearly know they cannot perform this task alone. The integration of Henry Ford's supply chain by virtue of ownership was virtually impossible then and remains financially infeasible today. Integrating operations with material and service suppliers to form a seamless flow of internal and external work overcomes the financial barriers of vertical ownership while retaining many of the benefits.

Evolving the structures to facilitate this integration is not easy or quick. Strategic alignment, operational fusion, financial linkage, and supplier relationship management capabilities must be developed. *Strategic alignment* requires that supply chain partners have a common vision of the total value creation process as well as shared responsibility for achieving it. Firms must carefully identify and select partners with complementary visions, strategies, and operational capabilities. Through *operational fusion*, supply chain partners must interface in ways that reduce duplication, redundancy, and dwell time while maintaining synchronization. *Financial linkage* spreads the risks and rewards of collaboration to solidify goal attainment. Finally, firms must extend management practices to include *supplier management*. In total, these capabilities reflect the recognition that a supply chain is only as strong as its supplier link. Exhibit 5-1 summarizes the concepts associated with material and service supplier integration.

EXHIBIT 5-1

MATERIAL/SERVICE SUPPLIER INTEGRATION

The competency linking externally performed work into a seamless congruency with internal work processes.

Strategic Alignment:	Development of a common vision of the total value creation process and planning clarity concerning shared responsibility.
Operational Fusion:	Linkage of systems and operational interfaces to reduce duplication, redundancy, and dwell while maintaining operational synchronization.
Financial Linkage:	Willingness to structure joint financial ventures with suppliers to solidify goal attainment.
Supplier Management:	Extended management to include hierarchical structure of suppliers' suppliers.

TECHNOLOGY AND PLANNING INTEGRATION

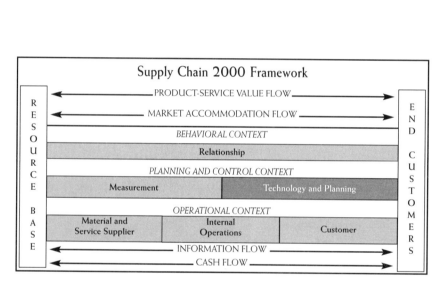

Supply Chain 2000 Framework

*A*s they pulled the pieces of the plan together, Charlie and the task force members noticed a theme running through each of the integration "gaps." It seemed no matter what the challenge, the solution boiled down to ensuring real-time, accurate, and accessible information. Whether it was working with customers to send and receive strategic and tactical data, integrating activities across internal boundaries, or collaborating with external material and service suppliers, information supported the control system that carried the message from planning to the operating extremities. A coordinated information system connecting all the players was required to enable the supply chain to provide high levels of value to end-users. Unfortunately, developing such a system was about as easy for most managers as *shooting a hole in one in the first round of golf of the spring.*

The most recent experience with the firm's information system, or systems, was an attempt to determine whether the logistics network was providing the best cost/service mix possible. Charlie had hired a consulting firm with powerful network modeling software to aid his analysis. The consultants and Albert Harris, Director of Information Systems, determined that accurate cost information, down to the transaction level, was needed from transportation, warehousing, and customer service as well as purchasing and production. Charlie gave his consent to gather the necessary cost data. The next time he wanted or expected to hear about the project was when the results were presented to him.

To his dismay, Charlie was dragged in several times over the next few months when problems arose regarding the availability of information needed to derive an accurate cost estimate. The network analysis required a breakdown of costs by activity. Although activity-based costing or ABC was often discussed at Spartan, the talk had yet to filter down to operating departments as a directive to collect the necessary data. Al Harris also explained that frequently it was difficult to determine which department had which information in which legacy system. Several times information that was believed sufficient to estimate costs for a particular activity yielded only one piece of the puzzle. Afterwards, someone had to spend time tracking down another piece, and another, until the rest of the pieces, or at least all that existed, were found.

The consultants eventually created a reasonable baseline estimate, but at the final presentation Charlie felt certain he was not the only one who was uncomfortable about making decisions based on the model recommendations. Amy mentioned information from customers and suppliers was needed for an accurate estimate of costs. Charlie noticed the senior partner from the consulting firm grimace after her comment.

Information was needed not only for operational decisions, but also for planning systems. The action and work plans used to guide operations depended on accurate data from supply chain partners. Charlie knew distribution and production often experienced shortages of popular products, and Amy had heard plenty of complaints about it from customers. Investigation usually revealed that a customer had failed to alert Spartan to an upcoming promotion that had increased demand dramatically. Most of the time the customer had a very good idea about what the effect would be but was unwilling, unable, or simply didn't think to pass that information along to Spartan.

Charlie had a hard time understanding why customers did not do a better job of letting Spartan know about sales spikes, especially since the success of a promotion ultimately depended on supply. Even more alarming was the lack of communication within the firm. Last March he had nearly gone to war with marketing for causing a huge service breakdown in the Northeast. The regional sales team had devised *a great promotion during the annual NCAA basketball tournament, but that infor-mation was never passed on to operations. There was also the regular and artificial end-of-quarter spike caused by the sales compensation system. The upshot was no prior planning for what amounted to an increase in demand of nearly 50 percent!*

Charlie knew it was essential to have a technology structure comprehensive enough to allow multiple supply chain members to exchange input about expected operating and environmental changes in real time so each could plan, schedule, and proactively adapt resources to meet customer needs. This capability would be partic-ularly important as the potential for electronic commerce began to be realized. His success in creating a supply chain organization that could rapidly respond to such sit-uations would depend on it.

Integrated management requires high-quality information to support the wide variety of operational configurations needed to create supply chain solutions for specific customers. Effective planning and operations requires thorough, accurate, and timely information from customers, material and service suppliers, and internal functional areas regarding current and expect-ed conditions. Only an integrated information system can provide the input needed for short-, mid-, and long-term plans that translate strategic goals and objectives into action and work to guide each operating area. The task is complicated since the systems must increasingly support global flows of product, cash, and information.

Firms with high levels of achievement on the Supply Chain 2000 capa-bilities have accepted the challenge to reengineer information systems according to customer-focused activities, such as managing customer inven-tory balances and providing inventory visibility as goods move through the pipeline. Traditionally, the increased speed of information technology was used to gain and maintain a cost advantage by increasingly processing trans-actions faster. The growing challenge is to integrate information technolo-gy with Advanced Planning and Scheduling (APS) systems. APS systems coordinate the use of firm production, inventory, storage, and transportation resources to minimize total supply chain costs. This enables information to be used as a service differentiator rather than simply a cost reducer. Managers with fingertip access to data throughout the supply chain, and the software needed to process it, are better positioned to gain rapid insight into demand patterns and trends. Such accessibility allows effective planning and operational decisions to be made in complex global supply chains.

The degree of information technology connectivity is critical to supply chain success. Poor information flow may be the reason data are not shared. Uncoordinated information systems pose a major obstacle to logistics integration. A firm must be able to transfer and interpret highly detailed data across internal and external organizational boundaries. Technology such as EDI and the Internet facilitate the two-way exchange of a wide array of rich data. However, the promise has not generally been realized for technology and organizational reasons. The technology issues often center on the ability to map data elements. The organizational issues concern the willingness to share information both within the organization and between partners.

What firms do with data after they receive it is no less important than the ability to exchange it. Processes for integrating data into analysis and decision making can make the difference between enhanced customer and cost performance and a missed opportunity. Effective information systems do more than provide access to data. They also provide the conversion and processing tools that transform it into usable information.

Simply investing in information systems and software will not result in integration. State-of-the-art technology cannot guarantee that the information exchanged is accurate, timely, or sufficiently comprehensive to be useful. Organizations must collaborate with key supply chain partners to develop systems and technology that enable them to share planning and operating data. The objective is to gain insight into complex operational and environmental situations. Promotional information exchanged between retailers and vendors, for example, frequently covers planned operational details but fails to share estimated sales effect. Relationships structured to exchange strategic marketing information do not always yield the full benefits of such collaboration. This often occurs because the supplier receiving the information cannot use it effectively.

Four capabilities are needed to achieve technology and planning integration: information management, internal communications, connectivity, and collaborative forecasting and planning. Each is discussed below.

INFORMATION MANAGEMENT

Traditional information management focuses on speed and automation in handling specific work, such as order processing and production scheduling. Increasingly, electronic solutions are replacing manual paper processing. Telephones, fax machines, and EDI now speed the order fulfillment process. The challenge for the future is to focus information management on decision support applications that facilitate supply chain resource allocation across the total order-to-delivery cycle. Core information processes must be reengineered to facilitate integrated marketing, procurement, manufacturing, and logistics operations. The key indicators of information management capability include enterprise systems, e-commerce, effective internal information sharing, and integrated planning systems.

Enterprise information systems require integrated hardware, software, and network capabilities. Hardware is the combination of mainframes, microcomputers, processors and storage technologies that manipulate and maintain information. Software consists of the programs that organize and analyze data. The network includes satellite, leased line, wide-area network (WAN), and local area network (LAN) technologies to transfer and coordinate information. Networking increasingly involves the Internet, thereby providing expanded linkages among suppliers, customers, and transportation intermediaries.

The goal of information management is to enable decision-makers to design and implement profitable customer solutions. Traditional cost-benefit analysis sought to optimize profit-and-loss performance within one functional area, but the focus in integrative management is total system cost and service. Information systems must help managers coordinate the supply chain through planning across such areas as: demand forecasting and planning, production planning and scheduling, raw material acquisition, work-in-process, finished goods inventory, and inbound and outbound transportation. The tremendous growth in Enterprise Resource Planning (ERP) applications and the more recent expansion to incorporate APS are reflective of the critical importance of information coordination and availability.

The second indicator of information system capability is the availability of data and systems to support e-commerce. The explosion of Internet based shopping for a wide range of product categories is placing heightened demand upon enterprise information systems. Managers are increasingly demanding systems that can accommodate Internet-based transactions and are capable of linking third party providers who provide such capability in a virtual environment.

The third indicator of information system capability is the ability to share standardized and customized information internally. Effective integrated management requires the ability to share information between all organizational functions involved in order fulfillment. While much of that sharing can occur in standardized formats, increasing demands from specific customers is driving the need for more flexibility and customization. This requires development and refinement of knowledge-based transaction systems to incorporate operational experience and expertise. In functional departments, advanced information technology and decision support systems can yield significant benefits due to more efficient and effective resource use.

The final indicator of information system capability is the shift to integrated planning. The total cost concept requires a shift in planning from a functional focus, such as materials requirements planning (MRP) and distribution requirements planning (DRP), to cross-functional integration, such as APS. Cross-functional and even cross-organizational APS requires coordinated information about inventory, transportation, and warehousing. The objective is to plan supply chain arrangements that consider lowest cost sourcing, plant production profiles, least total cost to customers, and overall resource deployment. Purchasing, operations, and customer service, for example, need to let the transportation department know when items are available for shipment and when they are needed at specific destinations. Transportation planners then can assess consolidation requirements and arrange inbound, outbound, and interfacility movement allowing products to flow seamlessly through the supply chain, especially in ways that combine lower costs and higher service levels. Executives frequently cite examples of APS applications with a payback of less than one year.

The Supply Chain 2000 research provides significant evidence that both high and average index achievement firms are placing a strong focus on implementing ERP and APS. The average achieving firms indicate that a majority are in the process of implementing ERP while the high achieving firms report almost universal application. In terms of the other three indicators, average index achievement firms report minimal application of these technologies with a substantially greater application by the high achievers. While the difference is not significant, the results indicate that both average and high index achieving firms place more focus on APS systems implementation than they currently are on developing e-commerce capability. However, recent attention to e-commerce potential may have shifted this conclusion since the field research was completed.

INTERNAL COMMUNICATIONS

Company-wide logistics decisions have often been fragmented due to data inconsistency. This inconsistency often has resulted from independently developed information systems characterized by data fragmentation and redundancy. Operational decentralization and geographical dispersion of facilities adds to the difficulty. The problems that have resulted from independent system development can be resolved through internal communication. Internal communication is the capability to exchange information across internal functional boundaries in a timely, responsive, and usable format. It specifically focuses on information and data communication rather than personnel communication. The indicators that demonstrate such internal communications capability include integrated databases, integrated applications, and more accurate and timely information.

Managers in isolated parts of a firm are frequently frustrated with their inability to know what is happening elsewhere in the organization. The first indicator of resolving this problem is movement toward common databases. The inability to share information between order fulfillment and purchasing often frustrates attempts to consolidate customer deliveries with inbound materials movements. Specific information regarding inbound freight movements is frequently unknown to firms since suppliers often control inbound movements. In these instances, transportation cost information may be rolled into the total purchase price of the supplied products. If firms do have specific inbound freight data, it is usually managed by a different information system than that used to manage outbound movements. It may be difficult or impossible to exchange information between the two systems.

Similar gaps are common between manufacturing operations and a firm's ability to accurately promise inventory to customers. For example, decisions are often made about finished goods inventory allocation with minimal consideration for the production plan even though both manufacturing and distribution were working with the same actual inventory. The disparity often results from the fact that each functional area is working with different plans.

Firms are attempting to resolve ambiguity by developing shared information or a data warehouse for both operating data, such as orders and inventory levels, and historical data, such as previous shipments, expenses, and sales promotion impact. The information warehouse will help make integrated operations possible because all functional users will have access to the same information. This universal availability implies that relevant parties can make decisions based on common and consistent information.

To illustrate the advantage of common information, a second internal communication capability focuses on integrated logistics applications. The independent operating systems of the past resulted in decisions that often were not based on the most timely information and often did not consider organizational or supply chain impact beyond individual functional boundaries. An example is the traditional firm's inability to use scheduled production or receipts as "available to promise" (ATP) for customer orders. It is increasingly clear that firms are attempting to enhance their internal communication through more integrated logistics applications.

The third indicator of effective internal communication involves information accuracy, timeliness, and formatting. While firms have previously felt that reasonable timeliness and above 90 percent accuracy are acceptable, the focus to reduce inventory is driving the need for better than 99 percent immediacy and accuracy. Managers at high index achieving firms frequently cite data accuracy and timeliness as a major issue when considering the application of enhanced APS systems.

The final indicator of effective internal communication concerns data timeliness. High achievement firms increasingly report sharing real time data with their supply chain partners. Real time access is facilitated through access to common databases that are updated by transmission of Point-of-Sale (POS) and in some select situations product consumption data. While the potential for POS data usage is high, many retailers are still reluctant to share the information.

High index achievement firms report a significantly better aptitude for all four of the internal communication indicators. A comparison of the relative indicators, however, reveals two interesting observations. First, while there is substantial difference between high and average achievement firms, all firms indicate a strong drive towards implementation of more integrated logistics applications. In essence, all firms are placing major emphasis on logistics system integration. Second, the largest differential between high and average index achieving firms is demonstrated in their ability to capture and maintain real time data. The high achieving firms demonstrate substantially more use of real time data as a means to reduce supply chain uncertainty.

CONNECTIVITY

A common internal database is tremendously important to integrated operations, but it is not sufficient to assure excellent service at the lowest total cost. Management generally recognizes the advantage of sharing information with supply chain partners. This sharing is facilitated by connectivity which provides the capability to exchange information with external supply chain partners in a timely, responsive, and usable format. Just as internal integration of information allows a single manager to coordinate resource deployment, accessibility to data across the supply chain facilitates interorganizational synchronization and improved resource use. For example, when retailers and manufacturers invest in technology that enables them to share data on item sales at store level by time of day, coordinated inventory availability and deployment become a possibility. This kind of connectivity is increasing in a variety of supply chains. The connectivity indicators include exchange technology investment, application of EDI standards, industry standards for data exchange, and the ability to share both standardized and customized information.

The first indicator of connectivity is the technology investment that firms have made and are continuing to make to enhance cross-organizational information exchange. These investments include the hardware and software to facilitate information exchange using dedicated and leased line, Internet, and satellite technologies. All firms in the sample report a substantial investment, with high index achieving firms indicating a very strong commitment.

The second indicator of connectivity is the use of industry EDI or Internet standards for information exchange. Historically, the barriers to connectivity have discouraged firms from pursuing strategies that depend upon frequent, timely data communication, using such technologies. Without a common industry communication standard, a virtual Tower of Babel was created as firms adopted various technologies to achieve data exchange. The result was that any firm with several supply chain partners was required to maintain several different communication systems. While accepted standards have improved the situation, there are still inconsistencies in the interpretation of the standards. The Internet has established a way around this problem. Issues of security, speed, and reliability, however, have until recently slowed its adoption. While there is substantial difference between the high and average index achievement firms when considering the use of EDI standards, the majority of firms report extensive commitment to industry EDI standards.

The third connectivity indicator augments the use of standards by extending their domain to include a broader range of information exchange. Expanded information types range from relatively tactical data, such as inventory status, shipment release schedules, warehouse shipments, and POS information, to more strategic data such as forecasts, production schedules, new products introductions, and marketing/promotion plans.

The final indicator of connectivity is the ability to share customized information with both suppliers and customers. High achieving firms are finding ways to encourage industrywide communication through EDI and the Internet. Industry and trade groups have made considerable strides to facilitate such transfer in recent years. Newer technologies including Applets, "agent technology," and Message Oriented Middleware (MOM) are now making it possible to exchange both the data and the processing capability across the Internet. Firms also are moving to establish "extranets" – secure Internet linkages – between themselves and supply chain partners. It is important to note connectivity does not necessarily require sophisticated technology. Telephones and fax machines can be used effectively. The key to connectivity is effective information sharing.

The research indicates that both high and average index achievement firms have placed a strong emphasis on connectivity. As stated previously, the vast majority of firms indicate increased use of industry EDI standards. While not quite to the same level, the majority of average firms report technology investment, use of industry standards for data exchange, and the ability to share both standardized and customized information.

COLLABORATIVE FORECASTING AND PLANNING

High achieving firms report supply chain efficiency is improved when customers and suppliers help them manage the business process. Constant communication and information flows must be maintained to avoid operational mistakes. Both effectiveness and efficiency can be improved when suppliers and customers play an active role in identifying and satisfying end-user demand.

Time-based techniques such as quick response (QR), just-in-time (JIT), and vendor managed inventory (VMI), as well as industry initiatives such as efficient-consumer response (ECR) and efficient health care response (EHCR) all support the conclusion that a coordinated supply chain can yield improvements in cycle time, order accuracy, and product availability. Better manufacturing efficiency and effectiveness, lower inventory levels, and sales increases also result from collaborative efforts. Such initiatives, however, may not facilitate true integration. For example, vendor managed inventory (VMI) programs may cut lead times and improve replenishment responsiveness but may not provide customers with sufficient insight to anticipate problems. At the same time, demand information provided by retailers may drive replenishment, but only a limited number of manufacturers report use of such information for advanced production planning. Without formal collaboration, suppliers and customers will continue to base forecasts on sales and allow their independent plans to drive production, promotion, and merchandising decisions. If plans are not shared operating results may be characterized by product shortages just when end-customer demand is high.

Supply chain success is increasingly dependent upon synchronization of information and product flow both within and across the firm's boundaries. Suppliers must collaborate with customers to develop a shared vision and joint plans. Collaboration can help ensure that the right amount of product will be available at the right place at the right time so stockouts are minimized and costs associated with inventory, expedited shipments, and rush production are reduced. Sales typically increase if the products being promoted are available on the shelves when consumers want them.

Implementation of collaborative forecasting and planning may require modification in traditional operating procedures. In many cases the planning processes exist but are not synchronized between supply chain partners. Typical planning and forecasting techniques used by both manufacturers and retailers aggregate demand at a brand or category level by region and by quarter. These forecasts are then disaggregated and used by independent operating units across companies to plan their activities. Joint planning and exchange of strategic information rarely occurs because of the traditional lack of trust between trading partners as well as a general a lack of understanding of the benefits. Using CPFR, suppliers develop strategic plans in collaboration with key customers. They may share strategic marketing information, such as when and what type of promotions will occur and the expected result. Also, other information that may affect sales such as product introduction and new store openings may be shared. When a manufacturer and its suppliers share information concerning retail promotional timing, they can each plan production accordingly. Collaboration also enables supply chain partners to simplify product and promotional offerings in a way that reduces ordering and invoice complexity.

The food and consumer products industries have pioneered the application of collaborative forecasting and planning techniques. These techniques have been referred to as collaborative planning forecasting and replenishment (CPFR). While certain industry characteristics have contributed to the success of CPFR in these two industries, it appears that the process can be leveraged by other industries as well.

Collaboration requires that trading partners actively develop a common set of expectations. These expectations establish common operating parameters so partners can implement changes without constantly consulting each other. Any change outside the parameters requires direct communication to renegotiate the plan.

In essence, collaborative forecasting and planning transfers end-customer demand information as far up the supply chain as possible to facilitate planning and to reduce guesswork. Once the partners agree on a product quantity for a specific time it is considered a confirmed order. The process requires technology to ensure information moves in real-time. Current information for operations usually can be provided by EDI. In contrast, data to support planning may not be as easily communicated by the firm's current transaction codes. CPFR, for example, bases the production plan on expectations regarding future promotions, but this information is exchanged via the Internet. Shared data warehouses are the growing way to facilitate collaboration. One food industry manufacturer reports greater than 50 percent sales increases for their brand through the use of CPFR.

There are four indicators of a firm's collaborative forecasting and planning capability. These include acquisition of direct customer data, active sharing of common expectations, joint strategic planning, and forecast/planning collaboration.

The first collaborative indicator is the commitment and ability to directly obtain customer POS, inventory, and promotional plans. This ability allows all supply chain partners to focus on the end-customer takeaway as the driver for supply chain activity.

The second collaborative indicator is the development of a common set of expectations with supply chain partners. Such expectations should include growth and profitability plans, marketing plans, category plans, and volume requirements. Creating a common vision results in a unified focus for the integrated supply chain.

The third collaborative indicator extends from common information. Not only do high achieving firms share a common set of expectations, they proactively develop joint plans with key customers. These strategic plans include unique product development and promotional offerings designed to enhance end-customer value and intermediate customer success.

The final collaborative indicator is the process of collaborative forecasting and planning. This includes the definition of a specific process, development of required technology applications, and the assignment of organizational responsibility. The Voluntary Inter-Industry Communications Standards Committee (VICS) has proposed such a process for the consumer goods industry (Information available on www.cpfr.org website). Exhibit 6-1 lists the CPFR process steps.

EXHIBIT 6-1

CPFR PROCESS STEPS

1. Develop front end agreement
2. Create joint business plan
3. Create sales forecast
4. Identify exceptions for sales forecast
5. Resolve/collaborate on exception items
6. Create order forecast
7. Handle exceptions for order forecast
8. Resolve/collaborate on exception items
9. Order generation

Research results indicate that high index achievement firms collaborate substantially more with their supply chain partners than average firms. Although all the indicators report a significant difference between the high and average firms, the indicators relating to sharing common expectations and joint development of strategic plans demonstrate the largest difference.

SUMMARY

Technology and planning integration requires information systems capable of supporting the wide variety of operational configurations needed to serve diverse market segments. Supply chain effectiveness depends on the exchange of timely and accurate information across customers, material and service suppliers, and internal functional areas.

Success of technology and planning integration rests upon four capabilities: information management, internal communications, connectivity, and collaborative forecasting and planning. *Information management* focuses on supply chain resource allocation through seamless transactions across the total order-to-delivery cycle. *Internal communication* uses technological systems to exchange information across functional boundaries in a timely, responsive, and usable format. *Connectivity* extends internal communications capability to supply chain partners. *Collaborative forecasting and planning* involves customers and suppliers developing a shared vision supported by a mutual commitment to jointly generated action plans. Exhibit 6-2 defines technology and planning integration concepts.

EXHIBIT 6-2

TECHNOLOGY AND PLANNING INTEGRATION
The competency of maintaining information systems capable of supporting the wide variety of operational configurations needed to serve diverse market segments.

Information Management:	Commitment and capability to facilitate supply chain resource allocation through seamless transactions across the total order-to-delivery cycle.
Internal Communication:	Capability to exchange information across internal functional boundaries in a timely, responsive, and usable format.
Connectivity:	Capability to exchange information with external supply chain partners in a timely, responsive, and usable format.
Collaborative Forecasting and Planning:	Customer collaboration to develop shared visions and mutual commitment to jointly generated action plans.

MEASUREMENT INTEGRATION

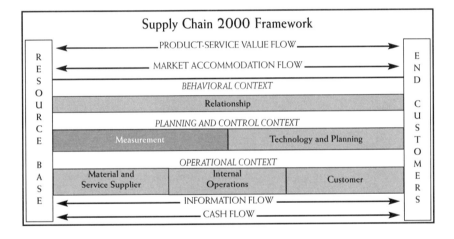

*I*nformation is needed not only for operational and planning decisions, but also for performance feedback. Each operating area must show its contribution to the goal of providing value to end-users. This was another issue on which the other VPs constantly agreed with Charlie – and constantly failed to act. Each department had various performance measures based on traditional goals and objectives, and often they performed quite well in those terms. Nevertheless, calls continued to come in from customers about service failures. As Amy observed, "customers don't care whether equipment use covers fixed costs or the warehouse meets efficiency goals. All they care about is whether we fill and deliver their orders, undamaged, and on schedule, 100 percent of the time." The task force concluded that measurement systems *ultimately have to assess whether customers are satisfied with the value produced by the overall supply chain.*

Furthermore, measures have to be translated into financial results. Both the previous CEO and Warren Thompson had discussed this need with Charlie many times during his quest for logistical excellence. Charlie knew that the board of directors – and the shareholders – would not get excited about change for its own sake. The improvements had to be tied to the bottom line.

Charlie remembered the financial problems Spartan confronted when his earlier restructuring plan was adopted. Production was slowed for three quarters to clear excess inventory from the pipeline. Wall Street analysts had downgraded Spartan's stock, failing to see the long-term benefits of integrated cost measurement. Back then, top management had taken a leap of faith that world class logistical changes would ultimately improve the bottom line. To his eternal credit, the former CEO had been willing to stay the course, and his experience had helped him convince the board. But it had almost cost him his job during the dark days, when the stock price fell for three consecutive quarters. Charlie knew that Warren didn't have that kind of power with the board. He would need quantifiable proof of the financial benefits of supply chain integration in order to get the board's approval to proceed.

Measurement is not solely a logistics or supply chain problem. There is general resistance throughout most firms due to its possible negative impact on compensation and career. Resistance in logistics and supply chain management, however, is particularly strong due to cross-functional and inter-organizational requirements. These boundary spanning relationship requirements also make the benefits of integrated measurement essential.

Creating competitive advantage through high performance logistics and supply chain capabilities requires integrated measurement systems. These systems must track the performance of operations across the borders of internal functional areas and external supply chain partners. Measurement systems must also reflect the operational performance of the overall supply chain and the financial performance of individual firms. Integrated performance measurement provides the basis for calibrating the many parts of the supply chain engine. Good metrics and strong measurement systems serve to provide timely feedback, so management can take corrective action, and drive superior results.

The goals of integrated measurement are simple. Accomplishing the task, however, is difficult, and it continues to challenge firms as they struggle to manage the innovative structures they create to ensure end-customer success. Specific functions must be viewed as contributing to the overall process as contrasted to stand-alone activities. This means that functional managers must be willing to guide operations toward the goal of lowering total logistics costs. Ultimately, measurement integration requires a comprehensive understanding of all the variables that affect a supply chain's ability to deliver value to the customer.

Measurement integration combines internal and supply chain performance metrics. Just as internal functions must be positioned to contribute to lowest total cost processes, similar trade-offs occur between firms in the supply chain. Throughout this research, five major measurement categories were used to reflect performance achieved from both an individual firm and a supply chain wide perspective. The measurement categories are: (1) customer service, (2) cost management, (3) quality, (4) productivity, and (5) asset management. These measures are discussed in detail later in this chapter and from a validation perspective in Chapter Nine. At this point it is important to stress the fundamental nature of comprehensive measurement in order to monitor progress and identify change necessary to maintain substantial success.

The four capabilities required to achieve measurement integration are functional assessment, activity-based and total cost methods, comprehensive metrics, and financial impact.

FUNCTIONAL ASSESSMENT

The starting point for managing and controlling supply chains is accurate assessment of functional performance. Managers need information about functional performance to identify problems and suggest ways to improve. Logistics performance measures focusing on customer service, cost, quality, productivity, and asset management are critical and require evaluation across a broad range of specific measures. The specific functional assessment indicators include measurement number, breadth, quality, and accuracy.

Most firms report substantially increased interest in functional performance measurement. Their interest focuses on a broader range of categories and individual metrics. Exhibit 7-1 lists frequently used measures to monitor customer service, cost, quality, productivity, and asset management.

EXHIBIT 7-1

	TYPICAL PERFORMANCE METRICS			
Customer Service	Cost Management	Quality	Productivity	Asset Management
Fill rate	Total cost	Damage frequency	Units shipped per employee	Inventory turns
Stockouts	Cost per unit	Order entry accuracy	Units per labor dollar	Inventory levels, number of days supply
Shipping errors	Cost as a percentage of sales	Picking/shipping accuracy	Orders per sales representative	Obsolete inventory
On-time delivery	Inbound freight	Document/ invoicing accuracy	Comparison to historical standard	Return on net assets
Backorders	Outbound freight	Information availability	Goal programs	Return on investment
Cycle time	Administrative	Information accuracy	Productivity index	Inventory classification (A,B,C)
Delivery consistency	Warehouse order processing	Number of credit claims	Equipment downtime	Economic Value Added (EVA)
Response time to inquiries	Direct labor	Number of customer returns	Order entry productivity	
Response accuracy	Comparison of actual versus budget		Warehouse labor productivity	
Complete orders	Cost trend analysis		Transportation labor productivity	
Customer complaints	Direct product profitability			
Sales force complaints	Customer Segment profitability			
Overall reliability	Inventory carrying			
Overall satisfaction	Cost of returned good			
	Cost of damage			
	Cost of service failures			
	Cost of backorder			

While most firms indicated involvement in functional assessment, high index achievement firms have a greater propensity to comprehensively measure how functions impact key processes. Such firms place a stronger focus on measurement breadth and quality. Unlike previous research findings, it is becoming increasingly clear that most firms have sufficient commitment to functional assessment to set the foundation for effective measurement integration.

ACTIVITY-BASED AND TOTAL COST METHODS

As noted earlier, leading firms build success upon their ability to synchronize and coordinate functions across the supply chain. This requires the ability to horizontally measure process efficiency and effectiveness. The bottom line in supply chain measurement is the ability to satisfy end-customers. True customer value can only be achieved by effective integration of many organizational functions across all firms engaged in the supply chain.

Firms must expand their measurement focus from functional related tasks or activities – such as cost of picking, picks per labor hour, or warehouse product damage rates – to systems that measure overall supply chain performance. This requires comprehensive costing, budgeting, and measurement to identify the cost/revenue contribution of specific customers, products, and services. Advances in costing methods have improved managers' understanding of the dynamics of integrating both internal and external functional activities. Total cost management, activity-based costing, and activity-based management provide the metrics firms use to support strategic and tactical decisions.

Total cost management embodies the perspective that specific functional costs are less relevant than overall cost. Expenditures on transportation, inventory, facilities, handling, and processing may be traded off to reduce total cost. The concept is simple, but practical applications can be monumentally difficult. Many enlightened managers believe they currently make decisions based on total cost. However, the real scope of such total cost is often is broader than they realize. In many situations significant procurement and acquisition costs are omitted from total cost assessments. Specifically, inbound freight costs may be excluded because firms cannot unbundle transportation from material or product purchase costs. Similarly, certain costs related to inventory, warehousing, and other areas are difficult to isolate. Such costs must be considered if decisions are to be based on the true costs of satisfying customers.

Activity-based costing (ABC) spans functional areas and focuses on costs associated with a specific activity or process. For example, order fulfillment often involves work by several departments in a complex organization. ABC identifies and tracks all relevant costs no matter where and by whom they are incurred, by identifying and measuring causal cost factors, called drivers. The drivers related to a specific process will differ according to the customer, product, or supply chain being examined. Firms using ABC can identify the true order fulfillment cost of providing a specific set of services for a product, individual business segment, or even individual customers.

Armed with such detailed cost data, executives can determine the performance effects of potential changes in logistical supply chain practice. ABC allows them to focus on specific product policy, customer service commitment, or supply chain design. Firms can then develop segmental supply chain strategies and solutions based on a specific cost-revenue analysis. For example, decisions to refine marketing and supply chain strategies can be based on the profit contribution of each SKU, customer segment, or channel.

Total costing and ABC methods enable firms to pinpoint the profitability of specific products, customers, and supply chains, as well as project cost-revenue outcomes for different programs and strategies. These approaches enable managers to set goals for specific actions and programs and to measure achieved performance. The use of total cost and ABC analyses to make decisions is called activity-based management. It has the potential to relate customer sales and related profitability based on exact costing of ordering practices and delivery expectations. This precise cost information can be used to modify supply chain practices. For example, managers can work with specific customers to develop new routines that simplify and streamline order placement, resulting in better service as well as lower cost.

When cost reductions cannot be identified within the existing supply chain, activity-based management can help identify alternatives. One manufacturer discovered that 50 percent of its profits came from its top 20 customers, and 99 percent of profit came from the top 100. The remaining 3,000 customers accounted for one percent of profit, and in some cases, accounted for substantial losses. In another case in the home furnishings industry, the top 20 percent of customers accounted for 88 percent of the profit contribution; the top 100 customers accounted for 110 percent of the profit contribution while the remaining 1900 customers accounted for an actual loss of ten percent. The supply chain structure to service these unprofitable customers was re-engineered. Order fulfillment was transferred to distributors, or a third party was contracted to perform fulfillment. This allowed the firm to focus on the 100 key customers, working out unique supply chain accommodations to service unique needs. There also are examples of firms using e-commerce to effectively serve business segments that previously had been unprofitable due to the high administrative costs required to support them.

Activity-based management also can be used to determine product profitability. This may reveal that relatively few products generate much of the firm's overall profit. This information can help firms reduce the number of products and/or product lines and allow firms to concentrate on the goods and services most important to future success. A significant barrier to implementing activity-based management is the belief that data must be measured precisely and validated to a high degree of statistical accuracy in order to support decision making. Precision is always desirable, but it is most important when accounting procedures are used to support legal and fiduciary reporting. In the case of activity-based management, data used to improve management operational decisions need not be precise. Firms should match desired precision to the sensitivity of the decision. In other words, you do not have to measure with a micrometer if you are going to cut with an ax.

Another barrier to activity-based management is a sensitivity of functions or organizations to have their data investigated or sniffed by someone outside. Managers are reluctant to have outsiders get into too much detail regarding their operations because they are concerned that a problem may surface. This barrier can only be overcome with top management's support of the analysis.

There is a significant difference between high and average index achieving firms in terms of their propensity to employ total and activity-based cost management. While average firms indicate relatively minor use in total and activity-based cost management, high firms report very strong use. Specifically, high achievement firms report strong use of total cost, management, segmental profitability, and relative logistics performance. While high achieving firms do not use ABC as much as total cost management, the relative difference between the high and average index achieving firms is the same. In summary, high index achieving firms report significantly more use of total costing, segmental costing, and activity-based management.

COMPREHENSIVE METRICS

Any measurement system is of limited usefulness unless it includes a standard of comparison. Most firms attempt to compare performance to that of the previous year or to what they feel competitors have accomplished. A hallmark of successful measurement integration is achieved when internal performance is compared with inter-enterprise and overall supply chain standards.

Firms are taking a hard look at currently accepted measures of costing, customer service, and quality. For example, effective inventory management has preoccupied logisticians for decades. Low inventory levels and rapid turns are goals for many organizations. Yet, existing inventory performance measures may not increase overall supply chain productivity nor ensure effective use of available assets, which should also be elements of effective inventory management. If a firm focuses solely on inventory turn, it may simply shift goods from its own warehouses to those of a supply chain partner with little or no reduction in total supply chain inventory days-on-hand. One government customer, for example, required that a supplier be capable of providing an inventory level equivalent to a six-month demand for a product at the time of contract negotiations. Once the sale was made, the supplier transferred the goods from its warehouse to the government's facility. The government, of course, did not use the product immediately, so there were no gains in supply chain inventory productivity. The overall supply chain inventory is the appropriate focus.

The primary indicators of comprehensive metrics are a commitment to zero defect logistical performance, application of extended supply chain measures, programs to externally measure customer satisfaction and external benchmarking.

A commitment to zero defect logistical performance is currently operationalized as the focus of the *perfect order*. Performance is tracked across a range of elements that reflect the number of orders delivered in full, on time, and totally error free (including documentation and invoicing). Traditional measurement systems monitor individual elements of total customer service such as fill rate. Single measures of customer service can provide a false picture. Customers may consider as many as 20 different logistics service elements to assess a perfect order. As a result, an increasing number of high performing firms report the development of measures which combine multiple customer service elements to measure integrated service performance. Exhibit 7-2 lists the multiple and expanding dimensions of the perfect order.

EXHIBIT 7-2

DIMENSIONS OF THE "PERFECT ORDER"

Correct order entry	Timely arrival
Correctly formatted EDI and transaction codes	Shipment not damaged
	Correct invoice
Items are available	Accurate overcharges
Ship date allows delivery	No customer deductions
Order picked correctly	No errors in payment processing
Paperwork complete and accurate	

The perfect order combines service accomplishment across service elements. In other words, a perfect order is the product of multiple measures. A firm that achieves 95 percent performance in each service area would appear to be doing very well. From the customer's perspective, however, orders are only delivered without some type of service failure $(.95)^{12}$ times, or about 54 percent of the time. Thus, performance across key measures is the key to zero defect performance.

The second indicator of comprehensive metrics is the development and application of metrics that extend across supply chain relationships. Specific measures are end-customer level sales, inventory dwell time, cash-to-cash cycle time, customer satisfaction, and benchmarking.

Tracking end-customer level sales highlights the recognition that speed and time synchronization in supply chains provide significant opportunities for competitive differentiation and enhanced financial results. End-customer level sales measurement requires each channel member to use actual sales to end-customers as the critical measure, regardless of position in the supply chain. Tracking end-customer level sales helps firms assess their attempts to increase inventory velocity and reduce the time required to complete the logistical process.

Inventory *dwell time* is a second extended measure reflecting overall supply chain performance. Inventory dwell time is the ratio of days inventory sits idle in the supply chain relative to the days it is productively being used. While it is sometimes necessary for inventory to sit in the supply chain for reasons of quality control or to buffer uncertainty, extended dwell time is generally not productive. Total supply chain inventory dwell time highlights the potential magnitude of non-productive inventory.

The third measure is the *cash-to-cash cycle time*. Inventory is reported as a current asset on the balance sheet. However, it may be offset by accounts payable depending upon the terms of payment. Bad debt aside, accounts receivable may not be paid for 30 to 45 days. Therefore, the physical possession of inventory is less important to asset productivity than tracking the flow of funds. This concept, called the cash-to-cash cycle, measures the time between expenditures to buy inventory and collection of revenue from sales. A retailer who receives terms of 2 percent net 10 from suppliers, for example, may sell the goods to end-customers long before the invoice is due. Some resellers have a velocity that results in a negative cash-to-cash cycle, meaning overall cash is received from end-customers for sales of inventory for which the corresponding accounts payable invoice is not yet due for payment! Sensitivity to cash flow dynamics is creating totally new business strategies.

The fourth comprehensive measurement indicator is a formal program to measure customer satisfaction. While the program may include ad-hoc activities such as surveys and interviews, high performing firms are employing more formal processes facilitated by information technology, third parties, and performance scorecards.

The final comprehensive measurement indicator is benchmarking. In addition to developing and applying new measures of integrated supply chain performance, top firms are comparing results to pre-determined standards. While benchmarking performance outcomes has been widely accepted, a large number of firms do not benchmark processes. Comparing both outcomes and processes to industry standards keeps management aware of state-of-the-art business practices.

A critical aspect of benchmarking is the choice of standards for comparison. Most firms compare the performance of internal business units involved in similar operations, or who operate in different regions. Since one business unit is frequently unaware of what occurs in other units within the corporation, internal benchmarking is a way to share experience as well as improve relative levels of performance.

Internal comparison, however, does not ensure that operations are keeping pace with those of competitors. A firm may be falling behind and not be aware of it. To guard against such a possibility, many firms make comparisons to competitors. Information on competitive performance helps firms identify *where* improvement is most needed because it is extremely difficult to obtain information about competitorsí operational processes. It seldom identifies *how* to improve.

Nonrestricted benchmarking refers to efforts to compare both process measures and outcomes to best practice, regardless of where the relevant practice is found. It does not restrict information sources or standards to internal operations or a specific industry. It is possible to learn from unrelated industries or organizations that have an outstanding reputation or use innovative strategies in a particular operating area. The warehousing and materials handling process of a leading mail order firm has, for example, served as a benchmark in industries as diverse as health and personal care and electronics. Although specific products may differ, firms often discover similarities between the operational characteristics and service requirements of unrelated industries.

To illustrate that benchmarking makes a difference, Exhibit 7-3 reports the percentage of high and average index achieving firms that benchmark various dimensions of supply chain performance. The results indicate that high firms benchmark on all performance dimensions significantly more than average achieving firms.

EXHIBIT 7-3

PERFORMANCE BENCHMARKING DIFFERENTIAL		
Performance Dimension	Percent of High Index Achieving Firms	Percent of Average Index Achieving Firms
Customer Service	92.5	56.0
Cost Management	80.0	47.1
Quality	70.0	31.0
Productivity	77.5	38.5
Asset Management	55.0	25.8

* All differences are statistically significant at .05 level

Benchmarking process and outcome metrics allows firms to track performance and identify improvement opportunities. The benefits of benchmarking are not easily achieved. Firms must make a large and continuous commitment in time and personnel resources. Top management involvement is essential to ensure that benchmarking receives sufficient cross-functional attention and is accurately considered in the planning and evaluation process. Firms that benchmark are more likely to meet goals because they can be proactive in a dynamic environment.

The comprehensive measurement capability is a strong differentiator of supply chain performance. While high index achieving firms report a substantially greater propensity on all indicators of comprehensive measurement, there were particularly large differences for benchmarking and comprehensive measurements. These results strongly support the notion that the leading firms employ benchmarking and comprehensive supply chain measures to enhance their supply chain performance.

FINANCIAL IMPACT

The three previous capabilities related to how well firms monitor operations and how measurement systems are used to drive operational improvements. Increasingly, however, managers must demonstrate how changes in supply chain practices and processes affect the overall financial health of their enterprise. Traditional performance measures do not describe achievement in the financial language spoken in the executive suite. Measurement systems must enable managers to link supply chain performance directly to financial performance. Exhibit 7-4 illustrates a comprehensive value model that considers both operational excellence and asset utilization. This model incorporates both operating considerations that are important from a firm competitiveness perspective and asset utilization dimensions that are important from a shareholder perspective. Application of the supply chain capabilities to achieve overall competency is only important if it can yield superior performance on at least one, but ideally more than one of these dimensions.

EXHIBIT 7-4

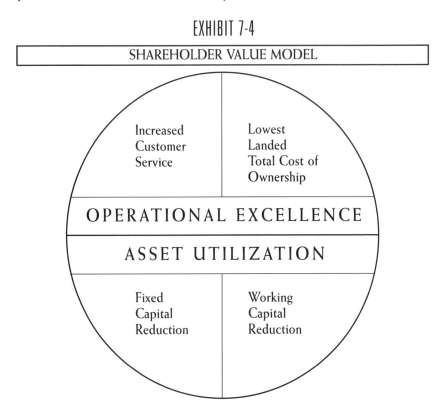

SHAREHOLDER VALUE MODEL

Increased Customer Service

Lowest Landed Total Cost of Ownership

OPERATIONAL EXCELLENCE

ASSET UTILIZATION

Fixed Capital Reduction

Working Capital Reduction

On the operational excellence dimension, the key metrics focus on increased customer service and lower total supply chain costs. The proper combination allows the supply chain to respond more precisely to specific customer needs.

Integrated customer service measurement concerns revenue and is achieved by developing a set of shared cross-functional and cross-organizational measures to guide and monitor work performed by multiple supply chain partners as they add value for the end-customer. Knowledge about customer perceptions of value is essential when creating proper measures. Traditionally, firms measure service in areas such as fill rate, cycle time, damage rate, and frequency of errors in terms of average performance in comparison to normative standards. While most firms continue to use such measures, top performers are expanding measurement to include more sophisticated methods and techniques. The growing consideration of this element is illustrated by the increased use of perfect order and end-customer sales as critical measures of overall supply chain performance. Also, it is critical to understand how the firm's customers (particularly major ones) measure customer service and respond to those measures. One software provider, for example, operates under a stated corporate goal of adding to the sales growth and cost savings of end-customers. Independent auditors validate the value they deliver for end-customers.

Leading firms are emphasizing absolute or specific performance in addition to averages. Furthermore, absolute performance is translated into specific customer statements. For example, rather than report that the firm provides 99.5 percent damage-free delivery, performance is expressed in terms of the number of damaged orders delivered to a specific customer during an operating period. Personnel on both sides of the relationship can better interpret specific figures. Performance goals are set to exceed customer expectations.

The second aspect of operational excellence is achievement of lowest total cost of ownership. Lowest total cost of ownership incorporates all basic product costs as well as all supply chain costs related to inventory financing, acquisition, processing, movement, storage, handling, and delivery. In general, the lowest total cost of ownership would reflect the best value from the end-customer's perspective. In addition to the individual cost elements, the dynamics of lowest cost are also influenced by shifts in logistics and supply chain productivity.

Asset value utilization reflects a supply chain's effectiveness in terms of fixed assets and working capital. Fixed capital assets include manufacturing and distribution facilities, transportation and material handling equipment, and information technology hardware. Working capital reflects the supply chain's inventory investment and the differential investment in accounts receivable relative to accounts payable. Overall asset utilization is a particularly important measure of firm and overall supply chain performance as viewed by the financial market.

Another aspect of asset utilization influencing firm capitalization is *free cash spin*. Free cash spin represents the decrease in cash requirements that can be attained through reduced inventory, facility, equipment, and receivables. For example, increased inventory turnover reduces the cash tied up in inventory and makes it available for other investments. High index achieving firms focus on ways to spin this free cash by reducing the level of assets employed to support logistics and supply chain operations.

The indicators of the financial impact capability include consideration of capital deployed in total cost measurements, supply chain influences on business profitability, and return-on-assets and economic valued-added. The first indicator is the inclusion of capital deployed as a component of total cost performance. The influence of supply chain operations on financial performance hinges on a better understanding of asset utilization. The central point is that traditional accounting procedures may not fully capture the cost of excess inventory. The traditional treatment of inventory as an asset ignores the holding cost, which includes opportunity costs (what the firm could earn if the resources tied up in excess inventory were invested elsewhere), depreciation, insurance, taxes and obsolescence of inventory. Estimates are that such costs range from 15 to 40 percent of inventory value per year. High index achievement firms develop segmental total cost analyses that consider inventory and accounts receivable components to focus efforts on satisfying their most profitable customers.

The second indicator is the ability to determine the revenue and profit impact of enhanced supply chain performance. Metrics currently used to track financial performance are not effective at monitoring operational costs or how operational improvements impact revenue. Financial managers frequently resist supply chain streamlining operations because of the short-term operating losses the firm may have to sustain over several quarters as pipeline inventory, which is reflected as a current asset in traditional financial accounting, is drawn down. Activity-based and total cost management attempt to overcome this barrier.

The third indicator is the application of measurement systems that can indicate the true influence of supply chain operations on financial performance. Two measures capture this concept. Return on net assets (RONA) is the ratio of net profit margin to asset turnover. Net profit margin measures a firm's effectiveness in converting revenue into profit. It is computed by dividing net operating income (NOI) by sales. Asset turnover measures how effectively a firm uses its invested capital, that is, how much business the firm generates on its asset base, including inventory. RONA is directly influenced by competitive intensity. Competition forces firms to follow pricing strategies that result in tradeoffs between profit margin and asset utilization. Managers and investors frequently consider RONA as a measure of the degree to which a firm strikes an effective balance between the two. This ratio is widely used to gauge a firm's operating achievement relative to competitors.

The long available Strategic Profit Model (SPM), also known as the Dupont Profit Model, continues to grow in popularity. The SPM relates operational measures, such as sales revenue and fixed and variable operating costs, to asset utilization measures, such as days of inventory on hand and inventory turn, to determine the overall return on assets. The results indicate how supply chain operating policies can drive asset utilization and overall financial performance. Appendix E provides more detail regarding the SPM.

The final indicator of financial performance is the application of Economic Value Added (EVA). EVA monitors the level of value created by a firm. It allows stockholders to determine whether management is creating or destroying wealth. EVA is calculated as annual operating profit after tax, minus a cost of capital charge. The measurement is a reminder to companies that increasing stock share prices does not justify growing earnings at any cost. Rather, earnings growth should be faster than new capital expansion. The theory is that no matter how good the books look, a company is not creating value to stockholders until it provides a profit greater than its cost of capital.

The research results show that more high achieving firms use EVA than average achievers. However, its use by even the high achieving firms is less than that of other financial measures. The lower use of EVA may reflect its relative newness. Low use may also reflect an honest disagreement regarding the appropriateness of the measure. Some firms have specifically rejected its use because it is not friendly to growth-related strategies. Long-term growth is difficult for firms operating under a strict EVA environment.

While the research found that all of the above indicators differentiate between high and average index achieving firms, the most significant contributors are the consideration of total cost including an element for capital and the application of EVA. Many firms indicate that they consider the logistics impact on the profit statement, so it is not a major differentiator of high versus average achievement. On the other hand, consideration of return on investments or assets does not appear to be particularly common for either high or average performing firms. This reluctance may be due to the attitude of some managers regarding the role of inventory. There are still many firms that do not consider inventory as a logistics cost responsibility.

SUMMARY

Managers are haunted by the phrase, "*If you can't measure it, you can't manage it.*" They frequently are frustrated by the inability of traditional measurement systems to monitor logistical processes that extend across functional and firm boundaries. Measurement integration is the competency required to assess performance throughout the supply chain. Expertise in four capabilities is needed: functional assessment, activity-based and total cost methods, comprehensive metrics, and financial analysis.

Functional assessment expands the number and categories of internal performance measures used and improves the quality, timeliness, accuracy, and availability of data. *Activity-based and total cost management* uses activity-based costing, budgeting, and measurement to obtain a comprehensive picture of the cost/revenue contribution of a specific customer or product. *Comprehensive metrics* capability establishes enterprise as well as overall supply chain performance standards and measures. *Financial impact* enables firms to link supply chain operational performance directly to financial measures in order to demonstrate how changes in business practices and processes will affect the overall economic health of the firm. Through measurement integration, firms can efficiently monitor supply chain processes and effectively identify and communicate the advantages of change. Exhibit 7-5 summarizes measurement integration and the four capabilities that comprise it.

EXHIBIT 7-5

MEASUREMENT INTEGRATION

Development and maintenance of measurement systems that facilitate segmental strategies and processes.

Functional Assessment:	The development of comprehensive functional performance measurement capability.
Activity Based and Total Cost Methodology:	Adoption and commitment to activity-based costing, budgeting, and measurement for comprehensive identification of cost/revenue contribution of a specific entity such as a product.
Comprehensive Metrics:	Establishment of cross-enterprise and overall supply chain performance standards and measures.
Financial Impact:	Direct linkage of supply chain performance to financial measurement such as EVA, RONA, etc.

RELATIONSHIP
INTEGRATION

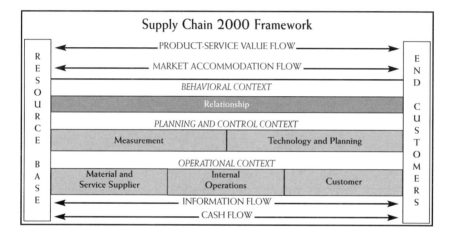

Supply Chain 2000 Framework

	PRODUCT-SERVICE VALUE FLOW	
R E S O U R C E **B A S E**	MARKET ACCOMMODATION FLOW	**E N D** **C U S T O M E R S**
	BEHAVIORAL CONTEXT	
	Relationship	
	PLANNING AND CONTROL CONTEXT	
	Measurement / Technology and Planning	
	OPERATIONAL CONTEXT	
	Material and Service Supplier / Internal Operations / Customer	
	INFORMATION FLOW	
	CASH FLOW	

*T*he task force was beginning to think it had covered all the bases of operational integration – not only operational linkages between customers, internal activities, and material and service suppliers but also the critical information and measurement systems that tied all the operations together. Yet, at the last weekly meeting Charlie said something was missing, a "human dimension," as he called it. "After all," Charlie told them, "what we're talking about doing requires change in people's behavior." The following Monday, Melissa Brighton volunteered that she thought she knew what Charlie was talking about.

Melissa began the meeting by telling about a service supplier relationship that had gone bad at her previous firm. Her former employer, a retailer, had decided to outsource the entire logistical process to a major third party service provider. The outsourcing process had been done by the book. The firm spent months collecting proposals and thoroughly interviewing prospective firms. Once they decided on a provider they spent an additional month carefully writing the agreement. It spelled out joint responsibilities, activities to be accomplished, performance standards, compensation, and reasons for discontinuing the relationship, among other things. Attorneys representing both parties reviewed the document, and there were numerous meetings between executives and managers at various levels in the two organizations.

Eight months into the agreement, misunderstandings had emerged about the cost and service benchmarks for performance evaluation. Furthermore, the logistics supplier's role with certain customers was not communicated clearly in the original document, which resulted in some heated exchanges between mid-level managers. It also became clear that the 150-page agreement provided insufficient structure to direct cross-firm operations, such as who talks to whom and in what circumstances, how to resolve conflict, and when to meet and how often. They also found that they often used different word definitions and implications thus resulting in further confusion. In addition, information required by the third party to make operational decisions was either passed along incorrectly or not at all. One manager in the logistics firm suggested that the retailer's transportation people were disgruntled about having their turf outsourced. Finally, the guidelines for gain and loss sharing were unclear. Within two years of signing the agreement, both parties were claiming millions of dollars in damages against the other.

Everyone on the task force knew of a similar story. Rich Watkinson, the Production Manager, told about a material supplier who had pushed for vendor managed inventory (VMI) as a way to improve service and cut inventory costs for both firms through better coordination. After considerable investigation, Rich and Javi Suarez (VP of Manufacturing) agreed to a pilot program for a limited number of materials. The vendor even committed a business manager who spent much of his time working with Rich's production team to ensure a seamless conversion. Things went well for the first quarter, but once the novelty wore off, the vendor focused attention on newer challenges, and service levels began to drop. Despite numerous meetings to address the situation, commitment to the program was not extensive throughout the vendor's operations. Somewhere, someone would make decisions that resulted in orders arriving short, or late, or with inaccurate information, or all three! Even the vendor's business manager assigned to Spartan was frustrated. Eventually it was agreed that the vendor organization simply could not achieve the commitment necessary to sustain the integrated relationship.

Despite all the press about the benefits of partnerships or alliances, in practice it seemed that you just couldn't trust someone who worked for another company to do the best thing for yours. Inwardly, the task force members admitted that their customers probably felt the same way about Spartan. Amy said as much, pointing out *that Super wanted the level of service that could emerge only from a strong multi-level relationship with Spartan, but Super either would not or could not provide the kind of information that was required to sustain that arrangement. One of their marketing managers had even suggested that Super was more than willing to provide promotional and sales data if Spartan was willing to pay for it. "Now there's a win/win attitude for you," Amy sighed. While this reluctance for trust has been an issue in the past, the current business environment requires a change in paradigm. The complexity resulting from such new realities as globalization, vendor managed inventory, and make-to-order arrangements require reevaluation of the willingness to trust.*

In a competitive environment, single enterprises acting alone cannot fully achieve all management goals. As customer demands increase and become more specific, high Supply Chain 2000 achieving firms undertake initiatives to coordinate responsibilities across the supply chain in order to improve service and lower total cost. The problem is that different firms typically operate under different management philosophies and pursue divergent goals. Successful relationships require managers to rethink the way they conduct business with suppliers and customers so the benefits of integrated and focused supply chain strategies can be achieved.

In most business relationships today, suppliers sell to customers. Often there is considerable conflict or lack of cooperation in these buyer/seller arrangements as each party seeks the best financial deal. Neither side fully trusts the other. Operations are inefficient because vendors must guess customers' needs since specific demand or planning information is not shared. In such situations, the potential for achieving overall supply chain efficiencies is limited as firms jockey for short-term benefits at the expense of their trading partners.

Relationship integration addresses the behavioral attitudes that firms need to instill if coordinated operations and strategies are to be developed and sustained. There must be a shared vision and shared objectives among customers and suppliers about interdependency and principles of collaboration. Efforts must focus on providing the best end-customer value regardless of where along the supply chain the necessary competencies exist. This collaborative perspective is the key to long-term supply chain viability. In order to pursue a competitive advantage, effective supply chain structures must be created to align the functional operations of multiple firms into an integrated system focused on satisfying end-customers. Relationship integration requires willingness on the part of supply chain partners to create structures, frameworks, and metrics that encourage cross-organizational behavior. This includes sharing proprietary planning and operational information as well as creating financial linkages making firms dependent on mutual performance.

The following sections introduce the capabilities that drive relationship integration: role specificity, guidelines, information sharing, and gain and risk sharing. These sections contain some information that duplicates content discussed under the topic of material and service supplier integration in Chapter Five. The topic of relationship integration, however, is sufficiently important to indulge this repetition.

ROLE SPECIFICITY

A major challenge in relationship integration is to develop a clear sense of the strategy, mission, and goals of a supply chain partnership. Close coordination means that resources are intermingled and corporate boundaries become blurred. In many situations, employees from the two organizations work side by side. While it is appropriate to share the objectives, role specificity clarifies the leadership process and establishes responsibility for activity completion among participating enterprises. The primary indicators of supply chain role specificity are joint clarification of roles and responsibilities among supply chain partners, identification of acceptable cooperative behavior ranges for suppliers and customers, and managerial belief in employee empowerment.

The first indicator of role specificity asserts the importance of stipulating the specific responsibilities of each partner in order to fix responsibility and accountability. Another aspect of this concerns the deal space or how do we both make money at this? This question is critical for the creation of a true win-win proposition. It is important at the start of the relationship to define the ground rules and gain commitment from engaged managers. All such relationships need a champion who is committed to making the engagement a success. The promotion or reassignment of that champion can be a major cause of failure. Role specificity defines responsibility for individual and shared work processes. Unilateral definition is at best useless and at worst lays the basis for serious misunderstandings and potential conflict. High index achieving firms work with supply chain partners to jointly define roles and responsibilities for specific jobs and processes.

The concept of relationship integration is based upon the belief that working together will achieve greater levels of customer-relevant performance than attainable by working independently. Partners in successful relationships must accept responsibility for specific work performance. Each firm should be committed to performing the roles that best focus their core competencies on creating value for the end-customer. That kind of special-ization leverages competency while simultaneously reducing duplication and waste. When expectations and tasks are spelled out, firms can more easily minimize delays emerging from uncoordinated operations and increase pro-ductivity. A number of firms, for example, share inventory management responsibly with suppliers to enhance coordination. Other firms have estab-lished relationships with third party providers to coordinate transportation load building, consolidation, and information management of finished goods being shipped to different customers.

Important elements of behavior specialization are functional absorption and functional spin-off. A manufacturer who assumes a nontraditional func-tion such as managing customer inventory exemplifies functional absorption. Functional spin-off occurs when a firm shifts some of its traditional respon-sibility to another member of the supply chain. Many manufacturers, for example, are spinning off warehousing and transportation activities to a third party. Managers who have been schooled in the importance of self-suffi-ciency and total hands on control do not easily accept such outsourcing. Firms are realizing that significant effort is needed to change or overcome such resistance.

Establishing acceptable practices for cooperation between suppliers and customers in different relational situations, the second indicator of role spec-ification, helps to maintain a balance of power. In traditional relationships one party typically dominated and called all or most of the shots. If that power was abused or exploited the relationship would only survive as long as the dominant firm maintained economic leverage. The typical result was that the subordinate firm would ultimately withdraw or be driven out of business. It is doubtful that the non-dominant firm would be motivated to develop or share innovations designed to benefit the relationship. If there were innovations by the non-dominant firm, they would almost certainly be defensive and self-serving. In contrast, an integrated relationship builds on a range of mutually acceptable practices to drive supplier and/or customer cooperation and establish the basis for effective leadership. Similarly, a range of acceptable behavior is clearly specified for situations in which the firm is not the dominant participant. Partners in successful relationships seek to have a clear understanding of these power dynamics. Increasingly, supply chain leadership is based more on knowledge, information, expertise, or other skill. However, there is seldom an equal balance of financial or market power between participating firms. Accordingly, leadership roles must emphasize guidance rather than specific authority within a realistic assess-ment of what each participating firm has at risk.

The third indicator of role specificity is senior management understanding that supply chain involvement requires significant empowerment of employees at the local operating level. This includes mentoring of the subordinate firm's management team to help them understand the benefits of integrated operations. Successful relationships involve substantial decision making at supplier and customer interface points. Decisions made at the regional or local level are better positioned to accommodate specific customer requirements. Empowerment requires defining clear roles and responsibilities so employees can act independently and quickly. All employees are expected to be able to handle routine tasks. Empowerment allows them to also deal with discretionary situations. This ensures rapid, effective response and frees management time for planning and other long-term duties. As a result, the supply chain becomes increasingly responsive to current requirements as contrasted to anticipating what may be needed based upon centrally planned forecasts.

Clear role specificity is a capability typical of firms that have achieved high levels of logistical integration. Firms achieving high index scores reported superior performance on each of the indicators of role specificity, particularly on joint specification of supply chain roles and responsibilities, employee empowerment, and development of clearly specified ranges of acceptable cooperative behavior in situations when they are *not* the dominant partner. High index achieving firms understand their role responsibilities within the supply chain context.

GUIDELINES

Although firms in general are favorable to building relationships, making inter-organizational integration work is another matter. A gap often exists between understanding what needs to be done and how to best do it. It is difficult for firms to deal with these relationship issues internally. It is even less common that firms consider them externally, and even then, the process is likely to be quite different. Firms consider relationship integration important to supply chain success but are unfamiliar with the ways and means or guidelines needed to accomplish the task. Guidelines are essential to facilitate inter-enterprise collaboration, leverage, and conflict resolution. Participants need to establish ground rules that clearly define a policy framework to guide behavior. Primary indicators of highly developed guidelines are the existence of plans to establish supply chain relationships and partnerships, and existence of a framework within which to pursue, establish, monitor, and terminate relationships and partnerships if and when they exceed their usefulness.

Since the essential capabilities for supply chain management are not resident in any single firm, considerable cross-organizational control and coordination is required in order to achieve desired relationship performance. Primarily, high index achieving firms develop and perfect policy guidelines that specify the conditions within which they pursue partnerships and alliances. These guidelines ensure that the goals and objectives of potential supply chain partners are complementary and are focused on shared goals. Guidelines that define joint operating policies and procedures for handling both routine and unexpected events focus attention on logistical activities that create value for end-customers. In addition, high achieving firms adopt guidelines jointly with partners to specify what to measure, who should measure it, how it should be measured, and how often.

It is also important to establish provisions for terminating relationships. Although most integrated relationships are voluntary and, in effect, can be dissolved at any point, setting formal exit procedures is advisable to prevent disputes over assets. These matters are best handled at the beginning of the relationship when all parties are cooperative and are amenable to setting fair and rational terms. A clause relating to duration and termination of the relationship ensures that it does not outlive its usefulness to the participants. Exit provisions are especially important when customized equipment or facilities are involved. Buy-sell agreements can be developed specifying who has the right or obligation to purchase or assume lease obligations. Strong and clear formal review and termination provisions actually strengthen an integrated relationship because both partners know the bounds of the arrangement.

Most of the firms in the Supply Chain 2000 database indicated that supply chain relationships are critical to achieving service and cost goals, but few have developed a formal set of policy guidelines for managers responsible for such relationship. High index achieving firms demonstrated much higher instances of developing formal guidelines than average firms. Exhibit 8-1 presents the percentage of firms that have developed formal guidelines. The indicator that was most substantial in differentiating high from average firms was the existence of guidelines for developing, maintaining, and monitoring supply chain relationships.

EXHIBIT 8-1

DEVELOPMENT OF FORMAL GUIDELINES			
My firm possesses Formal guidelines:	Percent of All Firms	Percent of Average Index Achieving Firms	Percent of High Index Achieving Firms
For developing, maintaining, and monitoring supply chain relationships.	30	23	77
For terminating partnerships/ alliances.	29	23	67
For defining the legal framework for involvement in supply chain collaboration.	24	19	58

INFORMATION SHARING

Cross-organizational exchange of information is fundamental to supply chain coordination. Partners must design and implement systems to facilitate integration of information and practices. Investment in technology is a necessary but not sufficient condition to facilitate information exchange. Unless a cooperative spirit exists between firms regarding information sharing, the arrangement will fail regardless of the technology available. The primary indicators of a high level of information sharing are maintenance of a database and access method to facilitate information sharing both between internal functional departments and with select external suppliers and customers. The information contained and shared within the database should be both operational and strategic if the supply chain is to achieve high levels of efficiency.

Effective supply chain integration is heavily dependent on trust beginning within the firm and ultimately extending to supply chain partners. Many managers still believe that sharing information such as forecasts, sales, inventories, costs, and promotional or development plans will compromise their organization's competitive position. This is particularly frustrating when managers interpret the organization as their specific functional department. For this reason, information is often not shared among departments of the same operating unit. A key indicator of information sharing capability is the degree to which operating and strategic information is shared among internal departments. If executives do not share internally its doubtful they will share information with supply chain partners.

Externally, some organizations will not share forecast or planning data under any circumstances, while others have adopted the practice of selling it to a third party provider of competitive data such as Nielson or Information Resources (IRI). Some retailers, for example, view point-of-sale data as a valuable commodity they own and from which they can extract a profit. This is a short-term mentality. The immediate gains that are generated from such information-hoarding pales in comparison to the cost savings and enhanced service that progressive firms feel is attainable by exchanging information with supply chain partners.

Firms that are committed to developing supply chain relationships must be willing to take some short-term risk in exchange for longer-term rewards. Information has traditionally been viewed as a source of power. This traditional perspective has developed a widespread cultural impediment to information sharing. While information should not be shared indiscriminately, it provides a way to cement important relationships. High index achieving firms generate a competitive advantage because of their willingness to exchange key technical, financial, operational and strategic information with partners.

Organizations that view sharing information as a key resource manage its exchange in a confidential manner to reduce conflict when conducting business with competing suppliers or in serving competing customers. For example, a number of manufacturers have established separate cross-functional teams to serve competing mass merchants. The teams include personnel from both organizations in such areas as sales, marketing, finance and logistics. Increasingly, shared confidential information is required to plan joint operations. To ensure that confidentiality is maintained, there must be credibility and trust between supply chain partners. Effective sharing of operational information with select suppliers and customers indicates high levels of information sharing capability.

Another key indicator of information sharing is willingness to share strategic data. Information sharing usually expands as trust is established. Initially, such tactical data as short-term forecasts and inventory availability may be provided to facilitate resource planning and product flow. Once the benefits of tactical sharing are realized, firms tend to become more open to sharing sensitive information on costs, product development plans, and promotional schedules. The automotive industry is a prime example of firms designating tier one lead suppliers who in turn coordinate and sequence the work of secondary suppliers. This supply chain strategy has significantly reduced cost and time of automobile assembly. Such benefits are totally dependent on sharing of information. Eventually, long-term plans and strategies are revealed in order to develop and integrate logistics processes and resources across the supply chains.

A final indicator of information sharing capability is maintenance of databases and the access methods used to facilitate exchange. Information sharing may take many forms. The most comprehensive is the exchange of data files and provision of direct access to databases. Shared employees, although not yet common, extends the process by providing a managerial conduit through which information flow between organizations can be coordinated and translated. Information also can be shared through third party logistics suppliers who assign dedicated employees to shipper locations to ensure coordination. High index achieving firms continue to seek innovative ways to share information necessary to streamline supply chain operations and deliver higher value to end-customers.

Information sharing clearly differentiates high index achieving firms from average firms. While high index firms had achieved greater scores on all critical indicators of information sharing, there were particularly large differences between high and average firms on levels of database maintenance and access methods to facilitate exchange.

GAIN/RISK SHARING

Rather than focus on internal improvements that deliver savings to the individual firm which is often at the expense of suppliers or customers who are continually pressed to make improvements that seldom benefit them, high index achieving firms are committed to sharing benefits from supply chain efficiencies. High achieving firms have discovered that sharing or mutually reinvesting the gains motivates partners to seek yet more ways to improve. Conversely, high achieving firms require that risks also be shared when appropriate. A policy of sharing mutual gain and risk reflects commitment to the belief that a firm's performance is closely linked to overall supply chain performance. Operationally, gain and risk sharing capability is indicated by supply chain arrangements characterized by sharing the benefits of superior performance with both material and service suppliers as well as customers.

Effective gain sharing depends on two factors. First, there must be a *willingness* to share benefits. That sounds simple, but gain is not always viewed as a two-way benefit. Partners must also be willing to share risk and cost. Everyone is happy to reap benefits, but it may be a different matter when operating results require reinvestment and joint shouldering of costs. All parties to a relationship must agree to allocate revenues and cost based on agreed-to responsibility and level of performance. Examples of gain and cost sharing include reinvestment of sales from capital equipment used by material or service suppliers in operations specific to the relationship and joint investment in shared resources.

Second, gain and risk sharing requires accurate performance measures and targeting as well as a consistent definition regarding inclusion of costs within the general ledger chart of accounts. Baseline cost and sales figures, for example, are critical to establishing fair compensation. Inaccurate or incomplete baselines have resulted in ugly court cases, with former supply chain partners suing each other to recover investments or costs. Performance metrics also have been used to motivate suppliers. In some cases material and service suppliers are rewarded according to product usage or consumption by end-customers. This focuses the supplier's account team on product availability and services that facilitate purchase by the end-customer, rather than on filling the intermediate customer's stockrooms. One retailer, for example, calculates replenishment cycles as the time elapsed from mechanically ordering to positioning on retail store shelves rather than arrival at receiving docks, as is traditionally the case. This encourages vendors to work with the retailer's personnel to develop innovative ways to speed transit as well as handling and storage to rapidly reach retail stores. Such measurement focus is a primary driver of direct store delivery and innovative cross-dock arrangements. While critical, target setting is also very complex. For example, should the vendor be punished for poor service even when the retailer is slow to place a replenishment order?

High index achieving firms had higher scores on all indicators of gain and risk sharing capability. The greatest difference between high and average firms was the development of behavior that encourages establishing supply chain arrangements with suppliers and customers that operate under principles of shared rewards.

SUMMARY

Relationship integration addresses the behavior that fosters supply chain coordination. There must be a shared mentality with customers and suppliers regarding interdependency and principles of collaboration. The ability to visualize and develop cooperative relationships throughout the supply chain focuses efforts on maximizing value to end-customers. This is the key to long-term superiority.

Role specificity, guidelines, information sharing, and gain and risk sharing drive relationship integration. *Role specificity* is the capability to clarify leadership processes and establish shared versus individual enterprise responsibility. *Guidelines* create the rules, policies, and procedures needed to facilitate collaboration, leverage, and conflict resolution between partners.

Information sharing involves the willingness to exchange key technical, financial, operational and strategic information with others in the supply chain. Finally, *gain and risk sharing* capabilities are derived from a willingness to apportion rewards and penalties appropriately across partner firms. High index achieving firms strive to develop behavior that provides the vision, willingness, and measurement structures that enable supply chain partners to creatively shift, share, and reward risk and responsibility. Exhibit 8-2 presents a summary of relationship integration and the four capabilities from which it emerges.

EXHIBIT 8-2

RELATIONSHIP INTEGRATION

The competency to develop and maintain a shared mental framework with customers and suppliers regarding inter-enterprise dependency and principles of collaboration.

Role Specificity:	Clarity concerning leadership process and establishment of shared versus individual enterprise responsibility.
Guidelines:	Rules, policies, and procedures to facilitate interenterprise collaboration, leverage, and conflict resolution.
Information Sharing:	Willingness to exchange key technical, financial, operational, and strategic information.
Gain/Risk Sharing:	Framework and willingness to apportion fair share reward and penalty.

WHAT'S IT ALL MEAN?

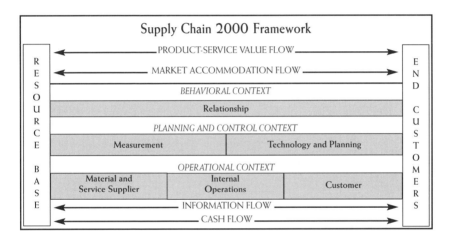

Supply Chain 2000 Framework			
R E S O U R C E B A S E	PRODUCT-SERVICE VALUE FLOW		E N D C U S T O M E R S
	MARKET ACCOMMODATION FLOW		
	BEHAVIORAL CONTEXT		
	Relationship		
	PLANNING AND CONTROL CONTEXT		
	Measurement	Technology and Planning	
	OPERATIONAL CONTEXT		
	Material and Service Supplier	Internal Operations	Customer
	INFORMATION FLOW		
	CASH FLOW		

*C*harlie and the members of the **Millennium** task force held a final review of progress. As a result of using the assessments Charlie had provided, as well as their discussions of a new way of doing business in the 21st Century, the task force had scoped Spartan's entire operations in detail. They reviewed activities involved in designing, sourcing, making, and delivering value to end-customers in an effort to uncover what they believed were significant problems in how internal planning and operations were integrated with one another as well as with customers and suppliers. They considered the firm's approach to relationships with partners up and down the supply chains. They also identified areas in which their information and measurement systems fell short of supporting their efforts, both now and those *planned for the future. Charlie felt it was now time to expose the groups findings to external critique. He invited the other VPs to attend a preliminary presentation to be held two weeks later.*

There was an air of nervousness in the room as the task force filed in to prepare for the presentation. Early in the process Charlie had convinced each of his counterparts to minimize their involvement until a draft had been developed. At Charlie's request, the task force members had provided their respective VPs with briefs of discussions at the weekly meetings. Now the task force members were anxious to show their bosses that their time had been well spent. If anything, the VPs were dubious. "At least Warren isn't here," Lawrence Ingram, VP of Finance and Administration, thought. "If I really hate what I hear, I can scuttle it before it gets to him. You never know when he's going to fall in love with a plan that could spell disaster for my department. And Charlie is just the guy to come up with one!"

The presentation of the Supply Chain 2000 framework sparked considerable discussion, most of which involved clarification and possible implications. Generally, discussion of each integration competency was met with nods of agreement. As soon as the entire model had been presented, Lawrence spoke: "This is all quite interesting. I'm not sure, however, what the benefits and costs will be and whether it will be worth the investment. Charlie, no offense, but these changes don't mean a hill of beans to the industry analysts that grade our stock. Unless we can quantify the costs and prospective benefits of change of this magnitude, I'm afraid the market – and our shareholders – will eat us alive. If this is really about improved service to customers, I don't think you've hit the winning note. We have always been able to improve our operational service levels; we just haven't been willing to lose money doing it! Despite the impressiveness of your proposal, I don't see how anything has changed."

*Charlie grinned. "I knew you wouldn't let me down, Larry. You know what? I think I can show you that this supply chain integration framework will enable us to move from the or world – lower cost **or** better service – to the and world – lower cost **and** better service. With these changes and improvements, we can improve our bottom-line position and increase sales. And you know what? With that combination I think we can be the industry leader!"*

Chapters Three through Eight introduced and described the six competencies and twenty-five capabilities that comprise the Supply Chain 2000 framework. Exhibit 9-1 summarizes the framework. Previously we have defined, described and explained the competencies and capabilities related to high index achievement. The framework can help managers identify and quantify improvement opportunities. The framework's overall credibility would be enhanced if it were conclusive that high index achievement had a direct correlation to superior operational and financial performance. The establishment of such a cause and effect relationship has long eluded logistical researchers. There are several legitimate reasons why the quantitative link between performance and best practice has not been achieved. In this research we have made a positive step toward such confirmation. Based upon careful analysis of senior management performance perceptions we offer substantial proof that having high achievement provides reasonable assurance that a firm will out-perform lower achievers.

EXHIBIT 9-1

SUPPLY CHAIN COMPETENCIES AND CAPABILITIES					
Customer Integration	Internal Integration	Material/Service Supplier Integration	Technology and Planning	Measurement Integration	Relationship Integration
Segmental Focus	Cross-Functional Unification	Strategic Alignment	Information Management	Functional Assessment	Role Specificity
Relevancy	Standardization	Operational Fusion	Internal Communication	Activity Based & Total Cost Methodology	Guidelines
Responsiveness	Simplification	Financial Linkage	Connectivity	Comprehensive Metrics	Information Sharing
Flexibility	Compliance	Supplier Management	Collaborative Forecasting & Planning	Financial Impace	Gain/Risk Sharing
	Structural Adaptation				

Chapter Nine confirms through statistical analysis that firms demonstrating high levels of supply chain competency report high-perceived performance levels on a number of different outcome measures. Overall, the statistical analysis strongly supports the senior executives' belief that customer integration has the single greatest influence on firm performance. The analysis substantiates the belief that effective supply chain management begins with a sound understanding of intermediate and end-customer requirements. Close integration with customers ensures that supply chain activities focus on critical elements of customer success. The analysis also supports the widespread belief that internal operational integration strongly differentiates firm performance. The remaining integrative management competencies contained in the Supply Chain 2000 framework have a somewhat lower influence level. While competencies related to supplier, technology/planning, measurement and relationship integration are meaningful influencers of performance, their impact is more as qualifiers rather than differentiators of high level achievement.

This chapter first establishes a measurement model to be used in the statistical validation. A set of 14 metrics is then related to the measurement model. The second part of the chapter covers the statistical validation analysis. The final section of the chapter generalizes the use of management perceptions to validate behavior and performance.

MEASURING SUPPLY CHAIN PERFORMANCE

The Supply Chain 2000 framework positions the capabilities that make a difference in firm performance. The step in establishing the link between Supply Chain 2000 capabilities and performance outcomes requires development of an appropriate supply chain measurement framework. Exhibit 9-2 presents a comprehensive measurement model that addresses both firm and supply chain performance. The model corresponds with the detailed listing of typical performance metrics presented in Chapter Seven.

EXHIBIT 9-2

COMPREHENSIVE SUPPLY CHAIN MEASUREMENT MODEL

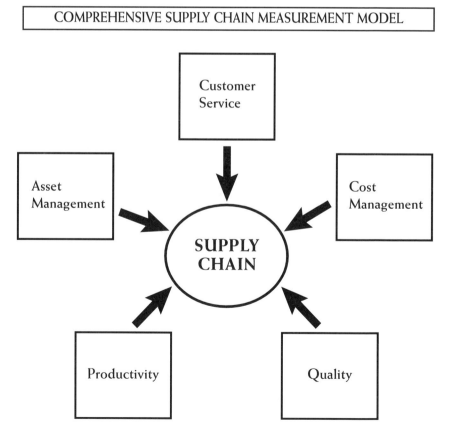

Customer service identifies the types of value provided to the customer. While there are a number of specific measures of customer service, the Supply Chain 2000 research focuses on customer satisfaction, product flexibility, and delivery speed. Cost reflects the functional and integrated logistics cost components used to facilitate supply chain financial operations. While there are a number of components of logistics and supply chain cost, the Supply Chain 2000 research uses a single comprehensive measure of total landed logistics cost. Quality reflects broader service measures used to enhance customer loyalty. The linkage is simple – superior service attracts and maintains key customers. The Supply Chain 2000 research focuses on delivery dependability, responsiveness, order flexibility, and delivery flexibility as the primary measures of quality. Productivity reflects how effectively material and labor resources are used to provide service. The Supply Chain 2000 research uses information systems support, order fill capacity, and advanced shipment notification as the primary productivity measures. Finally, asset management reflects the supply chain's effectiveness at using fixed assets and working capital. Overall asset utilization is a particularly important measure of firm and supply chain performance as viewed by the financial markets. The two specific asset utilization measures used for the Supply Chain 2000 research are inventory turn and return on assets (ROA).

Exhibit 9-3 presents performance metrics used for each measurement dimension to validate the Supply Chain 2000 Framework. In addition to 13 specific individual measures, an overall performance measure was created by combining individual measures. The validation procedure used this specific grouping because of ease of cross industry comparison. Information concerning each measure was obtained from senior management respondents during the survey phase of the research.

EXHIBIT 9-3

PERFORMANCE METRICS				
Customer Service	Cost Management	Quality	Productivity	Asset Management
Customer Satisfaction	Logistics Cost	Delivery Dependability	Information Systems Support	Inventory turn
Product Flexibility		Responsiveness	Order Fill Capacity	Return on Assets
Delivery Speed		Order Flexibility	Advanced Shipment Notification	
		Delivery Flexibility		

RELATING FIRM PERFORMANCE TO SUPPLY CHAIN COMPETENCIES

This section reports statistical analysis completed to relate the Supply Chain 2000 framework and perceived performance. The basis of the analysis is the executive rating of a firm's capabilities and its relative performance. The results of statistical analysis do not guarantee that a cause and effect relationship exists. The results do indicate the probability or likelihood that specific performance results from a firm's capability achievement. On the other hand, if managers generally believe that Supply Chain 2000 capabilities reflect best business practices and their implementation will likely improve supply chain performance, statistical confirmation that such a relationship exists is basis for concluding existence of cause and effect.

Three statistical methods were used to determine the relationship between capability achievement and perceived performance: correlation analysis, means testing, and regression analysis. The results and implications for each are discussed.

Correlation Analysis

Correlation analysis determines the magnitude of the relationship between two variables. In this case, the two variables are the firm's score on the overall Supply Chain 2000 index and the firm's perceived performance on the measures discussed previously. Correlation analysis produces an r value and a significance level. The Supply Chain 2000 index score reflects the firm's overall supply chain competency. The r value indicates the magnitude of the relationship while the level of significance indicates the likelihood that the reported relationship is simply due to random chance.

Exhibit 9-4 lists the correlation coefficients relating the Supply Chain 2000 index to the individual performance measures. If the correlation between the Supply Chain 2000 index and the performance measure is 1.0, it would indicate the supply chain competency totally explains perceived performance. In practical business situations, however, there are many different factors that influence performance other than supply chain strategy and competency. Such factors are marketing, manufacturing, product development, financial resources, and competitive behavior. Because these factors as well as others impact firm performance, one should not expect a perfect correlation between logistics and supply chain performance measures. The correlation coefficients reported in Exhibit 9-4 suggest that the metrics tested relating logistics and supply chain performance are significant determinants of firm success.

EXHIBIT 9-4

PERFORMANCE CORRELATION COEFFICIENT		
Performance Variable	Correlation Coefficient (r)	Coefficient of Determination (r^2)
Customer Service		
• Customer satisfaction	.394	.155
• Product customization	.181	.033
• Delivery speed	.306	.094
Cost Management		
• Logistics cost	.382	.146
Quality		
• Delivery dependability	.276	.076
• Responsiveness	.239	.057
• Order flexibility	.217	.047
• Delivery flexibility	.321	.103
Productivity		
• Information systems support	.533	.284
• Order fill capacity	.316	.100
• Advanced ship notification	.307	.094
Asset Management		
• Inventory turn	.285	.081
• Return on assets	.235	.055
Overall Performance	**.524**	**.275**
(All r and r^2 values are statistically significant at alpha=.05 level)		

Another statistic measured is the coefficient of determination or r^2. Mathematically, the coefficient of determination is simply the square of the correlation coefficient. Statistically r^2 measures the explanatory power of the relationship. The r^2 coefficient indicates the relative percentage of firm performance that is explained by supply chain competency. The r^2 column in Exhibit 9-4 indicates that supply chain competency explains from 3 to 28 percent of firm performance depending on the specified measure tested. In aggregate, overall supply chain competency explains 27 percent of the firm overall performance level. Explaining 27 percent of the variation in firm performance using logistics and supply chain performance is very relevant for managers.

The coefficients of correlation (r) and determination (r^2) reported in Exhibit 9-4 indicate little doubt that overall supply chain competency is related to the individual measures of firm performance. *For all performance measures except one, the r value exceeds 0.2 and r^2 exceeds 0.05 with all coefficients demonstrating statistical significance.* The levels of statistical significance indicate that there is less than 5 percent chance that such positive values would be observed if there was no actual relationship. In managerial terms, the correlation results support the conclusion that Supply Chain 2000 competency achievement contributes substantially to the firm's perceived performance.

Means Test

Means testing was the second statistical method used to illustrate the validity of the Supply Chain 2000 framework. The means test uses the firm's score on the Supply Chain 2000 index in comparison to the firm perceived performance measures. The concept behind the means test is to compare the performance means of the firms with the high index scores to the performance means of the firms with the average and lower index scores. The means test was completed by dividing the sample of firms into two groups. The first group consisted of the firms that scored in the top 15 percent as measured by the Supply Chain 2000 index. The second group consisted of the remaining firms. Firms were grouped solely on their Supply Chain 2000 index score.

The mean score for each performance metric was calculated for both groups. It was expected that the mean performance of the top 15 percent of firms as identified by the Supply Chain 2000 index would exceed the mean of the remaining 85 percent of firms. Such was the case.

Exhibit 9-5 reports the group mean for each perceived performance metric. The results demonstrate that the top 15 percent of firms based on the Supply Chain 2000 index reported substantially better performance than the other group across all metrics. The fact that the levels of significance are also all less than 0.05 indicates that the reported differences are not likely due to chance. The conclusion is that the Supply Chain 2000 index differentiates high performing firms from the average firms thus further validating the Supply Chain 2000 framework.

EXHIBIT 9-5

MEAN SCORES OF PERFORMANCE VARIABLES
FOR HIGH VS. AVERAGE INDEX ACHIEVING FIRMS

Performance Variable	Means for High Index Achieving Firms	Means for Average Index Achieving Firms
Customer Service		
• Customer satisfaction	4.19	3.54
• Product customization	3.95	3.51
• Delivery speed	3.95	3.47
Cost Management		
• Logistics cost	4.10	3.37
Quality		
• Delivery dependability	4.13	3.64
• Responsiveness	4.24	3.89
• Order flexibility	4.03	3.40
• Delivery flexibility	4.19	3.59
Productivity		
• Information systems support	4.12	2.79
• Order fill capacity	4.16	3.60
• Advanced ship notification	3.89	3.18
Asset Management		
• Inventory turn	3.63	3.17
• Return on assets	3.77	3.29
Overall Performance	**4.03**	**3.42**

(All differences are statistically significant at alpha = .05 level.

Correlation analysis and means differentiation testing provide ways to determine the relationship between two variables, in this case behavior competency and perceived performance. The results of these analyses provide an indication of the general influence of one variable on another as well as the positive or negative direction of that influence. The analyses concluded that overall competency achievement is directly related to perceived performance. These are significant findings that support the relationship between best practice behavior and perceived operating results. Additional confirmation was obtained using regression analysis to isolate how individual competencies influence various performance measures.

Regression Analysis

Regression analysis determines the relative influence a combination of variables has on a single dependent variable. In the case of the Supply Chain 2000 framework we sought to examine the relationship between the 6 competencies and the 14 metrics of perceived performance. The objective of the regression analysis was to determine the relative importance of each of the 6 competencies on each measure of performance.

Regression analysis computes two parameters that quantify the relationship between the independent variables and the dependent variable. The first is a ß coefficient that indicates the relative influence of the competency. The second is the multiple coefficient of determination or R^2 that indicates the relative explanatory power of the competencies on the performance variable. The R^2 in multiple regression is comparable to the r^2 used in the correlation analysis. The regression analysis attempts to relate supply chain competencies to each performance measure. The specific equation is:

Performance Measure = $ß_0$ + $ß_1$ (Relationship Integration) + $ß_2$ (Customer Integration) + $ß_3$ (Internal Integration) + $ß_4$ (Material/Service Supplier Integration) + $ß_5$ (Technology and Planning Integration) + $ß_6$ (Measurement Integration).

Exhibit 9-6 lists the statistically significant R^2 and ß values for each performance measure. The value in each individual cell indicates the relative influence of that competency variable on the performance measure. The first column, labeled Overall Performance, indicates that customer and internal integration have the most impact on overall supply chain performance. The R^2 value in the last row of the Overall Performance column indicates that the customer and internal integration competencies explain approximately 30 percent of the variation in overall supply chain performance with customer integration having a slightly stronger influence than internal integration. Blank cells indicate a particular relationship was not significant. For example, the blank cell for customer integration and return on assets indicates that customer integration either does not directly influence ROA or that there is not enough data to justify a relationship.

EXHIBIT 9-6

REGRESSION ANALYSES RELATING SUPPLY CHAIN 2000 COMPETENCIES TO FIRM PERFORMANCE

Competencies	Overall Performance	Customer Satisfaction	Product Customization	Delivery Speed	Logistics Cost	Delivery Dependability	Responsiveness	Order Flexibility	Delivery Flexibility	Information Systems Support	Order Fill Capability	Advanced Ship Notification	Inventory Turn	ROA
Customer Integration	.31	.26	.43	.33			.48	.24	.34					
Internal Integration	.28			.41	.50						.35		.32	
Supplier Integration							-.21							
Technology / Planning Integration											.61	.31		
Measurement Integration		.18				-.20								
Relationship Integration			-.20											.25
R^2	.30	.16	.09	.10	.16	.13	.12	.05	.11	.36	.12	.10	.10	.06

The regression analysis provides results for each of the performance metrics. The greatest amount of variance explained by the competencies is 36 percent in the case of information systems support. Combinations of competencies explained ten percent or more of variance in metrics related to customer satisfaction (.16), delivery speed (.10), logistics cost (.16), delivery dependability (.13), responsiveness (.12), delivery flexibility (.11), order fill capability (.12), advanced shipment notification (.10), and inventory turn (.10).

There are two explanations for competencies that do not demonstrate statistically significant relationships. The first is that the competency does not influence that dimension of the firm's performance. A second and more likely explanation is that the competency is not a *differentiator* on that particular aspect of the firm's performance. This condition would result when both high and average achieving firms reported similar index scores for a specific competency. This is interpreted that the specific competency is a qualifier with respect to that measure and that both high and average Supply Chain 2000 index firms had approximately the same level of achievement.

Customer integration, which is a significant predictor in six of the 13 individual performance measures, emerged as the dominant competency in terms of influencing firm perceived performance. Internal integration, which is significant in four of the thirteen measures, is the second most dominant competency. This result is consistent with the results of the correlation analysis and the means testing.

Interestingly, the regression results related to relationship, measurement, and supplier integration indicated significant negative influence on the individual performance measures. This should not be interpreted to mean these competencies negatively influence firm perceived performance. A more in-depth analysis indicated these competencies individually have a slight positive impact on firm performance. When combined with another dominant competency, however, multiple regression frequently assigns a negative influence to a relatively less important competency. A more appropriate interpretation of the negative ß is that the competency has a relatively minor but positive influence on the performance dimension.

MANAGERIAL PERCEPTIONS AS PERFORMANCE MEASURES

The statistical analysis demonstrated a strong relationship between the Supply Chain 2000 index and perceived firm performance. The rational for using perceived performance is based solely on persistent problems encountered when trying to develop a causal relationship between specific competency achievement and measured performance.

Few would disagree that it would be ideal if the Supply Chain 2000 competencies and capabilities could be positively correlated with actual measured performance. Even in situations where firms are willing to provide actual performance data it is difficult to generalize across firms and near impossible to compare industry groups.

Previous research attempting to establish causal relationships using published performance has not produced promising results. Such research generated, at best, a modest causal relationship between logistics and supply chain capabilities and publicly reported firm financial performance. The primary problem is that publicly reported performance does not directly reflect the effectiveness of logistics and supply chain capabilities. Publicly available financial data often combines performance results of multiple corporate divisions or strategic business units. It is difficult, if not impossible, to separate the performance of one division from another. Since most corporations have both high and low performing divisions, the reported performance is averaged and difficult to isolate to divisions scoring high on the Supply Chain 2000 index.

A second factor making such correlation difficult is that published financial data is designed to provide accurate information regarding publicly traded corporations. As a result, firms are expected to present published financials in the most positive light. Specifically, within the bounds of acceptable accounting practices, revenues and expenses are sometimes managed to present positive relationships and trends. The revenues and expenses may also be directly impacted through the use of pricing and promotion events. Similarly, acquisition and sale of assets can be timed to present the most positive financial perspective. These events are totally independent of the competencies that drive logistics and supply chain excellence.

To illustrate the wide variance in reported operating performance, Exhibits 9-7 and 9-8 present published data across 6 performance measures for 10 food manufacturers and 9 retailers. Each of these firms have publicly traded stock and report earnings according to Generally Accepted Accounting Procedures. It is clear that substantive variance exists in operating achievement. The Supply Chain 2000 framework has not been applied to these 19 firms. Therefore, no direct conclusion is possible concerning the relationship between high achievement and favorable operating results. The significant point in presenting the data is the wide variance in performance of competing firms operating in a single industry.

EXHIBIT 9-7

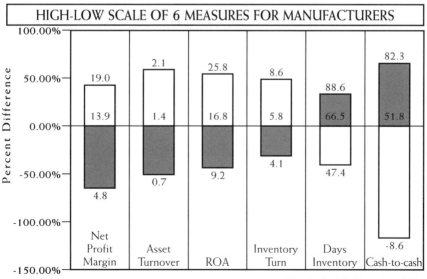

HIGH-LOW SCALE OF 6 MEASURES FOR MANUFACTURERS

EXHIBIT 9-8

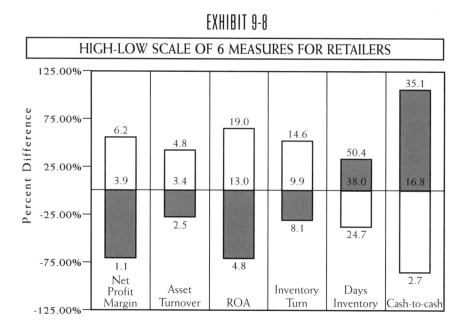

HIGH-LOW SCALE OF 6 MEASURES FOR RETAILERS

For the above reasons this research was designed to use perceived performance as its dependent variable. Each participating executive was requested to assess firm performance across 13 metrics. The comparisons ranged from much worse than competitors (rated as 1) to much better than competitors (rated as 5).

The use of perceived performance provides a meaningful way to validate the Supply Chain 2000 framework. *First*, the senior logistics or supply chain executive is intimately involved in and regularly views reports documenting divisional performance, they are very knowledgeable regarding actual divisional or firm performance levels. This knowledge provides a solid base for projecting perceived relative firm performance.

Second, the compensation of many senior supply chain executives is dependent on the firm's actual performance. Senior executives are thus strongly motivated to track and understand their firm's relative performance.

Third, executives are not typically promoted if they demonstrate lack of judgement or over-optimism. Any individual achieving senior executive status has most likely demonstrated good judgement regarding the strategies and relative performance of their firm and its competitors. This quality judgement and awareness of competition suggests that the senior supply chain executive's perceived evaluation is reasonably credible.

Finally, senior supply chain executives spend a substantial amount of time at conferences and in benchmarking discussions with key customers and supply chain partners. These discussions often directly or indirectly concern the relative performance of the firm or division. As a result, senior supply chain executives are typically very aware of their firm's relative performance.

While use of perceived performance measures to validate the Supply Chain 2000 framework may not in theory be as desirable as validation using actual measured performance, the above arguments support the approach used in this research. There is strong rationale to suggest that senior supply chain executives are both informed and credible sources regarding their firm or division's relative performance.

SUMMARY

Chapter Nine justifies the managerial relevancy of the Supply Chain 2000 framework. While the capabilities may have intuitive appeal, they are only relevant for managers if their impact on firm performance is real and can be documented.

Chapter Nine establishes the relevance of the Supply Chain 2000 framework by demonstrating a strong correlation and discrimination that validates that achieving the specific capabilities makes a difference in perceived firm performance. The statistical results indicate that the Supply Chain 2000 framework competencies and capabilities account for 20 to 30 percent of firm performance. The final segment of the chapter supports the rationale for using perceived firm performance to validate the Supply Chain 2000 framework.

CHANGE MANAGEMENT

*A*s *Charlie had anticipated, Lawrence Ingram raised the obvious question about quantifying the costs and benefits of supply chain integration. Hopefully, the task force had the information available to placate that concern. Now, Charlie knew, the really hard battle was coming. Javi Suarez and Gwynn Miller, the VPs of Manufacturing and Marketing, had remained relatively agreeable to what they had seen. Even Lawrence, whose department would be asked to implement changes in the way that information was measured and shared, was enthusiastic in his support for change as long as it could be shown to make good fiscal sense. The members of the task force were the managers who actually ran each of the firm's internal operating areas for the VPs. How could they refute the problems that the task force had compiled?*

*Charlie knew, however, that once the other VPs had time to really think about what was being proposed and how it would affect them, they wouldn't just get in line and start making wholesale change. After all, many of the problems outlined in the proposal could be traced to the fact that earlier changes proposed when the firm had realigned its logistical operations had not really received the commitment necessary to succeed. Now he was **simply** requesting a change in the way the company marketed, sold, sourced, produced, delivered, measured, and shared information! Charlie was sure that it would not, maybe could not, happen without some serious bloodletting and compromise. That was the nature of change.*

The last meeting of the task force before the presentation to the VPs had been spent trying to brainstorm possible objections to the proposed change. The experience of trying to implement integrated logistics had left a strong impression in the minds of those who had endured the process. It wasn't hard, therefore, to predict the all-too-human reactions to the proposed change. As before, the current proposal cited the need to be faster, more flexible, more accurate, and less expensive. Not only that, but as the experience with Super pointed out, customers were increasingly expecting fast, accurate, flexible service tailored to their specific needs. At a conceptual level, every-one knew what needed to happen to get that done. But making it actually happen on the front lines was another story. Charlie wondered how many of the managers in the room had the stomach, let alone the skills, to push through the ground level changes needed to impact how work was really done. Without their support Charlie knew that he had no way to ensure that the third shift shipping clerk in a DC in Indianapolis understood and was motivated to ship Super's orders in one unique con-figuration, another top customer's orders in a different way, and a less time sensitive customer's orders after everything else went out first. The thought of changing the work habits of everyone from purchasing agents to sales reps, as well as the external counterparts with whom they dealt, was daunting.

While operational change certainly presented a challenge, the potential organi-zational changes occupied much of the task forces' discussion during the final meet-ing. Structural change in the late 20th century had to overcome top management's fear of losing control. Structural change in the 21st century would have to overcome everyone's fear of losing his or her jobs. Charlie remembered the days during the early and mid-'90s when it seemed that each issue of the weekly trade journal, not to mention the evening newspaper, somberly announced the layoffs that accompanied some firm's attempt to restructure. He also remembered the knot he felt in his stom-ach when one after another of his peers at other firms called to ask if he had heard of any job openings since they had just been downsized or restructured out a job. People felt the sacrifices had already been made. To be confronted with another set of structural changes would send them running for cover.

Changing mindsets regarding relations with customers and material and ser-vice suppliers promised to be equally challenging. Decades old and tightly held philosophies regarding links to entities outside the firm would have to be converted. Marketing would have to learn that not all market share is profitable and sales would have to learn to walk away from select orders while collaborating more close-ly with profitable customers. Meanwhile, purchasing would have to learn that the lowest unit cost supplier might not be the most consistently valuable supplier. And operations managers that had come up from the trenches would have to part with some of their equipment and personnel and learn to manage relationships with the external providers that would control those assets. Finally, the command and con-trol systems that supported those philosophies would have to be reinvented to ensure that people could perform under the new rules and were compensated for complying with the new ways.

Could change of that scope and magnitude happen? How? Charlie realized that the success of the firm in the 21st century depended on the answers that the Task Force provided to those questions.

The Supply Chain 2000 Framework provides an assessment process for managers desiring to improve their supply chain logistics integration. Using the framework and diagnostic with comparison to the high achiever benchmarks offers a way for firms to identify performance gaps between assessment of their capabilities and those of high achievers. In the final analysis, change management leadership rests at the core of improving logistical performance. Change management was the major theme of the previous research reported in *World Class Logistics: The Challenge of Managing Continuous Change*. This chapter builds upon the foundations of that research to provide updated discussion of the important topic of change management.

Chapter Ten begins a three-chapter sequence related to managing effective change. In Chapter Ten we review the essential features of change management and provide an overview of the challenges related to successful change. A Supply Chain Change Process Model is presented to highlight the continuous nature of managing change. Chapter Eleven discusses procedural aspects of managing the change process. Finally, in Chapter Twelve, attention is directed to the most likely patterns of change logistics managers will face during the first decade of the 21st Century.

PERSPECTIVES ON CHANGE

Few executives have been trained in change management and most have limited experience with successful change. Since there are no Universities of Change Management it is important that executives understand the dynamics of change and take steps to self-develop their change management knowledge and skills. The education process starts with understanding the basic challenge of change.

The most fundamental point to keep in mind about supply chain change is that a business process that provides some level of performance is almost always in place. Rarely does change management commence from ground zero. Supply chain change improves a process or practice that isn't broken, and in the minds of some, doesn't need to be fixed.

Typically, supply chain change also requires the alignment of operations outside the direct control of a specific executive, and in terms of the supply chain, even the firm itself. One executive stressed the fundamental importance of change management leadership by estimating that only 20 percent of the scope of a typical logistical change initiative is within the direct control of a firm's logistics organization. The remaining 80 percent typically involve the responsibilities of managers from other business areas. Thus, logistical change leaders must sell ideas and serve as cross-functional catalysts. Managing change through others is a difficult task that logistics leaders need to master.

From the time a firm initiates operations it creates what amounts to a logistical legacy. Decisions are made concerning such items as facility location, inventory strategy, warehouse operations, and customer assignment. Countless other operating policies, procedures and systems are developed over time concerning how orders are processed, methods of transportation, service priorities, material handling methods, and cost allocation. These many decisions made at different times and motivated by different circumstances form a firm's logistical capabilities and overall competency. Typically, each decision was made logically, based on best available facts to accommodate the business need confronted. Like bricks in a wall, these individual decisions withstand time, framing organizational structures, operating policies, and practices. For example, a given procedure for handling orders or establishing service policy may be so widely accepted that it never is questioned. What once was a limited operational decision may, over time, become a central theme or key policy of an organization.

There is no reason to believe that the sequence of individual logistical system design decisions made over time will result in an integrated logistical process. In fact, executives who are not directly involved in logistics make many related decisions. Each individual decision, although a good solution at a particular point in time, may not fit well when viewed from a more holistic perspective. The operating focus and network structure that emerges from incremental decisions will typically lack integrated competencies related to customers, internal operations, material/service providers, technology and planning, measurement, and relationships. The supply chain that results from such a decision at a time approach may work, but the fundamental question is how well does it work in comparison to what is possible given contemporary supply chain knowledge and technology? These results are further stressed by increasing and more variant demand being placed by key customers. In the words of one executive interviewed, *"Why do people call what we are doing reengineering? Our system wasn't engineered in the first place. What we are really doing is reinventing the way we do business."* Supply chain change reinforces the need for comprehensive, long-term leadership and planning as opposed to the more free wheeling, non-integrated changes resulting from business process reengineering.

Managers have a natural tendency to want to continue doing or perpetuating what past experience has demonstrated works. There is tremendous uncertainty and pain related to change, and there often are not any cataclysmic events that clearly define the need for change. The problem is that the environment in and around the firm is changing. If a firm does not have the capability and inclination to change, it may find itself in the position of doing things extremely well that no one values.

Clearly, there are limits to the amount of change a firm can accommodate. Constant change can be dysfunctional and result in loss of momentum. One is reminded of the potential danger of change for the sake of change in the following quote:

We trained hard...but it seemed that every time we were beginning to form up into teams we would be reorganized. I was to learn in life that we tend to meet any new situation by reorganizing; a wonderful method it can be for creating the illusion of progress while producing confusion, inefficiency and demoralization.
Petronious, 200 B.C.

Thus, in a world characterized by accelerating change, the challenge becomes one of sorting, selecting and implementing meaningful change initiatives.

High achieving firms find that rethinking their supply chain competency can result in creative ideas to simultaneously improve service *and* cost. As a consequence, high achieving firms see change as a potential friend not an enemy. They are convinced that implementation of new and better logistics to support supply chain processes can help achieve competitive advantage. Managers who aspire to improve supply chain operations and planning need to know more about the challenges of change. Fortunately there are lessons to be learned from high achieving firms.

WHY CHANGE?

At first, the answer to why change, may appear obvious since the standard response is to gain and maintain competitive advantage. However, the real motivation for change usually results from one of four drivers: (1) crisis elimination; (2) waste reduction; (3) value improvement; and/or (4) external or environmental change. The initial motivation and driver behind each type of change are discussed below.

A crisis usually means that some significant part of a process is broken or simply not working up to expectation. Such crisis situations typically result from an organization's failure to meet expectations. The solution may be as visible as the crisis – do whatever it takes to get operations back on track. A wide variety of research supports the conclusion that crisis-induced change generally does not result in substantial modification of long-term behavior or performance. Most often, the crisis is resolved without any understanding of the underlying cause of the problem. Interviews with logistics executives over the years continue to indicate high levels of time committed to crisis-driven problem solving. Historically, logistics managers were often not included in customer meetings unless it was to explain an operational breakdown. Typically, the agenda of such crisis-driven meetings was to pinpoint blame and promise action to put out the fire. Fortunately in today's business environment senior logistics executives report they are frequent participants in top-to-top customer conferences and alliances. The focus of change management is shifting from crisis-induced to planned.

Elimination of duplication and waste is a fundamental reason why firms' plan new and improved supply chain processes. The broad discipline known as supply chain management and its supportive logistics processes have gained widespread reputation as being fertile ground for efficiency improvement. Over the past three decades, the challenge to improve logistics productivity has been embraced around the globe. During the 1980s, deregulation of transportation added fuel to the cost reduction crusade. Most senior managers saw deregulation as an opportunity to reduce transportation costs. Today, it is virtually impossible to find a firm with any degree of managerial sophistication that has not, in some meaningful way, improved logistics and overall supply chain efficiency over the past decade. The change that remains elusive is to capture efficiencies that flow cross-functionally within a company, and inter-organizationally between firms participating in supply chains. High achieving firms are making significant strides in attacking change related to these complex process improvement opportunities. The inefficiency has become particularly apparent as firms continue to integrate multiple domestic and international divisions. Managers frequently cite concern with the waste and duplication that occurs as products and information move between international supply chain partners. While the effort to eliminate waste and duplication is well underway, it is far from complete. Many firms still have significant opportunities to reduce waste, both internally and in cooperation with their primary customers and suppliers. Effective change management, however, is far more comprehensive than a search for ways to reduce cost.

Among leading firms, the most appealing change driver is the potential to improve performance. Managers in high achieving firms have a deep conviction that growth and profitability are directly related to outperforming competitors. This means committing to a constant search for new and unique ways to favorably impact customer value and thereby create a competitive advantage. Change aimed at value improvement is now widely perceived as the best route to long-term customer success. Exhibit 10-1 supports this conclusion by illustrating the relative focus on lowest total cost (score close to 1) versus highest customer service (score closer to 5) as a strategic driver of change across industries. Since the overall average and the score in 9 out of 10 industry groups exceed 3.0, it appears that most firms are focused on enhancing their service offerings.

EXHIBIT 10-1

RELATIVE FOCUS OF LOGISTICS STRATEGY	
Industry	Relative Focus
1. Mass merchandising and retail	3.57
2. Appliances, furniture and hardware	3.43
3. HBA and pharmaceutical	3.42
4. Food processing and distribution	3.39
5. Motor and transportation	3.35
6. Office equipment and supplies	3.35
7. Building and lumber, mining, metals	3.30
8. Clothing and textiles	3.25
9. Other	3.10
10. Chemical and petroleum	2.81
Overall Average	3.34

Scale: 1 = Primary focus on lowest total cost
5 = Primary focus on highest customer service

The final change driver is external and environmental change. The Logistical Kaleidoscope discussed in Chapter One documents the historical sequence of logistics' external and environmental change. The external drivers include market, industry, and competitive changes. Environmental changes include resource and technology availability, as well as the legal, social, and institutional environment.

Exhibit 10-2 captures the *why* of non-crisis motivated change. High achieving firms realize that supply chain change management must simultaneously yield improved performance and lower total costs. For example, many firms report substantial reductions in supply chain inventory while simultaneously improving customer order fill rates. This perspective creates a holistic vision concerning the sum of the supply chain functions and processes required to achieve successful change. It means developing ways to integrate operations both internally as well as between participating members of a supply chain. The goal is to jointly stimulate a continuous stream of unique and more efficient ways to attract and retain selected customers.

Typically, this requires establishing some strict improvement goals and objectives while continuing to improve basic operating capabilities.

EXHIBIT 10-2

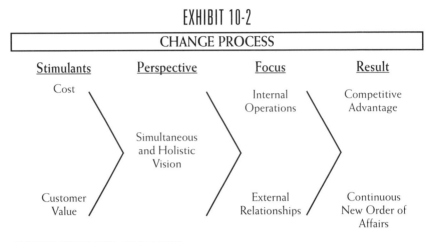

CHANGE PROCESS			
Stimulants	Perspective	Focus	Result
Cost		Internal Operations	Competitive Advantage
	Simultaneous and Holistic Vision		
Customer Value		External Relationships	Continuous New Order of Affairs

OBSTACLES TO CHANGE

It is becoming increasingly clear that high achievement supply chain management exploits change. While many executives interviewed did not refer to what they were experiencing and doing as *change management*, most talked about their vision of accomplishments and the methods they expected to use to achieve success. Executives cited many examples of successful change, as well as examples of failures. Because change management is a dominant theme of 21st Century logistics, readers might conclude that few if any obstacles to change exist within successful firms.

The reality is that the art of change management is difficult. As noted earlier, most supply chain change impacts other areas of a firm. Supply chain strategic or operational changes usually have substantial implications for the firm's marketing, financial, and information system operations. It increasingly impacts supply chain partners as well. Managers impacted by such change initiatives may resist for a host of reasons. However, one important point needs to be clarified. Because change is typically resisted, one should not jump to the conclusion that managers prefer the status quo. To the contrary, research suggests managers want and will support meaningful change. The problem is they often don't know how to position their area of responsibility in terms of the change initiative. Even if the proposed change is positive for the firm overall, selected individuals may resist for reasons of perceived self-interest. It is difficult for managers to shift behavior and responsibility to support an initiative that appears to primarily benefit other managers in the company.

In some cases managers may not have access to information essential to fully understanding the impact of the proposed change. Most managers view change as risky because they have difficulty projecting results or envisioning the end state. They realize they may be held responsible if the change initiative is not successful. In many cases executives have difficulty visualizing how the change will occur. As a result, many managers react to change by focusing on what is being lost or given up as opposed to what might be gained. Most people fear the unknown or unpredictable. It is often difficult to change things even when everybody agrees they should change.

Another potential obstacle centers on the timing of change. Managers often express frustration with decisions regarding the appropriate time to make change. It is difficult to effect substantial change while maintaining ongoing business operations. Unfortunately, firms cannot simply hang out a sign saying "Closed for Repairs" and expect customers to wait for the new and improved logistical competency.

Supply chain change challenges and seeks to modify well-ingrained practices and procedures that are often cross-functional and inter-organizational. Managers prefer the status quo because they understand how it works, it's comfortable, it is often viewed as secure, and it avoids confrontation. They understand the accepted rules of the game that generated success in the past. In a sense, past success creates a complacency, even a loyalty, to protecting and maintaining what works. This loyalty creates a high hurdle for the acceptance of new ideas.

This research update and discussions with managers confirm the obstacles to change as originally reported in *Logistical Excellence*. Exhibit 10-3 lists the most commonly stated obstacles.

EXHIBIT 10-3
OBSTACLES TO CHANGE

- Lack of real focus on the customer
- Lack of information that has strategic value
- Lack of understanding of overall supply chain dynamics and relative economics
- Information not organized and distributed to facilitate strategic use
- Difficulty in revamping organizational structure and tasks
- Overcoming the deadly inertia created by the accepted way of doing things
- Lack of a business case for action
- Lack of senior leadership sponsorship
- Not invented here syndrome
- Lack of a clear, commonly understood, and appropriate strategy and mission

During interviews conducted earlier in the research stream, managers frequently expressed a growing concern for how change would impact their personal security. One executive called this concern the *sand box mentality* – a desire to protect the status quo. The significant difference today in comparison with previous research is that more managers are finding ways to break change-resistant barriers. Three guidelines are widely accepted among leading logistics executives.

- Total organization involvement is essential for effective change. This means the change process must have senior management support, functional management endorsement, and buy-in from those who must do the work. Approval or direction from senior management is important and required, but not sufficient to result in meaningful change in a process as comprehensive as logistics. Functional managers need the support of workers to achieve change goals. Workers will be supportive once they understand the change and how it will impact their careers.

- To effectively meet end-customer requirements, the change process must consider the capabilities and limitations of the entire supply chain. Since a chain is no stronger than its weakest link, change initiatives must be coordinated among supply chain partners to take advantage of each party's core competency. Inter-organizational change management requires the identification of the competencies of each partner and then orchestration to achieve a synchronized supply chain.

- Successful change must be planned and proactively managed to avoid or prevent loss of logistical competency. The change process must start long before the need to modify behavior is generally recognized. Most of all, crisis-induced change will not result in long-term competitive advantage. Once the change itself is underway, the success of the process itself will be highly dependent on the quality of information and feedback shared among the participants.

MAGNITUDE OF CHANGE

It seems clear that industry leaders are those firms that master translating research and technology into new processes, products, systems and services. At least three magnitudes of supply chain change are widely observable: (1) continuous improvement; (2) reasonable change; and (3) radical change. Supply chain managers at different times are likely to be involved in any or all of the three.

Continuous improvement is the solidly established legacy of the quality revolution. Throughout the world, commitment to quality is essential. Unless a firm has a rigorous quality commitment, it is highly unlikely that a customer will give it serious consideration as a preferred supplier. Every executive must be responsible for continuous improvement within all operations and processes managed. This means maintaining momentum and not allowing initiatives to get bogged down. Therefore, when leading firms talk about change management, they normally focus on something larger in scope than continuous improvement. Measurement tools, a reporting framework, and a zero defects mentality are critical for continuous improvement.

Reasonable change describes significant change that is relatively easy to envision. For example, a logistics group undertakes an evaluation of the number and location of distribution warehouses in an effort to improve its facility network. The potential revisions are relatively easy for managers to visualize and illustrate the type of change required to improve performance. Most managers would agree it is within the realm of reasonable change to simultaneously reevaluate all facility locations on a systemwide basis. Such evaluations could result in change that most managers consider reasonable. In other words, the most likely outcome and accompanying recommendations fit their vision of what the business should be doing.

Radical changes are much more out-of-the-box than either continuous improvement or reasonable modifications. Radical change seeks to reinvent the fundamental way a firm does something that is widely considered by managers to be important. In fact, radical change typically puts in question the basic reason for specific behavior that is currently accepted as reasonable practice. The radical change process starts by asking, what is the purpose of the work? not, how we can do the current work better? Radical change management starts with the fundamental belief that business as usual has been cancelled. The challenge is to seek maximum breakthroughs in an effort to better serve customers without reservation or protection of existing practice. Therefore, a new solution may totally challenge every aspect of the prevailing way of performing all or part of a business process.

The fact is that radical means *extreme*. Naturally, the more radical a proposed change, the greater both the risk and level of resistance. In some extreme situations, a radical change proposal may be resisted by every means possible including government regulatory action. The status quo could well be the preferred state of affairs for almost everyone involved except the change leader. To illustrate, only a few progressive food retailers are willing to embrace the impact consumer home delivery might have on the nature of today's supermarket. This failure to embrace the potential of home delivery seems to ignore the fact that all the required technology to implement such a service is currently available. The accepted rules of the game may be outdated and even dangerously counter-productive to meeting the challenges of a new competitive situation. The phenomenal growth in e-commerce exemplifies the radical supply chain changes that are actually occurring today.

Few question the persistence and magnitude of the challenge of change that managers confront. Learning how to be an effective change leader may be the difference between average or superior performance for today's manager. What is less clear is how to proceed with change. Most managers interviewed expressed frustration in conceptualizing and operationalizing effective change management.

These change management perspectives focus on the need and challenge of creating a new order of affairs. Exhibit 10-4 provides a Supply Chain Change Process Model that illustrates the dynamic challenge faced by logistics change managers. The ball portrayed in motion suggests the need for the firm to constantly track and accommodate changes in end-customer requirements and competitive capabilities.

EXHIBIT 10-4

| SUPPLY CHAIN CHANGE PROCESS MODEL |

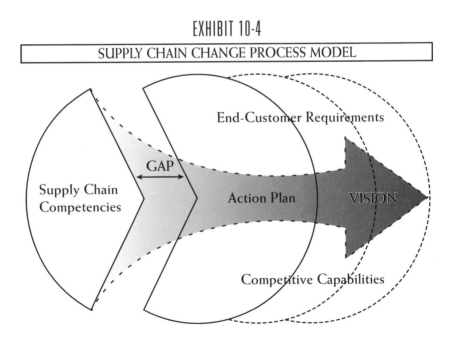

Most managers have a reasonable perception of the current business situation and how they feel it should be modified. This perception is driven by assessment of their supply chain competencies, which can be achieved using the Supply Chain 2000 Framework and diagnostic methodology. The wedge on the left captures the current status of supply chain competencies. The difference between the current assessment and their vision of desired achievement represents the gap. This opportunity gap describes the performance and financial benefits attainable from improved integrative management. To be meaningful, these performance and financial measures must be quantified to initiate and drive change. In this respect, leadership is essential to help simplify operating complexity by identifying and focusing on relationships and practices that, if modified, have the potential to enhance performance. Change management leadership is the art of creatively identifying, articulating and guiding a shared vision of the opportunity gap and the way to improve. While leaders astute in change management may be able to identify an opportunity and scope its potential, the existence and magnitude of a gap is typically not so obvious to managers who are deeply involved in day-to-day operations. The balance between vision, current reality, and resource opportunities creates the essence of a change management action plan.

Visioning is a process of creativity and innovation. Change leaders must develop a *big picture* perspective that conceptualizes the dynamics and influence of complex interrelationships. Leaders see an integrative pattern of connectiveness where others may see only specific events and problems requiring resolution. Change managers are able to create a vision of future market requirements and then identify refinements in operations, facilitation, or application of external resources to achieve such visions. Such leaders are also able to articulate the reality of the present, thus identifying the comparative gap between vision and reality that motivates change.

The role of visioning is to conceptualize the supply chain situation and identify desirable and achievable system modifications consistent with overall enterprise objectives. To enhance the current situation, the vision must be shared and adopted by a wide range of individuals and groups who must be involved if meaningful change is to result. Thus, visions with a high degree of perceived legitimacy and offering substantial opportunity are more likely to be accepted over those proposing radical change. For some types of supply chain change, reasonable modification of current practices and relationships is sufficient. The truly difficult change management challenges are those proposing that well-established practices or relationships be discarded or radically modified. As noted earlier, resistance to new practices and relationships that challenge a sense of individual and business security can force a serious, if not terminal, resistance to the change management process.

Successful supply chain change leaders must be able to communicate the benefits and risks associated with the vision in a credible manner if widespread support for any initiative is to be generated. Leaders who successfully enable change are masters at creating legitimacy for visions in terms of detailing future directions and conceptualizing the capabilities and resources necessary to get there. Most important, such visions must be aligned with overall enterprise and supply chain goals.

The visioning process builds on understanding three in-depth elements of the supply chain environment. The first is understanding current and future supply chain requirements of the end-customer. This includes understanding service dimensions and performance levels that will be necessary to satisfy intermediate and end-customers in the future. For example, a visionary executive would have anticipated the trend to e-commerce and the resulting need for modified logistical competency.

The second understanding concerns competitive capabilities. A supply chain visionary must anticipate and understand the current and likely strengths and weaknesses of key competitors. Such understanding is critical to allow a firm and its related supply chain partners to match competitive threats and target weaknesses. However, information and understanding regarding the supply chain environment is often difficult to obtain. Leading firms are using benchmarking and educational programs to achieve this understanding.

The final understanding concerns the firm's current and likely future capabilities. An accurate vision of current reality is critical to provide credible and effective direction regarding the need for change. The procedure to undertake this assessment and change development is discussed in depth in Chapter Eleven. Exhibit 10-5 provides a perspective of the competency structure that constitutes the Supply Chain 2000 Framework. In this exhibit the six integrative competencies have been formed as the wedge that fits the gap identified in Exhibit 10-4 (the Supply Chain Process Change Model).

By way of assessment, managers must determine the gap that exists in current competencies. The gap is defined as the difference between current capabilities and those needed to achieve the change vision. Change initiatives and plans offer a blueprint to close the gap. Since the supply chain environment is always changing, the transformation of the end-customer requirements and competitive capabilities is dynamically displayed. This dynamic posture serves to highlight the fact that change is a continuous challenge.

EXHIBIT 10-5

SUPPLY CHAIN COMPETENCY STRUCTURE

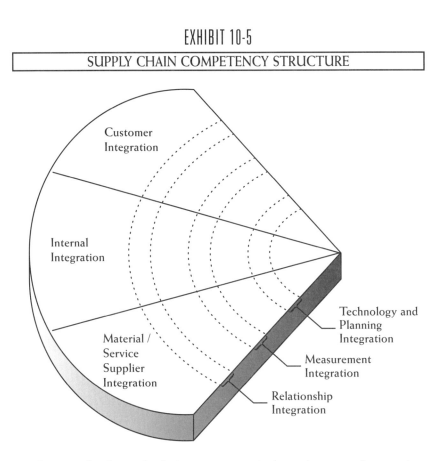

Customer
Integration

Internal
Integration

Material /
Service
Supplier
Integration

Technology and
Planning
Integration

Measurement
Integration

Relationship
Integration

Just as a firm's supply chain competency is dynamic, so are the associated visions. Since visions are about the future, they frequently change. In fact, visions must undergo constant refinement if they are to remain relevant. Once a vision is widely shared, it immediately impacts current decision-making. In essence, the shared vision becomes part of the present as well as the desired future.

In a matter of time, some leaders in an organization will conclude that sufficient potential exists to justify undertaking change. It is difficult to pinpoint exactly what triggers the perceived need to change. Certainly each organization has unique trigger points. In theory, when the gap between the current and desired performance becomes sufficiently large to overcome the perceived risk of change, the process is triggered. In reality, some firms respond much more quickly to change opportunities than others. Clearly high achieving firms have a greater propensity to embrace and accommodate change than more average firms. It is also true that some organizations have a culture that seems to thrive on change. Quoting one executive: *"When things are going well, we get together and figure out ways to do them better. It's assumed that no one wants to get comfortable with the way we are doing things."*

SUMMARY

Chapter Ten discussed the fundamental importance of managing supply chain change. The chapter began by reviewing why firms change and then documented the primary stimulants that motivate such change. Typical obstacles to change were briefly noted. The chapter contrasted three approaches to change management – continuous improvement, reasonable change, and radical change. While many firms have adopted ongoing continuous improvement initiatives, effective supply chain change often requires more extensive reasonable or radical change. Finally, Chapter Ten produced a Supply Chain Change Process Model to provide an overview of the dynamic change challenge. The Supply Chain 2000 Framework provides a benchmark to define the capabilities and competencies that are to be the focus of change. The change itself was viewed as closing a *gap* in pursuit of a vision of future improvement. The blueprint to achieve the desired vision was identified as the change initiatives and action plan. Finally, the entire change process was cast in terms of a dynamic supply chain environment consisting of rapidly changing end-customer requirements and competitive capabilities.

BENCHMARKING SUPPLY CHAIN INTEGRATION

*U*sing the Supply Chain 2000 framework as a guideline for directing the task force as it searched for areas of integration breakdown, Charlie had been able to lead the operational directors into crafting a proposal for change. Since the members of the task force worked for – and frequently collaborated with – each of the VPs, the latter had given their blessing to the plan. One critical piece of the puzzle, however, was still missing. Warren Thompson, the CEO, had received weekly progress reports from Charlie, but he had not been fully briefed on the details. Charlie did not want to take that step until he could ensure that his data could be verified by a cross-section of Spartan's top executives. He knew that ultimate implementation success hinged on his ability to sell each initiative and then measure and present data upon which everyone could agree. Any sign of significant dissent could sink the whole project before it had a chance to start. He knew he would not have a second chance to make these changes.

Although Charlie had completed the supply chain diagnostic himself when the project first began, he decided he needed a management consensus regarding perceptions of current firm capabilities. He wanted to incorporate the perspectives from a broad range of managers and groups, both within and outside the firm, to have a solid and relatively indisputable basis of comparison and justification for future initiatives.

Charlie orchestrated an assessment process to guide the development of management consensus and relevant change initiatives. The assessment process used the Supply Chain 2000 diagnostic, which is structured to probe the firm's achievement levels on the twenty-five capabilities that form the six integration competencies.

Charlie employed a two step process. The first aimed at identifying and reach-

ing managerial consensus regarding current logistical competency. For this step, a diverse group of managers independently completed the diagnostic. Since Charlie wanted to determine the assessment differences by management level and major functional area, he requested a number of managerial groups to complete the questionnaire independently. He desired specific input from senior management, sales, marketing, logistics, production, procurement, finance, and third-party providers. Each manager completed the questionnaire independently and the results were tabulated for each group. Each group was presented with their summarized results. Managers were then asked to discuss the rationale for the differences in their specific responses and jointly resolve any perceptual gaps. In essence, they were seeking a consistent perception regarding Spartan's logistical performance. Charlie wanted each perspective developed independently to ensure that he was receiving a fair overall assessment.

The second process step compared each group's consensus to the average of firms in comparable industries as well as to a benchmark based on high achieving firms. After the consensus responses were received from each group, Charlie compared Spartan's results against the high achiever benchmarks provided in the diagnostic. The purpose was to identify gaps that could serve as the basis for change management initiatives.

The supply chain diagnostic tool had provided invaluable guidance as the task force sought clues to integration gaps and performance shortfalls. Charlie pulled out his copy of the new assessment results and began noting how the data could be used in conjunction with the change management procedure to develop and present a cohesive and powerful argument for change. Then he scheduled a meeting with Amy Thornton and Bill Wingate. With their help, and with input from the other task force members, he felt certain they could prepare a presentation that was sure to convince corporate management and the board of directors.

Due to the complexity of activities and organizations involved, it is critical that supply chain change be managed as a proactive process. The objective of supply chain change management is to ensure that the firm's logistical competency is making an acceptable contribution toward achieving both firm and supply chain goals and objectives. The change management process seeks to identify and prioritize potential action plans aimed at increasing value through refinement of a firm's capabilities.

Prior to initiating change, managers within a firm must develop a common and consistent understanding of their current situation. This chapter describes a procedure to conduct an assessment of a firm's performance with respect to the logistical and supply chain capabilities. To support this procedure, the compact disk, available with this book, includes a diagnostic tool. Appendix F provides specific details on using the diagnostic. Once the assessment is completed managers are better positioned to determine:

- Level of internal functional integration and perceptual differences between key managers;

- Management consensus concerning future direction and areas of change;

- Comparison of the firm's relative position to benchmarks; and

- Opportunities for intermediate and long-term improvement

THE CHANGE MANAGEMENT PROCEDURE

The generalized change management procedure is designed to direct the change initiative, as well as develop a comprehensive understanding of the benefits, costs, and risks associated with the proposed change. Logistical change management itself has been generally understood since the early 1950s. *The Logistical Excellence* research and the *World Class Logistics* research, as well as Chapter Ten of this book, expanded specific application of change management to logistics. Exhibit 11-1 presents a synthesized change management procedure built upon the practice of managers in high achieving organizations. The sections of this chapter outline logistics-specific activities in the change management procedure.

EXHIBIT 11-1

CHANGE MANAGEMENT PROCEDURE

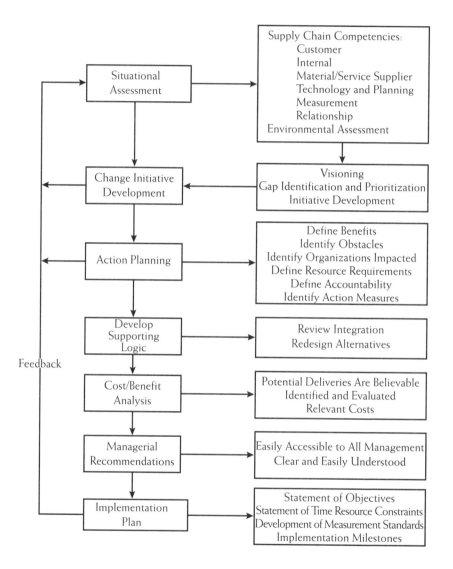

SITUATIONAL ASSESSMENT

Situational Assessment is the first step in the change management procedure. Logistics situational assessment determines both firm and supply chain competencies and scopes the existing operating environment. The Supply Chain 2000 Framework serves to develop a common structured perception of a firm's current supply chain competency.

Supply Chain Assessment Procedure

The Supply Chain assessment centers on a diagnostic tool containing a detailed questionnaire, an analysis spreadsheet and high achiever benchmarks. The questionnaire is structured to probe achievement levels for each of the twenty-five supply chain capabilities. The assessment utilizes a 108-item questionnaire. The questions are presented in random order to facilitate data collection accuracy. The spreadsheet is organized to relate specific questions to capabilities and then aggregate achievement perceptions concerning the capabilities.

The assessment methodology includes two exercises. The first is aimed at identifying and reaching managerial consensus regarding current logistical and supply chain competency. The second consists of benchmarking assessment comparison to results reported by industry and high achiever respondents. A description of each methodology follows.

Exercise One: Developing Group Consensus

The first exercise serves to identify perceptual differences and develop a common understanding regarding the firm's capabilities and competency. The power of this exercise is to perform the self-assessment with a diverse group of managers within the firm who are involved in providing, or are impacted by, logistical and supply chain performance and integration. The diverse group of managers having a broad range of responsibilities assures a variety of perceptions and experiences. Based on the previous research, many managers have found this exercise to be extremely valuable because it served to synthesize and develop a common understanding of logistics and supply chain mission, beliefs, and processes. From this consensus information, participating managers are expected to gain basic understanding and knowledge of logistical and supply chain capabilities leading to areas for potential improvement.

Since it is important to determine the perceived differences for each management group or functional area, managers are asked to complete the questionnaire independently. Each manager is asked to complete the questionnaire by circling the response that most closely matches his or her perception regarding the question. The participant group size should be sufficiently large to incorporate variation in perception and background in order to highlight similarities and differences across functions or departments. A minimum of 8 to 10 participants is recommended to generate a range of responses for consensus generation. A key point regarding participant composition is to ensure cross-functional representation. Participants should ideally represent different functional/departmental areas to encourage creative ideas and suggestions. A group with various backgrounds and knowledge will generate in-depth understanding of the firms supply chain activities.

The administrator inputs the individual responses into the diagnostic spreadsheet, which is programmed to summarize the results by management group, including the mean, group minimum, and group maximum for each question, capability, and competency. The means, minimums, and maximums are used to isolate and quantify areas of perceptual agreement and disagreement. Managers then are asked to discuss the rationale for their specific responses and jointly debate the validity of whatever perceptual gaps exist in the range of responses. In essence, the managers are resolving perceived differences in assessment of current logistical and supply chain capabilities, as well as reaching consensus regarding a common understanding regarding how well the firm currently performs logistics.

Often perceptual discrepancies develop because information is not available to specific managers or not disseminated throughout the company. In other situations, managers in one department may be unfamiliar with activities managed in other departments. As reported in the research, many logistics executives have begun to participate in high-level customer visits. On such visits, it is not uncommon for them to see evidence of a lack of communication between their own firm's departments. Sales executives are often surprised to discover that their company can offer logistical options, such as next day delivery, direct-store delivery or cross-docking. A sales manager who is unfamiliar with such options may perceive the company as being inflexible to customer needs and indicate this perception on questions concerning flexibility and accommodation. When this perception is discussed with the consensus-seeking group, a learning process occurs. Differences of opinion may be resolved or at least understood to provide the basis for an improvement action plan.

A group consensus-building discussion focused on discrepancies may also highlight areas of deficient communication and awareness. Differences that result from lack of communication and awareness may represent areas for significant improvement without need for extensive resources.

Once the group has discussed the discrepancies and reviewed mean scores, it is often useful for the participants to complete the questionnaire a second time. The new information obtained through the consensus-building process may cause participants to change their perceptions on a significant number of questions. Much like a Delphi panel, the mean responses and discrepancies from the revised questionnaires will highlight areas appearing to have been resolved. The second round quantification will reinforce areas of remaining significant difference and may pinpoint new areas of concern not apparent during the first round.

The basic assessment procedure outlines the recommended use of the diagnostic. The procedure can be creatively employed using different respondent groups. For example, an assessment could be completed using dealers or distributors as a response group. Variations could also include employees at lower or higher organizational levels. For example, front-line employees could be included to gauge the perceptual discrepancies between the strategic and operational levels of an organization. Mean responses between such divergent groups and results from follow-up discussions could introduce totally new and significant understanding. Another variation might be to include customers and suppliers to complete the questionnaire. Here, the focus would be to compare scores of participating groups to determine if large discrepancies exist and to position the firm to better understand how it is perceived by its customers and suppliers.

Exercise Two: Benchmarking

Once the first exercise is complete and the group has achieved consensus, a second aspect of the assessment is to benchmark results to those of firms in comparable industries as well as to those of high achieving firms across all industries. Benchmarking translates the assessment into a competitive evaluation. A quantifiable standard serves to determine objectively how a firm's competencies compare to those of other firms. The high achiever benchmark is based on a score that differentiates the top 15 percent of firms in the database from the remaining 85 percent. In effect, the top 15 percent achieved scores greater than one standard deviation above the mean. This top 15 percent of all respondents are identified as high achieving firms. The diagnostic provides a high achiever benchmark for each question, capability and competency. To facilitate comparison, the spreadsheet displays the research-determined benchmark score in a column immediately to the right of the firm's consensus score. Questions, capabilities or competencies that are substantially below the benchmark are areas in which managers perceive their firm lags perceptions of managers from high achieving firms.

The research provides a second type of benchmark allowing firms to compare their results to firms in the same and other industries. Exhibits 11-2 through 11-7 illustrate comparative industry performance for each of the six Supply Chain 2000 Framework competencies and respondent index score. Exhibit 11-8 combines all 6 competencies by industry group. Each exhibit provides the average score for all firms on the competency index. For each industry, the exhibit provides the mean, minimum, and maximum assessment of all firms in each industry. In addition, the size of the bar above and below each industry mean illustrates the standard deviation or variation around the mean for each industry. For each industry, the majority (67 percent) of the firm assessment scores are within the range included by the bar.

A comparison of industry assessments highlights two observations. First, there are significant industry differences in average assessments. Some differences from the mean are statistically significant thus indicating that managers from some industries perceive substantially superior or inferior achievement levels (Exhibit 11-8). Specifically, the health and beauty aids and pharmaceutical industry reports the highest mean perception, whereas the building, mining, and metals industry reports the lowest. While there were significant differences between industries, the second observation supports the premise of this and prior research that there are high performing firms in all industries. These exhibits indicate that each industry includes firms ranging from very low to very high achievers. The results strongly support the conclusion that there are supply chain excellence and laggards in every industry.

The Supply Chain 2000 diagnostic, along with the two step assessment procedure, serves as a platform to synthesize and organize management perceptions regarding current firm capabilities and competencies. A second contribution is the quantitative evidence that compares firm achievement to other firms in the same industry and to a cross-industry group of high achieving firms. The combination offers a solid and justifiable case for action.

EXHIBIT 11-2

CUSTOMER INTEGRATION

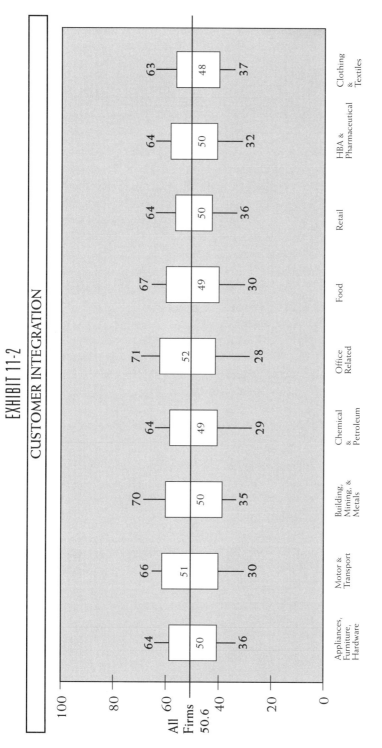

Industry Group

EXHIBIT 11-3

INTERNAL INTEGRATION

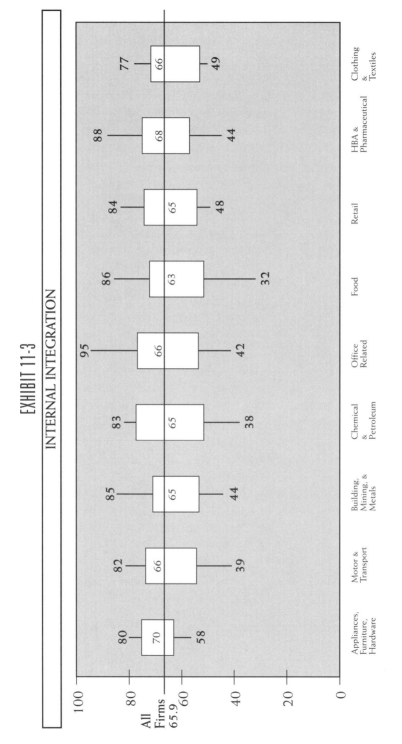

Industry Group

EXHIBIT 11-4

SUPPLIER INTEGRATION

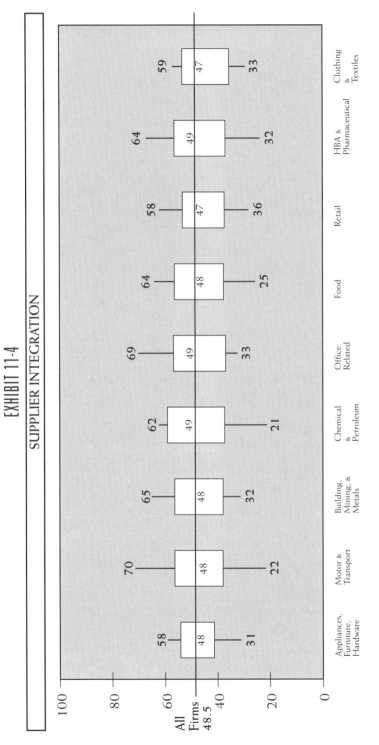

Industry Group

EXHIBIT 11-5
TECHNOLOGY AND PLANNING INTEGRATION

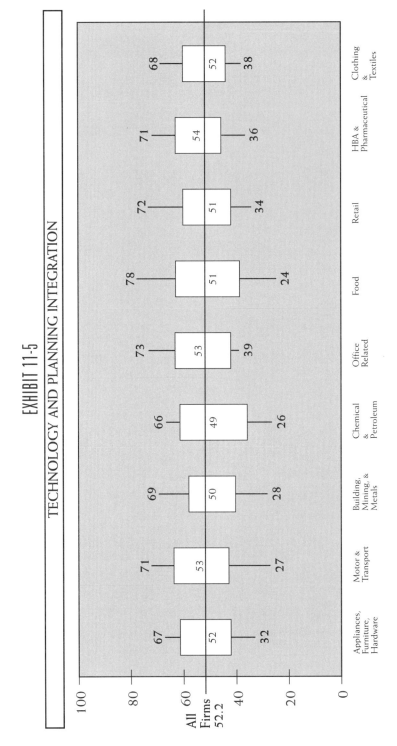

EXHIBIT 11-6

MEASUREMENT INTEGRATION

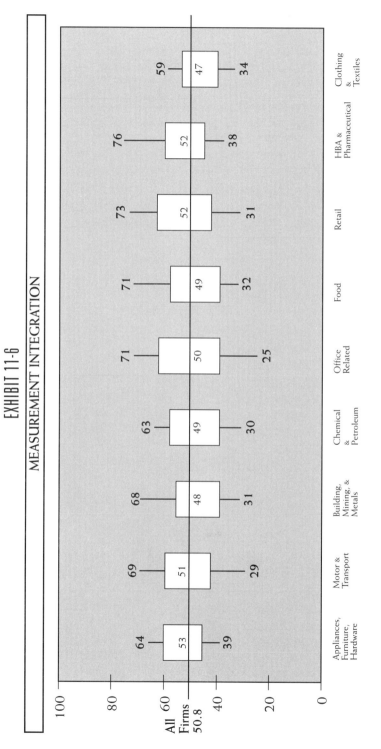

Industry Group

EXHIBIT 11-7

RELATIONSHIP INTEGRATION

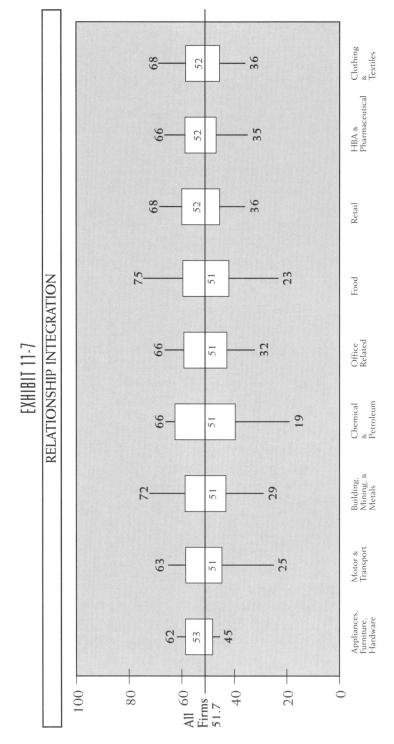

EXHIBIT 11-8

OVERALL SUPPLY CHAIN INTEGRATION

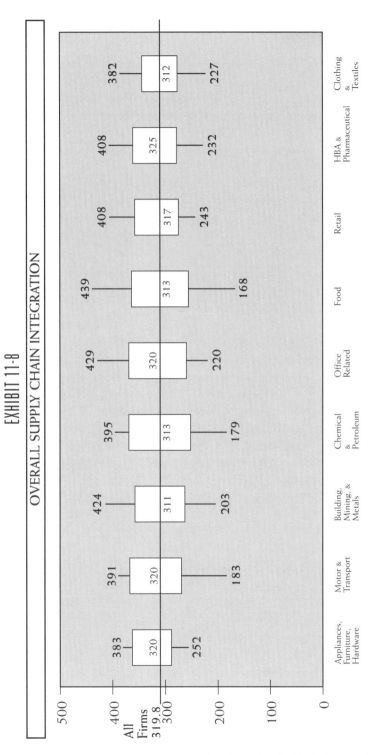

Industry Group

Environmental Assessment

While effective change management requires a common understanding of the firm's relative achievement concerning each supply chain capability, change management must consider environmental demands and constraints and position change initiatives in terms of available resources.

Demands / Constraints

Demand considerations reflect intermediate and end-customer supply chain requirements. To be successful, a firm must develop or retain the capabilities to meet ever-increasing end-customer requirements. These demands are reflected in such factors as increased expectations for perfect orders that meet precise requirements. In addition to near zero defect performance, customers are expanding the range of operational concerns they deem critical. Firms aspiring to high achievement status must understand the dynamic dimension and magnitude of these demand drivers.

In addition to customer demand, there are also constraints that limit the magnitude and direction of supply chain change initiatives. Such constraints might include material or capacity limitations, systems or process capabilities, and physical or geographic operating structure. These constraints represent external forces outside the control of the logistics and supply chain managers that must be considered when considering change. The constraints may be actual or imposed as a matter of policy.

Demands and constraints form the supply chain's external operating environment. Effective change management requires consideration of these demands and constraints as part of the situational assessment. This consideration will enhance change management effectiveness.

Resources

While demands and constraints are generally external and outside the control of the firm, resources controlled by the firm's management must also be considered to achieve effective change. Typical resources include capital equipment, capacity, personnel and information. Historically, logistics managers have focused primarily on internal firm resources.

However, to achieve the vision while recognizing the current level of capabilities and environmental situation, change managers are increasingly considering the creative application of external resources such as alliances and partnerships. Examples of these external resources include the use of contract or third party logistics providers. It is important for firms to consider the potential leveraging of external resources that expanded supply chain relationships can provide. Consideration includes a creative evaluation of the enhanced capabilities and/or reduced resource commitments that such external sources might bring to supply chain performance.

CHANGE INITIATIVE DEVELOPMENT

Once the situational assessment is complete, the second procedure step is change initiative development. This step includes visioning, gap assessment and prioritization, and initiative development.

Visioning

The creative aspect of change management is the leadership to envision new and improved ways to provide value to end-customers. Prior to initiating change, the goal must be crystallized and documented by those involved in the change process. The resulting vision drives change management activities.

The essence of visioning is the leadership ability to justify the need for change accompanied by the ability to provide direction and enthusiasm to motivate the change. Such change should result in improved performance and enhanced overall competitiveness. Ideally the vision will be shared among all firm employees and supply chain partners involved in the change process.

Gap Analysis And Prioritization

The second change initiative development activity reviews and prioritizes the gaps between the firm's assessment in comparison to high achievers. Exhibit 11-9 illustrates the diagnostic report used for the gap analysis.

EXHIBIT 11-9

SUPPLY CHAIN 2000 GAP ANALYSIS REPORT
Diagnostic Results

Capability Results

Supply Chain 2000	High		
Scale: Strongly Disagree 1 2 3 4 5 Strongly Agree	Firm Mean	Achiever Benchmark	Gap
Segmental Focus	13.62	15.36	-1.74
Relevancy	12.76	16.10	-3.34
Responsiveness	14.10	14.88	-0.78
Flexibility	12.65	14.99	-2.34
Cross-Functional Unification	14.65	16.54	-1.89
Standardization	15.11	16.14	-1.03
Simplification	13.26	15.10	-1.84
Compliance	13.78	15.68	-1.90
Structural Adaptation	14.51	16.18	-1.67
Strategic Alignment	12.61	15.94	-3.33
Operational Fusion	13.32	14.86	-1.54
Financial Linkage	12.02	13.82	-1.80
Supplier Management	12.37	14.33	-1.96
Information Management	14.31	16.32	-2.01
Internal Communications	14.51	15.59	-1.08
Connectivity	12.89	16.76	-3.87
Collaborative Forecasting and Planning	12.58	15.61	-3.03
Functional Assessment	14.79	17.66	-2.87
Activity Based and Total Cost Methodology	12.56	14.05	-1.49
Comprehensive Metrics	13.98	15.91	-1.93
Financial Impact	13.09	15.01	-1.92
Role Specificity	12.78	15.26	-2.48
Guidelines	13.34	15.26	-1.92
Information Sharing	12.98	16.04	-3.06
Gain/Risk Sharing	13.67	15.93	-2.26
Overall Score	336.24	370.37	-34.13

Competency Results			
Supply Chain 2000	High		
Scale: Strongly Disagree 1 2 3 4 5 Strongly Agree	Firm Mean	Achiever Benchmark	Gap
Customer Integration	53.13	59.69	-6.56
Internal Integration	71.31	76.56	-5.25
Material/Service Supplier Integration	50.32	56.98	-6.66
Technology and Planning	54.29	62.39	-8.10
Measurement Integration	54.42	60.15	-5.73
Relationship Integration	52.77	60.62	-7.85
Overall Score	336.24	370.37	-34.13

Once the gaps are identified, they are prioritized to focus the firm's efforts. While there are a number of methods to prioritize these gaps, one approach is to focus first on the largest gaps. The Supply Chain 2000 assessment diagnostic facilitates this approach by allowing the change manager to sort and sequence the gaps to identify which capabilities lag the high achiever benchmark by the greatest amount. The logic supporting this approach is that the firm should focus its efforts on the capabilities that demonstrate the largest gaps. Action plans need to be formed based on paybacks achievable by closing specific gaps.

One could argue that the smaller gaps should be the initial focus for change since it may be possible to close these gaps quicker and with fewer resources. However, focusing only on the small gaps would most likely lead, at best, to minor or incremental improvement. In today's competitive marketplace, substantial performance improvement often requires at least reasonable, if not radical, change. If significant performance enhancements are desired, firms need to focus on the larger gaps. The goal of gap prioritization is to develop a consensus regarding which capability improvement will most help the firm to achieve high performance status.

Initiative Development

Once the gaps have been identified and prioritized, the individual capability and competency gaps must be synthesized into change management initiatives. Although there could be one initiative for each capability indicating a gap, capability gaps can usually be grouped to form logical management initiatives. For example, there may be a number of gaps such as responsibility, flexibility, and segmental focus that involve the broad need to improve customer integration. To maintain focus and effectiveness, customer integration might represent the overall initiative. While competencies often provide the common basis for individual initiatives, it is not always the case. Some change initiatives may be formed using individual capabilities while others may involve multiple competencies. The objective is to define a relatively limited number (4 to 6) change initiatives to maintain firm focus while still making a difference in supply chain achievement level. Once the initiatives have been identified, the next step is action plan development.

ACTION PLANNING

The combination of vision, capability assessment, and environmental assessment focuses and prioritizes the direction for change to ensure long-term supply chain viability. Effective change management uses this focus and priority to develop specific action plans to affect enterprise and supply chain change. The action plan consists of individual change management initiatives. The initiatives include an array of activities that can be broadly categorized as business process redesign or resource utilization. Business process redesign initiatives include changes in the way that supply chain activity is performed. Examples include supply chain organization changes, information system redesign and metric refinement. Resource utilization initiatives seek to improve use of physical resources such as facilities, equipment, and personnel. Examples include operational consolidation with other supply chain partners to jointly use facilities and equipment with common customers and suppliers. Other examples of resource utilization initiatives are shifts in information and inventory management responsibility to enhance supply chain scale economies.

Leading firms organize their initiatives into integrated action plans to guide the firm through change management. Successful change managers must have the vision to position believable future propositions and the capability to achieve a consensus so that both executive and operational management will support the initiative. To achieve such support and to guide individual activities, the specifics for each initiative must be defined. Exhibit 11-10 outlines the key items related to each initiative. To formalize and justify change initiatives, managers typically document a formal action plan proposal to define each item contained in Exhibit 11-10.

EXHIBIT 11-10

DEVELOPMENT OF CHANGE INITIATIVES

- Benefits anticipated
  - Service
  - Performance
  - Productivity
- Obstacles to overcome
- Organizations impacted
- Resources required
- Accountability
- Action measurements

First, the change manager must identify the expected benefits for each initiative. The benefits likely are in the form of service, performance or productivity improvement. To the extent possible, such benefits should be quantified in terms of the five measurement areas detailed in Exhibit 9-2. The harder the numbers supporting the proposed action plant, the more likely support will be generated for the initiative. The rationale for documenting the potential benefit is to justify the organization's change effort in terms of return on required resources. Effective change management requires a common and credible vision regarding why the pain of change should be endured.

Second, it is important to identify potential obstacles that could inhibit the change initiatives. While the obstacles may apply to any of the integrated competencies and capabilities, they most often are related to intra- and inter-organizational responsibilities, existing information systems and current operating policies and procedures. Specific examples of obstacles that inhibit change management include inconsistent measurements, conflicting organizational responsibilities and inflexible information technology. Effective action planning requires that potential obstacles be identified to focus management and employee efforts to overcome them.

Third, the action plan should identify the internal and external organizations that are likely to be impacted by the change initiative. This is necessary to identify modifications in organizational structure and responsibility necessary to accommodate the change initiative. Since supply chain integration often requires organizational cooperation and collaboration, a critical step is to identify what managers and organizations will be involved.

Fourth, the action plan should specify resources required to achieve change. In addition to corporate human and financial resources, change initiatives may require outside expertise, external physical capacity and technology enhancements. Once the resources have been identified, change leaders need to specify how they plan to generate essential resources.

Fifth, to keep the change initiatives on track, leading change managers assign accountability for individual activities. Each initiative is assigned to a responsible individual and the feedback or reporting process is specified.

Finally, appropriate accomplishment milestones and measures must be established for each initiative. The milestones focus the time expectation to increase the likelihood of timely change. The measures are critical to direct the change process and for monitoring the benefits of change. Appropriate milestones, supported by before and after measures, significantly increase the probability that change management will stay on schedule and will indeed make a difference.

Once the action plans are documented and rationalized, effective change management requires continued review and justification of change benefits to impacted managers. A fundamental need exists to reinforce the change initiative and its projected benefits to assure interest continues to peak as the detailed phases of the change procedure are completed.

The last four steps in the Change Management Procedure (Exhibit 11-1) outline activities involved with developing supporting logic for change, cost/benefit analysis, managerial recommendations, and implementation planning. These steps go beyond the scope of this book. They are discussed in great detail in Chapter Eighteen of *Logistical Management: The Integrated Supply Chain Process*. The specific citation is included in Appendix G, which also lists a selection of other work related to this topic.

21ST CENTURY SUPPLY CHAIN MANAGEMENT

*F*rom the Supply Chain Management assessment and diagnostic, Charlie learned that Spartan Enterprises was doing very well in some areas but it was losing the benefit of that performance due to uncoordinated operations across other activities. Also, the assessment showed significant problems at the boundaries between Spartan's internal operations and those of key customers and suppliers. The results provided a baseline for where they were and indicated the areas in which they needed to improve to fulfill the vision of true integration with customers, internal functions and activities, material and service suppliers, technology and planning, measurement systems, and relationships. Charlie was ready to present the plan to Warren Thompson.

Warren was impressed. He had increasingly been hearing about unrest among customers, and also had noted the increasing references to supply chain management by top executives and in publications. "In fact, Charlie, I put you in charge of devising our plan because I knew you would tackle that issue. I'm an old accountant, so I'm certainly no expert on the topic, but I think if we want profitable growth at rates that will please our shareholders, we've got to figure out a new way to compete in the coming years and how we can be among the best in our industry. This type of thinking has worked for other companies in other industries. I think we have the kind of organization that is flexible enough to reinvent itself to allow us to compete this way. Let's tell our board what we can do."

Charlie enjoyed a spectacular view overlooking Lake Michigan as he sipped his coffee in the lobby of the resort that hosted the board meeting. The morning was crisp and clear – the sort of morning where you feel almost like you can see the future, Charlie mused. Now, to convince the board.

After the introductory session to review the most recent operating results, Warren briefed the board members on the goals he had set for the task force and relinquished the stage to Charlie. Charlie began by discussing the need to enter the

21st century with a new vision, one in which innovative firms could create value by cutting costs **and** improving service and sales to key customers rather than having to settle for one or the other. The trick, he cautioned, was having the vision and motivation to drive the changes necessary to make it happen. He promised to present them with a cross-functional, cross-enterprise (this raised a few eyebrows) plan to accomplish this.

To the board's surprise, the presentation began with a discussion of the customer base led by Gwynne Miller, the VP of Marketing. Charlie was determined that this would not be interpreted as an operational plan, but rather be seen as a new vision for the entire business. Gwynne identified different value segments in the market and highlighted those most attractive to Spartan. Amy Thornton, Director of Order Fulfillment, followed with an operational vision for serving each target segment. Javi Suarez, VP of Manufacturing, painted a more in-depth picture of internally integrated operations plus the key relationships with suppliers and customers that would have to be forged and cultivated to ensure the seamless flow of product, information and cash. Next, Larry Ingram, VP of Administration and Finance, discussed technology and planning and measurement systems requirements to support the plan. Finally, Charlie closed the presentation with a financial impact statement and vision of new work behavior fostered by an evaluation and compensation system that would encourage win/win relationships across the internal and external supply chain.

The room was silent as Charlie sat down. The members of the management team exchanged nervous glances. During rehearsals, each felt excited to be part of what they believed was a detailed panorama of the future and the role Spartan Enterprises would play. Could it be possible that this vision was too radical for this group of distinguished senior business people?

What seemed to Charlie like an eternity passed before David Hodges, the board chairman, spoke. "Folks," he began in his slow, south Texas drawl, "I first have to say that I'm impressed that we could have four VP's present us with a plan that all seem to agree upon!" This was greeted with appreciative laughter. "What you have just proposed," Hodges continued, "will require a dramatic change in the way the people that work for you view the jobs that they get up for every morning. I happen to believe, however, that change is called for and that if you're going to make change you're better off making it significant and doing it before the rest of the field does so there can be no mistaking who the leader is. If you can make this happen – and have no doubt that this board will be looking over your shoulder every step of the way to monitor your progress – I think that we will be positioned for the kind of profitable growth that becomes the subject of Fortune magazine cover articles." A wave of smiles cascaded through the room. Charlie caught Warren's eye – he was beaming!

The question and answer session that ensued was a blur to Charlie. He did remember the board's vote to adopt the plan. Before he knew it he found himself with a glass of aged scotch in his hand and Warren Thompson leading him by the elbow to an isolated corner of the country club dining room. "Charlie," Warren began when out of earshot of the crowd, "I wanted to wait until I saw how this meeting came out to discuss something with you. I've been planning on stepping down when the timing was right, and I think now is the time to do that. I've spoken extensively with Dave Hodges about it, and he and I both agreed that if we came from this meeting with a solid vision of Spartan's future that this next year is the time for me to go home. He and I both think you would make an excellent candidate for the job. You need some seasoning in corporate strategy, so we would like you to attend a corporate executive management program at a top-notch university in the next few months. I think that insight, in addition to the experience you've gained working as a member of my team the last few years, will enable you to put an impressive package before the board."

"On another issue," Warren continued, "we think Amy Thornton is a fast-tracker for a top level management position. If you move up the ladder you'll have plenty of other things to keep you busy and you'll need someone who thinks like you to make these changes you've proposed. I would like to see her get some additional insight concerning the broader picture of integrated supply chain operations so that she could replace you as VP at some point in the not too distant future. What do you think?"

Charlie felt his knees get wobbly. Was he – the guy who started out with the company as a "trucker" all those years ago – really capable of being CEO of Spartan Enterprises?

Back in his office the week after the meeting, Charlie sat and stared out the window, reflecting on the changes that he had seen in politics, society, and business since he had first entered the profession. When he started with Spartan, the United States and its allies were engaged in The Cold War against a nation that no longer exists. Ronald Reagan was a former actor and the governor of California. The war in Southeast Asia was a recent and bitter memory. The nations of Western Europe got along but the European Community was just a pipe dream. Japan was beginning its economic rise, but most of the "Tigers" of the Pacific Rim were still third-world economies. Bell-bottoms were popular, there were only three major networks on TV, and you had to leave your chair to change the channel! Music was only heard on the radio or on a record player, Dr. J. was the only person who could fly, the Dallas Cowboys still "couldn't win the big one," and you could only cook popcorn over a stove.

In business, manufacturing and marketing ruled the corporation and everyone else supported those efforts. A person might work in transportation or warehousing, but logistics was something only the military did. Only the Japanese had heeded the lessons of Deming and Juran, but everyone was reading what Peter Drucker and Michael Porter had to say about strategy and competitive advantage. Most people still drove cars made in Detroit and watched TV sets made in America. Fred Smith was still the owner of an idea for overnight package delivery that had netted him nothing more than a "C" in a college class. Reports were still done on typewriters *because computing was done on room-sized mainframes accessed through punch cards and paper tape. And anyone who didn't work for your company was regarded suspiciously and certainly was not trusted with information about your upcoming product launch! No one was talking about core competencies, business process reengineering, or supply chain integration.*

Charlie smiled when he thought of how much money he could have made if he had predicted even a hundredth of the changes since then. He never really had time to think much about what things would be like in the future. He was too busy trying to make it through today. He had heard someone say, however, that things were moving so fast that a manager in his position should spend most of his time thinking about tomorrow to be successful. The people he hired should worry about today for him.

With that thought Charlie decided to summarize a list of the assumptions of what the business world would look like in the 21st Century that the task force had used as a basis for their vision. After all, it was only a couple of months away. What are the mega-trends that will shape the future competitive landscape?

Attempting to predict the shape and content of the future is a challenging assignment. Few who prognosticated about the last decade were able to capture the dynamic rate of change and the ultimate shape of the 20th century. Those close to the logistics profession fully appreciate that more change took place during the last ten years than in all decades combined since the industrial revolution. Where will it all lead to 10 years out? Our look to the future starts with a discussion of four major paradigm shifts that will shape the character of business in the 21st century. These paradigm shifts are now firmly rooted and will expand during the foreseeable future. Next, attention is directed to 10 mega-trends that are supply chain specific and are likely to shape how the work of logistics will focus during the formative decade of the 21st century. Using a 10-point scale, the research team provides our estimate of where the profession is in 1999 thereby positioning the needed rate of change in each mega trend space. Finally, the book is concluded with a brief discussion related to the growing context of logistical professionalism.

THE COMPETITIVE ENVIRONMENT

Looking back from the threshold of the new millennium, it is clear that the competitive environment within which supply chains have emerged and begun to flourish has been characterized by at least four basic paradigm shifts which continue to shape the essence of business competition: (1) globalization; (2) responsiveness (3) financial sophistication; and (4) information relevance. Each paradigm is briefly reviewed to frame the landscape within which the logistical mega-trends are projected to mature. It is important to remember that paradigm shifts are viewed as long-term and will be sustainable for the foreseeable future. They are the elements that will cast and shape the character of doing business in a technology driven information age.

GLOBALIZATION

It is unequivocal and irrevocable that business is and will increasingly become global. Over the last decade industry after industry from automotive to pharmaceutical to retail grocery has been recast into a hyper-competitive global context. The business model of successful global operations is characterized by centralized strategic planning combined with regional production and local flexible operations. The global challenge is to orchestrate operations to leverage the economic benefits of specific geographic markets, natural and human resources, and unique legal and tax structures. Awareness and competitive positioning is rapidly moving firms from basic import/export operations to greater international local presence and inter-regional operations. As a result, management and shareholders are increasingly viewing their business challenges in a global as contrasted to a national context.

The globalization of business has a profound impact on many facets of traditional operations. However, no operational area is more critical to globalization than logistics. Going global is primarily a logistical challenge! Timely and economical movement of goods and materials on a global basis as contrasted to national operations means: (1) Longer and more volatile performance cycles; (2) Far greater operational diversity; (3) Complex system integration and, (4) Formation of multi-cultural alliances. Each of these global logistics vectors could be the subject of a dedicated chapter. For the present purpose, suffice to say that the global paradigm is highly dependent upon logistical competency. These globalization challenges are being met by precision transportation supported by sophisticated satellite and internet communication.

The paradigm shift is resulting in a shrinking global competitive environment characterized by the death of distance as we knew it during the 20th century.

RESPONSIVENESS

As illustrated throughout this book, flexibility and agility increasingly characterize logistical operations. In today's competitive world, technology driven time-based competition is reconfiguring distribution channels that were developed prior to the 19th century into goal-directed 21st century supply chains. In essence, the distribution processes of the world are being rapidly reinvented to meet the needs of a new millennium society.

Quick information passage upstream coupled with fast and dependable product delivery characterize the new breed supply chains. Illuminated by information technology, the new pattern of responsiveness is characterized by substituting information for anticipatory process forecasting and inventory.

For decades, the traditional business model was dominated by a sequence of events that were characterized by purchasing components, building products, storing products, selling products and then delivering products. Driven by information technology and the rapid acceptance of e-commerce, new business models are emerging. These new models incorporate principles of postponement in terms of timing when essential value-creating activity takes place. As a general rule, the timing of purchase commitments and strategic movement, as well as the finalization of product configuration, are increasingly being postponed to as late as possible in the sales cycle. Hence, the business model sequence of selling products, buying components, configuring and delivering products is increasingly being perfected. While many readers will recognize this new business model as the traditional concept of customized build-to-order, the new paradigm evolves around the speed and variety with which a customer's need can be accommodated. In comparison to past practice, many firms today are delivering customized products faster, with substantially less risk and with fewer total resources deployed. What is occurring is a fundamental shift from an *anticipatory* dominated business model to one characterized by high levels of *responsiveness*. This new business model necessitates a common understanding of end-customer values and requires substantial collaborative planning across the supply chain.

Logistical systems in the new millennium will be characterized by collaborative endcasting as contrasted to extensive forecasting. Working closely with trading partners, emphasis will be placed on continuous flow of material. Information sharing will allow product dwell times to be minimized and synchronized to facilitate maximum value added during dwell. Techniques such as mix, sort, segregate, sequence and reconfigure during the distribution process exist today and will grow in the future. Products will be designed for rapid accommodation using standard components during logistical processes. As much as 50 percent of final manufacturing customization will take place within selected supply chains.

This responsiveness paradigm shift is resulting in the growth of alternatives to the traditional forecast driven channels of business that dominated the 19th and 20th centuries. The result will not be the replacement of all traditional distribution with demand driven logistical solutions. The end state will be a balanced approach to business operations that introduces a recasting of traditional notions concerning economic efficiency and market effectiveness to include customer relevancy. The balance approach must include a supply chain management organization integrating marketing, procurement, manufacturing, logistics, and order fulfillment.

FINANCIAL SOPHISTICATION

Perhaps the paradigm shift, related to financial sophistication, is currently more a dream than a reality. However, there is increasing evidence to suggest that senior management, shareholders and the so-called street are all anxiously ready to take the cure for the *end of disease*. Almost as predictable as night and day, end of period, quarter, and year pushes to make sales projections have long dominated business practice. This remains true despite the fact that most business executives realize the practice often sacrifices long-term profit. Perhaps the single greatest cause of logistical system redesign failure is the lack of managerial fortitude to stay the redesign course and allow the newly configured supply chain to achieve economic stabilization. During the course of this research we have encountered numerous examples wherein the transformation from a traditional push to a more responsive pull system has required numerous operating periods to fully wean channel inventory. The target of less total inventory moving to end-customers faster and fresher is a highly desirable goal, but the sacrifice and pressure related to failure to meet short-term sales and profit projections may be fatal to one's career.

The paradox is that the yardstick being used to measure business success is based on metrics and rewards that drive short-term sales and earnings. Few who take the time to fully understand the competitive process would question a long-term approach to operational excellence that is asset utilization sensitive. The challenge for operational managers, including those who direct logistics, is to develop a widespread understanding of the financial benefits of superior performance. Such attributes as shorter cash to cash cycles, reduced and strategically positioned dwell time, and zero operational variance all have long-term financial benefits. All serve to reduce total landed cost of operations and have the potential to systematically release or free spin capital out of the logistics capitalized asset base. In addition, a fine-tuned logistical competency can reduce the cost and risk of non-performance with key customers.

The paradigm of financial sophistication may seem like an unattainable dream to many managers who have watched countless efforts to improve long-term competitive positioning sacrificed in favor of short-term earnings. One firm interviewed saw their market valuation drop more than 20 percent overnight as a result of pre-announcement that quarterly earnings per share would fall short of analyst's (not the company's) projected earnings. The result was the scuttling of a long-term supply chain strategy that was being implemented in favor of a robust price promotion aimed at expanding short-term sales. As an endnote, it's interesting to report that the firm soon became a victim of a street driven merger. While progress is slow, evidence suggests that an increasing number of financial analysts are looking to long-term supply chain positioning and logistical competency as key aspects of valuation. We are sufficiently optimistic to cast financial sophistication as a new millennium paradigm shift.

INFORMATION RELEVANCE

While information technology has always facilitated commercial operations, its use as an enabler is a significant paradigm shift. During the last three decades of the 20th Century, the role of information technology has been to exchange information and process transactions quicker and more accurately. At the dawn of the new millennium, information technology is shifting to become the enabler of radically different business practices and relationships. Three aspects of information will have particular relevance for the ways that supply chain management is practiced in the 21st Century.

First, hardware, software, and data communications technology allows connectivity on an unprecedented scale. More and more end-customers are being linked through the supply chain using the Internet. This level of connectivity facilitates interchange of both requirements and shipping information. This capability for information exchange will make individually developed operating plans increasingly less relevant.

Second, the continued development and application of advanced decision support systems will alter the business paradigm as they shift the *who* and *where* of decision-making and the criteria used to make them. While supply chain managers have always made decisions regarding resource utilization, requirements for improved financial performance drive the need for more comprehensive and integrated decision systems. New systems, commonly labeled Advanced Planning Systems (APS), are typically focused on integrating production, inventory, storage and transportation decisions.

Third, in addition to providing substantial connectivity, the Internet is re-writing the rules regarding supply chain design. A local firm can rapidly become regional or global with a web site and a business relationship with a third part logistics service firm. The Internet is opening more channel alternatives for some firms and is threatening the relevance of others.

While information technology has had a dramatic impact throughout our lives, these aspects of information technology will shift the way firms operate. Information technology is becoming the enabler of new and innovative supply chain arrangements.

2009 - A LOOK AHEAD

In this section, 10 mega-trends are discussed within the context of the 4 basic paradigm shifts. The mega-trends are cast within the perspective of the long-term transition taking place as we move from an industrial to an information technology driven society. Our belief is that the best of the best firms in terms of logistical achievement will increasingly modify practices to perfect their supply chain arrangements to accommodate these trends. The mega-trends are not presented in any order of importance.

Customer Service To Relationship Management

Focusing on customer relevancy will increasingly become the key strategic commitment of leading corporations. Whereas traditional customer service measures are metrics based on internal operating activities, a truly relationship driven supply chain focuses on key elements of customer success. For many customers, such operating features as cycle time compression, exact point in time delivery performance and perfect order-to-delivery may be the prime drivers of supplier acceptability. In contrast, other customers may not be willing to shoulder the cost of day-to-day 6-sigma logistics support. Their preference may be for a high level of average logistical support fortified by immaculate logistical recovery when and where needed. Supply chains designed to achieve clear-cut customer value propositions have the potential to turn commodities into value-added solutions. Given an understanding of what drives end-customer purchase behavior, a supply chain based on relationships has the greatest potential to result in unique logistical solutions. A sound relationship foundation can result in supply chain arrangements that are simultaneously effective, efficient and relevant. This implies that firms will likely participate in multiple supply chains and unique logistics solutions to support different customers.

Adversarial To Collaborative

The composition and day-to-day conduct of the relationship driving a supply chain is critical to its ultimate success. The concept of integrated supply chain management serves to highlight the leveraged benefits of firms working together. Examples of increased overall efficiency as a result of reduced duplicate work and elimination of non-productive redundancy are truly mind-boggling. The notion of focused responsibility, coupled with a true *cradle to grave* accountability, are serving to revolutionize the ways that firms work together to streamline the distributive process. But at the heart of collaboration there must be trust and value. True collaboration must be driven by a framework to guide the collaborative process that is not at its core dominated or self-serving to one party in the arrangement. Rules and agreements must drive mutually agreed to policies concerning such critical aspects as risk and benefit sharing, as well as clarify contingent liability. Finally, participating firms must be willing to address difficult issues related to relationship de-integration far in advance of actual need to dissolve a supply chain arrangement. To be truly effective, collaborative arrangements must be highly sensitive to the potential *dark sides* of interlocking agreements.

Forecast To Endcast

A key feature of collaboration is the ability to share both operational and strategic information. As noted earlier, the prevailing distribution model is to drive operations based on forecasts. In essence many firms continue to forecast things that other participants in the supply chain already know. At the center of collaborative management is the ability to jointly develop supply chain plans to best service end-customers. In addition to sharing information itself, participating firms must redesign products, processes, and facilities to fully take advantage of the power of quality information. While forecasts will remain an important step in planning future activity and gauging requirements, they should not be used to direct day-to-day operations. A concerted effort must be made to reduce the number and horizon of forecasts.

Experience To Transition Strategy

For years, the so-called Experience Curve has dominated strategic accommodation to market and competitive situations. Increasingly, firms confront unique situations about which they have zero or at very most limited experience. For example, just a few months ago no firm designed or conducted operations to achieve a negative cash-to-cash cycle. Today, however, several firms are scrambling to duplicate the ways new competition have entered their traditional supply chains using a combination of e-commerce and direct logistics to in fact operate on less than zero capital investment. The point being that all the experience in the world concerning how the traditional distribution model worked was of little or no value in developing a strategy to confront this new competitive pattern. In fact, during periods of intensive change, experience and existing infrastructure become one of the most difficult barriers to overcome. Firms are increasingly confronting a need to reinvent processes that are adequately working when gauged in terms of history, but are being dramatically out-performed by new and better solutions. The capability to identify new strategic patterns and manage continuous transition is becoming the leading edge model.

Absolute To Relative Value

The key to long term success is doing those things well that attract and maintain the most profitable customers. The traditional measure of success has been absolute market share typically measured in gross sales dollars. A more sophisticated approach to measuring success may be the relative value share a supplier enjoys in the terms of key customer success. Profits are and always have been the difference between revenues and cost. Many firms have pressures for increased sales only to find that escalating costs fully erode marginal profits. The notion of relative value is to grow a larger share of dollar revenue available in a business arrangement by a willingness to perform a broader range of value-added services. Thus, the true measure of successful growth may not be so much the absolute size of dollar sales as it is the relative share of sales received for value rendered. It is the notion of relative value that drives such common logistical practices as multi-customer transportation consolidation, cross-docking, mixing in-transit, and other operational innovations that improve customer efficiency.

Functional To Process Integration

One of the oldest and potentially most productive trends is the continued migration from functional to process integration. As noted throughout the research, the work of logistics itself has remained relatively the same over the past decade and will continue to remain the same during the first decade of the new millennium. What has changed dramatically and will continue to change rapidly is *how* we do the work. Increasingly, management realizes that functional excellence is only important in terms of the contribution that function makes to the process it serves. In terms of organizational structure the concept of functional departments is as obsolete as punch cards are to information technology. As pockets of power and control developed within organizations the notion of a department became synonymous with being *departed* from the rest of the organization. While departments may remain the preferred method of managing work, the reality is that process-oriented, self-directed, work teams are increasingly the solution to significant break-throughs in efficiency. The reality and potential of meaningful metrics based on one plan, which in turn is based on one forecast, will increasingly become reality. It should not come as a surprise to some managers that most employ-ees will do what they are measured on and what they are paid to do. The challenge is to convert metric and reward structures from department relat-ed budgets to coordinated process-related incentives.

Vertical To Virtual Integration

The logistics industry is blessed with a highly developed service indus-try. Typically called Third Party Logistics Integrated Service Companies, (3PL), the reality is that these integrated service companies typically work on behalf of either the shipper or the customer. Few 3PL's serve to orchestrate the supply chain arrangement as a true catalyst for *both* the shipper and the customer. However, such collaborative focused 3PL arrangements will grow in the future as supply chains seek new levels of efficiency. The advent of 3PL's providing integrated or cross-functional logistical services does repre-sent a significant departure from traditional practice. Historically, service providers specialized in a single service such as transportation or warehous-ing. Today, a vast network of service companies specializing in multi-func-tional services is available. Some such firms specialize in providing services that require physical assets whereas others specializing in providing integrat-ed information services to facilitate the logistical process.

At the root of 3PL specialization is core competency. Most firms do not consider logistics their core competency. Such firms may find the use of third party logistics specialists as a way to enjoy shared benefits of economy of scale and scope with other shippers. Others may find that the critical nature of logistics to their business success makes performance a core neces-sity. These firms may decide to by-pass the potential benefits of using hired specialists. Each firm also faces a range of logistical requirements that may justify the use of specialists to perform selected logistical services. For exam-ple, it is common practice to use 3PL's to manage distribution of relatively slow moving products or to handle the challenge of reverse logistics.

While traditional 3PL's have focused on physical processes, there is a growing trend to outsource knowledge processes as well. Staff and process design activities are being outsourced to consultants. Information design, collection, maintenance, and analysis is outsourced to information integrators. Knowledge specialization will increasingly become an activity considered for outsourcing by the virtual enterprise. The benefits of obtaining core logistical competency in order to focus on core business requirements will continue to drive firms from vertical to virtual integration.

Information Hoarding To Sharing

Implicit in several of the mega trends is the need for supply chain participants to share information. The shift from a need to know mentality to open information architecture is a difficult transition for old school managers. Most, with years of experience in the trenches, have learned the hard way that information is power. However, technology has changed the information landscape and it is becoming increasingly clear that those who hoard information can only exploit it – they cannot leverage it. The open deployment of information across the supply chain is the catalyst that enables effective integration. It serves as the key that unlocks the power of supply chain integration. Managers are slowly learning to share information. New concepts of data warehouses that can be accessed by all authorized members of a supply chain are opening the door to information required for effective collaborations. As noted earlier, information sharing is an important part of most mega-trends. However, the concept of free information access is sufficiently powerful to qualify as its own mega-trend.

Training To Knowledge-Based Learning

In the foreseeable future the logistic process will remain human centric. However, effective management of the logistics process is complicated by the fact that over 90 percent of all logistical work takes place outside of the vision of any supervisor. No other employees within the typical business enterprise are expected to do so much critical work without direct supervision as those who make the logistical process blossom. For example, a truck driver performs almost all value-added work between a shipping location and arrival at the customer. In addition, truck drivers may spend more time face-to-face with key customer representatives than any other company employee. In fact, the truck driver may not even be an employee of the firm who is making the shipment to the customer. A second example is the need for customer representatives and inventory planners that understand supply chain dynamics and can use information-based tools to develop and implement effective strategies.

The challenges of effective human resource management are being complicated by increased globalization. Senior management must improve capabilities to manage a diverse workforce. The key to success is found in a shift from emphasis on individual employee skill training toward the development of knowledge-based learning. For sure, a truck driver needs to be skilled in all facets of driving. However, they also need to be skilled in much more. They need to possess knowledge concerning how they fit into the logistical process and how to access expert data warehouses and adaptive decision support systems to resolve and prevent operating problems. Some forms of knowledge generation are as simple as learning how to cooperate. Others may require astute skills to identify emerging trends or observe competitive superiority. It is becoming increasingly clear that firms need to build the knowledge capabilities of key employees. In a world where all logistical employees are relatively high paid specialists, the firms who achieve human resource integration will exploit the winning formula. Among all the megatrends the development of effective knowledge based learning systems may be the least developed.

Managerial Accounting To Value Based Management

For decades firms have been managed by the numbers. Managers have also been sufficiently aware of the limitations of Generally Accepted Accounting Procedures (GAAP) to be willing to spend significant resources on managerial accounting such as activity-based costing. Today managers are seeing a need to extend their measurement to an assessment of how the work they perform impacts stakeholder value. Value-based management is closely related to the basic paradigm shift toward financial sophistication. In fact, value management is appropriately viewed as the implementation of financial sophistication. To frame the challenge of value management the operative questions become who benefits from a specific initiative? how do we measure the benefit? and, how do we report the achievement? Until very recently, those in management possessing the greatest ability to help develop meaningful value measurement have been far too committed to maintaining the status quo. As the need for precise costs became apparent, the tendency was to try to convert activity-based costing into activity-based accounting. While conversion was an effort to improve control, it was far too complicated to meet day-to-day operational needs. More recent developments, driven in part by widespread adoption of Enterprise Resource Planning (ERP) and Advanced Planning Systems (APS), are resulting in integrative frameworks to implement value-based management. The key is to identify and support activities that create value as contrasted to those that only increase revenue or decrease cost. The drive toward value management remains in its infancy.

WHERE ARE WE NOW?

Given the 10 mega-trends presented above and the 4 basic paradigm shifts they are based upon represent an accurate view of the challenges logisticians and supply chain executives will face during the emerging decade. A reasonable question is: where are we now? In the opinion of the research team, the current maturity of the mega-trends is uneven. Using a scale of 1 to 10, with 10 being total adoption and 1 representing no meaningful acceptance, the research team offers an assessment of an average North American firm's realization of each trend. A meaningful exercise for your firm would be to poll executives in your firm to see how their assessment of your firm's achievement stacks up.

Customer Service to Relationship Management.
- The most advanced of the mega trends
- Typical concern in well managed firms
- Growing in commitment
- ◆ Average Score 5 to 6

Adversarial to Collaborative
- Subject of great deal of discussion
- Not well defined in most firms
- Some firms talking more than doing
- ◆ Average Score 2 to 3

Forecast to Endcast
- Attracting a great deal of attention
- Widely acknowledged as way to reduce supply chain cost
- Experiencing implementation difficulty
- ◆ Average Score 3 to 4

Experience to Transition Strategy
- Management beginning to realize potential benefit
- Key to effective change management
- Requires a new approach to problem solving
- ◆ Average Score 3 to 4

Absolute to Relative Value
- Enlightened managers tend to agree
- Extremely difficult to measure
- Being exploited by a few advanced firms
- ◈ Average Score 1 to 2

Functional to Process Integration
- Validity of trade-off concept beyond questioning
- Difficult to measure on a multi-functional basis
- Being supported by sophisticated costing methodologies
- ◈ Average Score 4 to 5

Vertical to Virtual Integration
- Most firms have taken initial steps
- Relatively few firms have full scale implementation
- Expansion currently slowed by reported failures
- Service providers being carefully qualified
- ◈ Average Score 4 to 5

Information Hoarding to Sharing
- Being driven by technology
- Ease and cost of Internet is driving rapid change quickly
- Hard transition for managers measured and rewarded on traditional metrics
- ◈ Average Score 3 to 4

Training to Knowledge-Based Learning
- More theory than practice
- Enlightened executives acknowledge need
- Those who desire to implement are having operational problems
- ◈ Average Score 1 to 2

Managerial Accounting to Value Based Management
- Late to gain senior management attention
- Being driven by commitment to ERP implementation
- Likely to take off now that supply chain management concepts are receiving increased acceptance by financial community
- ◈ Average Score 1 to 2

Based on over a decade of researching the development of integrated logistics and the change management process, we have developed a deep appreciation of just how difficult it is to effectively redirect long standing practices. The crisis mentality of the early 1990s has given way to a feeling of: Let the good times role. Until recently, shareholder value has risen to record levels based on growth and acquisition. As a result, senior management has been reluctant to implement basic changes necessary in supply chain design, relationships, and operations. The reluctance may be partially due to a lack of vision and motivation. While many firms espouse the principles of integrated supply chain management, a majority of them continue to conduct business in traditional ways using traditional channels and relationships.

While these mega-trends should enhance supply chain performance over the next decade, they also introduce some risks. These risks merit some consideration as change is contemplated. Three specific risks include: (1) dependence on real time connectivity; (2) channel balance of power; and (3) vulnerability of global operations.

First, real time connectivity enables reduced supply chain uncertainty and inventory. Lack of inventory buffers, however, reduce availability of critical items when communication or transportation systems become disabled. Second, while there has been a significant shift in the balance of distribution channel power from manufacturers to retailers, it is still reasonably balanced. Increased Internet usage has helped to maintain that balance. Continued consolidation of mega-stores, however, could shift that balance. Finally, global operations introduce substantial supply chain vulnerability. In addition to distance and time, global operations introduce significant diversity in the political, legal, labor, cultural, and economic environment. This vulnerability reduces firm control and frequently removes managers from their areas of competency. The result is enhanced potential for supply chain failures.

LOGISTICAL PROFESSIONALISM

At the end of the day, the value of research is its usefulness in helping practitioners make improved decisions and to assist academics to better understand and teach the related subject area.

Over the past three decades, logistics has emerged as a substantial force in business. To achieve discipline status, logistics needs to move beyond passive description and develop a coherent body of knowledge that explains its scope and relevancy. Such a body of knowledge builds on constructs that relate functions, explain structural relationships, and quantify trade-offs. Finally, a coherent theory of logistics must continuously identify and update what constitutes best practice and offer a fair degree of outcome predictability.

The research reported by the Michigan State University Team, as well as a wide range of meaningful investigation completed by our colleagues throughout academia and industry, combine to generate such a coherent body of knowledge. This knowledge details the specific work of logistics and how it is best performed across a wide range of operational conditions. This knowledge also specifies the relevancy of logistics in terms of financial and service outcomes. Logistical performance across the supply chain has the potential to significantly impact end-customer relevancy. Superior logistical performance can be a major source of competitive advantage. The process of logistics is costly and consumes significant financial resources. It also follows then that meaningful financial benefits are likely when logistical operations are well managed.

The constructs of logistics in a supply chain context are documented by the Supply Chain 2000 Framework as six competencies which include 25 capabilities. These constructs generalize the well-established functions of logistics into a universal framework that transcends industries and even national boundaries. The framework facilitates abstraction and integration of the specific work and functions that constitute day-to-day logistics. Functions such as transportation, warehousing, order processing, material handling, and inventory management are generalized in terms of the business need they serve. This abstraction integrates structural relationships between functional areas, allowing them to be quantified at the process level. The use of general systems theory allows integration of relevant processes. Thus, cost-to-cost and cost-to-revenue trade-off quantification becomes the source of integration behavior.

Superior performance should be the reward for adopting and implementing integrated logistics. Evidence is rapidly accumulating to support the conclusion that highly competitive supply chains have well established logistical processes. Less well documented is the direct link between being logistically superior and out-performing competition. Many different factors drive business success. However, it is significant that senior executives in companies who were high achievers, as well as their less accomplished counterparts, jointly agree that having superior logistics and supply chain capabilities provide a competitive difference.

MSU LOGISTICS MANAGEMENT RESEARCH STREAM 1989-1999

This book is the culmination of more than ten years of research conducted by Michigan State University faculty and doctoral students concerning logistics management. Hence, publication of *21ˢᵗ Century Logistics: Making Supply Chain Integration A Reality* is the next step in our understanding of an ever-growing body of knowledge. Readers not familiar with the previous publications may find some concepts discussed in this book novel and unique. However, most new insights and refinements find their roots in previous research. The following sections briefly review the overall research stream from *Leading Edge Logistics* (1989), *Logistical Excellence* (1992), *World Class Logistics* (1995), *World Class Logistics: A Two-Year Review* (1997), and *Food Supply Chain Management: Differentiating Through Effective Logistics* (1999). The scope and key findings of each research initiative are highlighted.

LEADING EDGE LOGISTICS (1989)

The Leading Edge Logistics research commenced in 1986 and concluded in 1989 with the publication of *Leading Edge Logistics: Competitive Positioning for the 1990's*.[1]   This initial research was funded by grants from Digital Equipment corporation, A.T. Kearney, Inc. and the Council of Logistics Management. The main focus of the research was to expand general understanding of what constituted best practice in the emerging logis-

---

[1]Donald J. Bowersox, Patricia J. Daugherty, Cornelia L. Dröge, Dale S. Rogers and Daniel L. Wardlow, *Leading Edge Logistics: Competitive Positioning for the 1990's* (Oak Brook, IL: Council of Logistics Management, 1989).

tics discipline. The initial assumptions were that best logistical practice could be generalized across North American industries as well as between firms at different levels in the channel of distribution, and that best practice was transferable. A major conclusion of the *Leading Edge Logistics* research was that best practice was remarkably similar regardless of industry, channel position or firm size. The fundamental belief emerged that firms exhibiting selected observable and measurable qualities were most apt to be high performance logistics organizations. Thus, a best practice model was generalized concerning organization structure, strategic posture and managerial behavior that reflected leading edge logistical status.

At the conclusion of the research the characteristics of leading edge performers were summarized in ten behavioral propositions:

- Exhibit an overriding commitment to customers.

- Place a high premium on basic performance.

- Develop sophisticated logistical solutions.

- Emphasize planning.

- Encompass a significant span of functional control.

- Have a highly formalized logistical process.

- Commit to external alliances.

- Invest in state-of-the-art information technology.

- Employ comprehensive performance measurement.

During the *Leading Edge Logistics* research, considerable attention was devoted to developing a better understanding of the growing importance of logistics alliances. The book reported the emerging importance being placed on developing closer relationships between all types of buyers and sellers. It was observed that such special relationships led to the formation of alliances that transcended the channel of distribution, creating supply-chain-wide organizational arrangements. Such close working relationships led to comprehensive offerings, which often included tailored and value-added services. The research identified that leading edge users and service suppliers were the most likely to linkup in alliances. As the initial research concluded, many questions remained unanswered concerning how such cooperative arrangements would evolve and to what extent such behavior would become common practice among retailers, wholesalers, manufacturers as well as service and material suppliers.

LOGISTICAL EXCELLENCE (1992)

Before *Leading Edge Logistics* was off the press, new research initiatives had been launched to expand, update, further analyze and enhance interpretation of the database. This expanded research was funded through a supplemental grant firm Digital Equipment Corporation. The continuing research commenced in late 1989 and resulted in the publication of *Logistical Excellence: It's Not Business as Usual* in 1992.[2] The primary motivation behind *Logistical Excellence* was to weld together the generalized capabilities of leading edge performers into a relational model that could help guide managers in the process of logistical renewal. To better understand what was occurring across maturing alliances, new case studies were conducted regarding the formation and operation of such cooperative arrangements. The data from the *Leading Edge Logistics* research were subjected to extensive statistical analysis regarding the development of trading partner and service supplier alliance relationships. The result was the model shown in Exhibit RA-1.

EXHIBIT RA-1

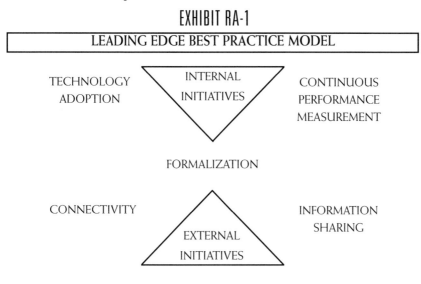

| LEADING EDGE BEST PRACTICE MODEL |

TECHNOLOGY ADOPTION — INTERNAL INITIATIVES — CONTINUOUS PERFORMANCE MEASUREMENT

FORMALIZATION

CONNECTIVITY — EXTERNAL INITIATIVES — INFORMATION SHARING

---

[2]Donald J. Bowersox, Patricia J. Daugherty, Cornelia L. Dröge, Richard N. Germain and Dale S. Rogers, *Logistical Excellence: It's Not Business as Usual* (Bedford, MA: Digital Press, 1992).

This initial best practice model, based on research synthesis and generalization, postulated that best practice resulted from initial integration of internal logistical processes followed by development and integration of external supply chain relationships. Internal integration was viewed as resulting from commitment to formalization of logistical processes, technology adoption and continuous performance measurement. External to the enterprise, supply chain integration required commitment to information sharing, connectivity and formalization of interorganizational logistical processes. A high state of internal and external formalization resulted in logistical flexibility.

The primary goal of achieving logistical excellence was the competitive advantage that flexibility engenders. A soundly designed and implemented logistical capability was viewed as being so well *"adapted to handling the countless details and complexity involved in satisfying customers that it creates an in-place capacity to surge and capture extraordinary opportunities. Flexibility is the ready and waiting reserve to perform the extraordinary that enables the use of logistical competency to gain competitive advantage."* [3]

The *Logistical Excellence* research concluded with eight propositions regarding the projected direction and magnitude of leading edge logistical practice into the 1990s:

- The basic demand for logistical services will expand.

- Environmental and infrastructure constraints will become increasingly restrictive.

- Human resources will be a critical concern.

- Logistical competency will increasingly be viewed as a strategic resource.

- Logistical arrangements will become more relational.

- Technology will continue to reshape conventional logistical processes and channels.

- Management emphasis will focus on process accountability.

- Logistics organizations will become increasingly transparent.

---

[3]Ibid., p. 165.

The propositions reflected how the best companies accommodate the simultaneous impact so speed, quality and organization change.

By 1992, the challenges of change management were becoming central to logistical excellence. Attention was focused on reconfiguring a firm's logistical competency. The following excerpts from *Logistical Excellence* capture the final vision of that research:

> In retrospect, a case can be made that the decade of the 1980s was a logistical renaissance. During the 1980s, logistics practices underwent more change than in all of the years since the Industrial Revolution. Some lessons learned are:
>
> • To significantly improve performance of a process that is not broken, takes considerable time and will often be resisted by those who are having the most to gain.
>
> • The majority of business managers simply have neither the training nor the work experience to position themselves to manage true integration. As a result, the vast majority of available technology capable of facilitating process integration is underutilized.
>
> • Improving quality is illusive in a service such as logistics that is performed across a global playing field, and is difficult to measure. Therefore, the early advantage favors those who are critical of proposed change. Getting buy-in and ownership when long-standing paradigms are being challenged is most difficult.
>
> • Finally, the process of improvement must be a continuous effort – the job is never done.[4]

WORLD CLASS LOGISTICS (1995)

To further understand the emerging logistical discipline, a third book, *World Class Logistics: The Challenge of Managing Continuous Change*, was published in 1995. The World Class Logistics research was conducted primarily under grants from The United Parcel Service Foundation and the Council

---

[4]Ibid., pp. 174-75.

of Logistics Management. The overall thrust was to better understand how the world's best firms achieve and maintain their logistical excellence. In addition to general confirmation of prior research conclusions, the initiative focused on four goals. *First*, generalization – to elaborate and better understand the fundamental aspects of superior logistics performance. *Second*, universality – to confirm the growing belief that the capabilities and supporting practices of world class logistics are fundamentally the same throughout industrially developed nations. *Third*, dynamics – to better understand how logistics managers accomplish high impact change; and *fourth*, relevancy – to develop factual and circumstantial evidence to support the contention that being world class matters.

The overall research design generated three sources of data: (1) a baseline survey administered by mail in eleven countries; (2) in-depth interviews and supporting workbooks from firms perceived to be superior logistics performers in North America, Europe and the Pacific Basin; and (3) three doctoral dissertations focusing on the development and maintenance of logistics alliances. Each is briefly discussed.

Base-Line Survey

The objective of the base-line survey was to: (1) identify trends and perceptions related to global logistics management; (2) confirm universality; and (3) prioritize logistics research concerns and issues. Prior to completing in-depth interviews regarding logistical practice, it was important to develop an appreciation of logistics issues on a global basis.

The first phase of the base-line survey focused on professional assessment of best practice trends and company status updates regarding United States logistics. The survey was mailed in May 1993 to 6,417 members of the Council of Logistics Management. A response of 1,255 surveys (19.6 percent) was achieved without follow-up. To extend the research globally, the identical base-line survey was administered to the membership of 10 logistics professional organizations in North America, Europe and the Pacific Basin. This resulted in 2,438 additional responses for a total of 3,693. This represented a 17.1 percent overall response rate.

Initial results of the base-line survey were reported at the 1994 Council of Logistics Management Annual Conference and a synopsis was published in the proceedings of that meeting.[5] Michigan State University published an expanded version of the analysis in 1994 under the title, *Global Logistics Best Practice: An Intermediate Research Report.*[6]

Interviews

Interviews formed the in-depth understanding of world class practice. The interview sample consisted of 111 firms from North America, Europe and the Pacific Basin. In total, firms headquartered in 17 different nations were interviewed. All firms selected were pre-judged by a group of logistics experts to have a high potential of world class logistical capabilities. Half the sample was selected from North America, with the balance equally divided between Europe and the Pacific Basin. Twenty-five of the North American firms interviewed had participated previously in the *Leading Edge Logistics* research. The firms interviewed included 22 manufacturers conducting business on a global basis. These global firms have business in each of the three developed regions and achieve 40 percent or more of total sales outside their headquarters country.

The interview process was structured as a dialogue that began in early 1994 and concluded during Spring 1995. Firms were asked to identify their business unit for having the best logistics capability for in-depth study. The interview process involved completion of an extensive background data workbook, in-depth interviews and follow-up contact when necessary to fully achieve research objectives.

All firms interviewed were scored using an index to reflect commitment and achievement with respect to specific logistical capabilities and competencies. The index was developed by the research team. Researchers scored the companies they interviewed. The index used for statistical analysis was structured around 10 basic capabilities, each of which was comprised of four subcomponents or drivers.

It is important to note the difference between the index data and the data obtained from the base-line survey. The index data were scored by the interviewers using their notes from in-depth interviews, the content of workbooks completed by company representatives and any other information gathered about the firms. The result was an independent score from an expert that rated the achievement of a particular firm on the range of capabilities being researched.

At various times throughout the *World Class Logistics* book, analyses were conducted using the indexed interview results. A typical procedure com-

---

[5]Donald J. Bowersox, David J. Closs, M. Bixby Cooper, Stanley E. Fawcett, Edward A. Morash, Lloyd M. Rinehart, Steven R. Clinton, David J. Frayer, Robert E. Bowles, Hans van der Hoop and Heon Deok Yoon, "Global Logistics Best Practice: An Intermediate Research Perspective," *Proceedings of the Council of Logistics Management, Vol.* 1 (1994), pp. 27-42.

[6]Michigan State University Global Logistics Research Team, *Global Logistics Best Practice: An Intermediate Research Report*, 1994.

pared the upper one-third with the lower one-third of the index scores. In total, 108 firms were ranked using the index, with scores ranging from a high of 185 to a low of 70 on a total scale of 200 points. Analysis of interviewer grading patterns revealed no bias patterns or other irregularities. All graders had substantial representation of firms interviewed throughout the index range. Statistical comparison of index ratings of the upper one-third to the lower third of the scored firms revealed significant differences for all capabilities and drivers in favor of the highest scored third.

Doctoral Dissertations

An important dimension of university-based research is support for doctoral students. Specific "windows of opportunity" were defined within the overall initiative that allowed students to demonstrate individual research competencies and encourage development of distinct research streams.

Three doctoral dissertations were completed to compare logistics alliance practices among North American companies in the grocery industry. Funding was provided by Mercer Management Consulting, Inc. and the Food Industry Institute at Michigan State University. These independent, but interrelated, dissertations utilized a dyadic case study approach to examine the alliance building and maintenance process among: (1) manufacturers/merchandisers; (2) manufacturers/material suppliers; and (3) manufacturers/service suppliers. The importance and practical relevancy of this facet of the research is demonstrated by the fact that the combined dissertation contributions have been synthesized and published as *Best Practice Model for ECR Alliances: Guidelines for the Development, Implementation and Maintenance of Alliances*.[7] This report was prepared for the ECR Best Practices Operating Committee of the Joint Industry Project on Efficient Consumer Response. Other dissertations are anticipated as part of the overall research.

World Class Logistics Results

The World Class Logistics research was successful in achieving its four basic goals. The results are briefly summarized.

Goal One
Generalization: To elaborate and understand in a more specific way the fundamental aspects of superior logistics performance.

---

[7]Judith M. Schmitz, Robert Frankel and David J. Frayer, *Best Practice Model for ECR Alliances: Guidelines for the Development, Implementation and Maintenance of Alliances*, a report prepared for the ECR Best Practices Operating Committee of the Joint Industry Project on Efficient Consumer Response, 1995.

Based on survey and interview research, a far more specific understanding of what the best-of-the-best logistics firms do to achieve world class status was compiled. The Leading Edge Best Practice Model (Exhibit RA-1) was replaced by a far more precise World Class Logistics Model. The key focus of the model was the simultaneous achievement of the four key competencies illustrated in Exhibit RA-2.

EXHIBIT RA-2

WORLD CLASS LOGISTICS COMPETENCY MODEL

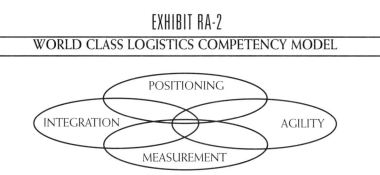

Positioning is concerned with the selection of strategic and structural approaches to guide logistical operations. *Integration* deals with internal achievement of logistical operating excellence and boundary-spanning development of solid supply chain relationships. *Agility* relates to a firm's competency with respect to relevancy, accommodation and flexibility. *Measurement* is concerned with internal and external monitoring of results. High achievement in all four competencies requires comprehensive and continuous improvement. When a firm perfects and fuses positioning, integration, agility and measurement, customer loyalty is engendered and logistics has the potential to become a core competency. World class firms are far more apt to exploit logistics as a core competency than are their less advanced competitors.

The World Class Logistics Model was, of course, far more detailed than simply describing four critical competencies. The model identified 17 measurable capabilities that were integral to logistical superiority (see Exhibit RA-3).

EXHIBIT RA-3

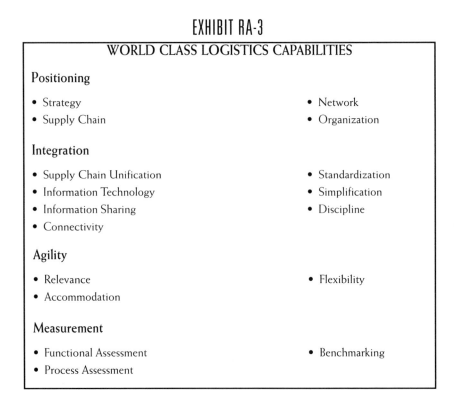

WORLD CLASS LOGISTICS CAPABILITIES

Positioning

- Strategy
- Supply Chain
- Network
- Organization

Integration

- Supply Chain Unification
- Information Technology
- Information Sharing
- Connectivity
- Standardization
- Simplification
- Discipline

Agility

- Relevance
- Accommodation
- Flexibility

Measurement

- Functional Assessment
- Process Assessment
- Benchmarking

The capabilities represent the ways and means of being world class. No individual firm identified throughout the world achieved superior status in all 17 capabilities. All firms had substantial room for improvement in most capability areas. However, firms that achieved world class status had a better across-the-board capability than more typical firms. *World Class Logistics* delved deeply into the determinants of excellence in terms of practices and behavior.

In conclusion, the first goal of the research was achieved in that a World Class Logistics Model was generalized that mapped specific practices and behaviors into four resultant competencies, which combine to create superior logistics.

Goal Two
Universality: Confirmation of the growing belief that the capabilities of world class logistics are fundamentally the same throughout developed nations.

The basic premise of the universality of leading edge behavior was previously confirmed for North America. One goal of the *World Class Logistics* research was to confirm that the same capabilities transcended national boundaries and existed throughout highly diverse cultural settings.

Confirmation of the universality of world class logistics capabilities was based on analysis of the base-line survey data and was further confirmed from the interviews. World class firms were identified in all countries that participated in the base-line survey. While firms in selected areas of the world appeared superior in the achievement of selected capabilities, firms from other areas excelled in different ways. World class firms were sufficiently accomplished in all 17 capabilities to stand well above less logistically sophisticated firms in all area of the world.

In conclusion, the second goal was achieved. The capabilities that led to world class status were independent of industry, position in the channel of distribution, size and country of primary business domicile. The capabilities resulting in world class logistical competency were universal.

Goal Three
Dynamics: To better understand how logistics managers accomplish high impact change.

Logistics executives increasingly perceive the need to create substantial change in the way they conduct their operations. During the course of the *World Class Logistics* research we gained substantial insight into how the challenges of change were managed. The best firms logistically perfected their management procedures to accommodate a continuous capability to envision and achieve change. These capabilities were enhanced by the creation of a shared information resource that was maintained as part of their continuous performance measurement. The result was the ability to achieve planned change with far less vulnerability than when crisis-induced.

World Class Logistics introduced four aids to help firms determine logistics performance: (1) the World Class Logistics Model of logistical competencies; (2) an assessment process; (3) a diagnostic spreadsheet; and (4) benchmarks of world class achievement. The World Class Logistics Model described the interaction between the logistical capabilities and the stages of effective change management. The assessment process provided firms with a process to determine their current level of performance with respect to logistics competencies and capabilities. It required evaluations from a range of functional and process managers and included data collection, data analysis and the interpretation of results. The diagnostic, presented in the form of a Microsoft Excel spreadsheet, facilitated the assessment process. It provided the questionnaire for collecting the data, the forms for entering the data, and the summary reports that compared firm statistics to world class benchmarks. Inclusion of world class or high achiever benchmarks provided a quantifiable standard to determine objectively how a firm's competencies compared to those of leading firms. The high achiever benchmark was defined as a score that divided the top 15 percent of firms in the sample database from the remaining 85 percent. In effect, the top 15 percent of firms had a score greater than one standard deviation above the mean and were defined as the world class firms.

In conclusion, the third research goal was achieved in that we created a bridge between general change management knowledge and specifics related to logistics. The result was a comprehensive guide for undertaking and achieving logistical renewal. The World Class Logistics Model and its supporting structure represented the key contribution of *World Class Logistics*.

Goal Four
Significance: To develop factual and circumstantial evidence that being world class matters.

The *World Class Logistics* research sought to link explicit logistical behavior to achievement. The logic guiding this goal was the belief that pursuit of excellence is simply reflective of good management practice. Confirmation of such linkages could provide justification for why firms should seek logistical excellence.

The results of our ambitious efforts were mixed. The correlation between perceived and benchmarked performance with achievement in logistical capabilities offered positive results. World class firms simply did things better and achieved better results. The direct link between publicly available financial data and world class parameters was not conclusively established. However, some interesting linkages among United States interview firms were identified at both the firm and the general economy level.

In conclusion, the fourth goal was at least partially achieved. Being world class mattered. This conclusion was based on more than just an intuitive feeling that it is the right thing to do. An array of insights were accumulated to give credibility to the significance of achieving world class status.

Conclusion

The research concludes with some general propositions concerning emerging challenges of the late 1990's:

- Logistics for the foreseeable future will be dominated the challenges of managing change.

- Logistics will become increasingly global.

- The universal World Class Logistics Model will continue to evolve and describe a maturing discipline.

- Logistics strategies will increasingly achieve competitive advantage by being finely tuned to specific customer requirements.

- Increasing emphasis will be placed on establishing and maintaining strong supply chain relationships.

- Considerable management priority and effort will be focused on next-generation facility networks and operations arrangements.

- Information technology emphasis will continue to shift from a general change management and control enabler to a developer of the means to achieve specific customer-driven ends.

- Organization structures will become increasingly difficult to generalize and turmoil will continue as firms shift from functional to process management.

- Measurement will significantly increase in scope and importance.

- Reward and recognition systems will be revamped rapidly to encourage meaningful work.

WORLD CLASS LOGISTICS: A TWO-YEAR REVIEW (1997)

This investigation "re-searched" some of the North American companies that had participated in the 1995 study to reexamine their position two years later. The research broadly examined sample firms in terms of their logistics strategy, organizational structure, measurement, and performance.

A number of significant conclusions emerged from the research. With regard to strategic direction, world class firms in particular shifted toward a channel strategy, embracing the full supply chain perspective. These firms were de-averaging and customizing their logistics systems to meet the needs of key channel customers. Firms also were shifting back toward an emphasis on lowest total cost though still favoring a customer service orientation. This assessment was based on the assumption that service levels were to remain constant while improving system efficiency and flexibility. Firms that had achieved high levels of customer service were searching for ways to maintain the service level, but at a lower cost.

Despite substantial investment in information technology, both world class and norm firms expressed dissatisfaction with their information technology operating and planning systems. While the systems have facilitated an increased span of control at the operational level, room for improvement clearly exists. If the move to channel strategy is to be successful, firms will have to improve their system's capability. External connectivity remains a formidable hurdle for most firms.

A major conclusion of the research contradicts the general belief established by a substantial body of organizational science research that formalization decreases as environmental dynamism and hostility increase. In the face of intense change and competitive response, sample firms in this research opted for more written procedures and processes. The outcome supports the earlier finding from the *World Class Logistics* research that routinization leads to logistics flexibility. Being flexible implies that a firm can make operational adaptations in the face of unexpected circumstances. In order to achieve flexibility, however, all other normal activities must also be handled. Routinization, therefore, should be introduced to as many recurring processes as possible. Any commonly occurring logistics situation can be rapidly addressed without hesitation and in a consistent fashion, thus assuring that overall effectiveness is maintained. By routinizing recurring functions, the goal is to dispatch with those activities as quickly as possible. In principle, this frees up time for the unexpected occurrences and creates a flexible logistics enterprise. Flexibility is attainable because normal day-to-day transactions are handled in an efficient and routinized fashion.

Bearing that line of reasoning in mind, higher levels of formalization in the face of increasing environmental change and hostility are desirable. The written procedures and rules of formalization are a building block of routinization, providing a reference for all employees to consult if there is any question concerning repetitive functions or activities. Reliance on standardized, written procedures has the counter intuitive result of creating the desired end state – flexibility.

Sample firms also reported mixed trends in the pursuit of system simplification. There was evidence that world class firms had begun to focus their logistics simplification efforts on reducing marginal products, while the norm firms were emphasizing a reduction in the number of marginal customers. Significant differences in perceived relative performance that existed in 1995 between benchmarkers and non-benchmarkers had disappeared in 1997. Similar findings are reported in a number of areas for world class and norm firms. World class firms, however, indicated higher relative performance in aggregate than norm firms and non-benchmarkers do.

FOOD SUPPLY CHAIN MANAGEMENT: DIFFERENTIATING THROUGH EFFECTIVE LOGISTICS (1999)

An analysis of the financial and operating performance of firms primarily engaged in the grocery industry since the inception of Efficient Consumer Response (ECR) and other supply chain integration initiatives reveals individual companies are achieving widely different operating results. Some firms have demonstrated significant financial improvement. A larger group of firms exhibit flat or declining financial performance. At specific levels of the food supply chain, wide variance also exists between the comparative performance of individual firms. Supermarket operators are discovering that price and assortment alone do not generate sufficient value to maintain consumer loyalty.

Financial and operating analysis reveals that selected food firms have changed the fundamental way they operate based on integrated supply chain best practices. While many have espoused these principles, only a limited number of senior managers have had the motivation and foresight to guide their companies through the stages of application and implementation of these best practices. A large number of food industry participants continue to pursue strategies based upon the principles of forward buying and diversion. Financial and operating analysis indicates that firms who adhere to supply chain management (SCM) principles enjoy significantly higher net profit margin, asset turnover, and return on assets as well as superior inventory performance in comparison to those who continue to follow traditional buying strategies. Integrative supply chain operating principles, as advertised, represent best practice. More importantly they result in financial gains or "free cash spin" that can be reinvested to counter growing competitive challenges.

The financial and operating analysis is supplemented by independent research of food industry logistical practices. Using the World Class Logistics Model developed by Michigan State University (MSU), a 1998 survey comparison of logistical practices was compiled for food firms, health and beauty aids and pharmaceutical drug (HBAP) firms, and firms from all other industries. Food industry logistics practices were generally benchmarked inferior when compared to those of the HBAP industry and generally scored lower in performance when compared to a cross-section of respondents from all other industries. Whereas the food industry has individual firms with logistical competencies that rank among the best of the best, the number of such high achievers is comparatively small. The framework provided by the MSU World Class Logistics Model offers a competency-based blueprint to guide managers who seek constructive change.

The following represent the major conclusions of the research:

- ECR and SCM best practice operating principles work. They represent practices based on leading edge concepts that are being applied throughout the business world.

- Only a limited number of food supply chain participants are aggressively implementing these principles. Therefore only a few firms are generating results essential for improving competitive positioning.

- Meanwhile the traditional food industry's landscape is changing in at least two significant ways:

  - Consumer value expectations are extending beyond price and assortment to include life cycle accommodation.

  - Competitive formats are emerging that are directing value-added service to areas that accommodate consumers' life style demands better than the solution offered by traditional supermarkets.

- The future will belong to those firms capable of aligning their product/market positioning to most effectively accommodate a significant segment of consumer demand. In the world of precise consumer value expectations no firm will be capable of being all things to all consumers.

RESEARCH STREAM PUBLICATIONS

The following are publications from 1986-1999 that are based on this overall logistics research stream.

Books

1. The Global Logistics Research Team at Michigan State University

(1995), *World Class Logistics: The Challenge of Managing Continuous Change* (Oak Brook, IL: Council of Logistics Management).

2. Bowersox, Donald J., Patricia J. Daugherty, Cornelia L. Dröge, Richard N. Germain and Dale S. Rogers (1992), *Logistical Excellence: It's Not Business as Usual* (Bedford, MA: Digital Press). Translated into Italian (1993).

3. Bowersox, Donald J., Patricia J. Daugherty, Cornelia L. Dröge, Dale S. Rogers and Daniel L. Wardlow (1989), *Leading Edge Logistics: Competitive Positioning for the 1990's* (Oak Brook, IL: Council of Logistics Management). Translated into Japanese (1991).

Journal Articles, Chapters, Monographs And Proceedings

1. Bowersox, Donald J., David J. Closs, Theodore P. Stank, and Devin C. Shepard (1999), *Food Supply Chain Management: Differentiating Through Effective Logistics* (Washington, DC: The Food Marketing Institute).

2. Bowersox Donald J., David J. Closs, Theodore P. Stank, and Thomas J. Goldsby (1998), "World Class Logistics: 1998 Study of North American Processes." *Proceedings of the 1998 Council of Logistics Management* Annual Meeting (Anaheim, CA: Council of Logistics Management).

3. Bowersox, Donald J. (1997), "Integrated Supply Chain Management: A Strategic Imperative," *Proceedings of The Council of Logistics Management*, 181-190.

4. Bowersox, Donald J. (1997), "World Class Logistics: A Korean Assessment," *Hanjin Group Transportation and Logistics Institute*.

5. Bowersox, Donald J. (1997), "Developing a World Class Logistics Competency," *University of Wisconsin, Grainger Center for Distribution Management*.

6. Clinton, Steven R. (1997), *Context-Strategy-Structure-Performance in Logistics: A Contingency Approach*, an unpublished dissertation, Michigan State University.

7. Clinton, Steven R., and David J. Closs (1997), "Does Logistics Really have Strategy?" *Journal of Business Logistics* 18:1, 19-44.

8. Closs, David J., Thomas J. Goldsby, and Steven R. Clinton (1997), "Information Technology Influences on World Class Logistics Capability," *International Journal of Physical Distribution and Logistics Management* 27:1, 4-17.

9. Closs, David J., M. Bixby Cooper, Steven R. Clinton, and Stanley E. Fawcett (1997), "World Class Logistics: A Two-Year Review," *Proceedings of the Council Logistics Management Annual Meeting*, 191-202.

10. Closs, David J. M. Bixby Cooper, Steven R. Clinton, and Stanley E. Fawcett (1997), "Les Nouvelles Dimensions World Class Logistics: Qhel Enseignements pour une Europe en Mutation?" *Logistique & Management* 5:2, 35-43.

11. Closs, David J. (1996), "World Class Logistics: The Challenge of Managing Continuous Change," *Proceedings of the 1996 Contemporary Logistics Management Conference* (Taipei, Taiwan) 39-56.

12. Schmitz, Judith M., Robert Frankel and David J. Frayer (1995), "Logistics Alliance Formation Motives: Similarities and Differences Within the Channel," *Journal of Marketing Theory and Practice*, 4:2, 26-36.

13. The Global Logistics Research Team at Michigan State University (1995), *World Class Logistics: The Challenge of Managing Continuous Change* (Chicago, IL).

14. Bowersox, Donald J. and Patricia J. Daugherty (1995), "Logistics Paradigms: The Impact of Information Technology," *Journal of Business Logistics*, 16:1, 65-80.

15. Clinton, Steven R. and Edward A Morash (1995), "Channel and Logistical Integration: A Comparison of North American and Asian-Pacific Practices," *Proceedings of the Facing East/Facing West Conference* (Western Michigan University), 9.

16. Fawcett, Stanley E. and Steven R. Clinton (1995), "Enhancing Logistics Performance to Improve the Global Competitiveness of Manufacturing Organizations," *Proceedings of the Third International Decision Sciences Institute Conference* (Puebla, Mexico), 256-259.

17. Frankel, Robert (1995), *A General Alliance Model: An Examination and Design of Alliances Between Manufacturers and Service Suppliers*, an unpublished dissertation, Michigan State University.

18. Frayer, David J. (1995), *The Alliance Process: An Examination of Logistics Alliances Between Manufacturers and Merchandisers in the Grocery Industry*, an unpublished dissertation, Michigan State University.

19. Morash, Edward A. and Steven R. Clinton (1995), "Channel Management and Relationship Marketing: Some Global Comparisons," *Proceedings of the AMA Summer Educators' Conference*, 1, 23-30.

20. Pfohl, Hans-Christian, Hans van der Hoop and David J. Frayer (1995), "Logistical Excellence in Germany: A Research Report Examining Managerial Perceptions of Best Logistics Practices," *Unternehmensführung und Logistik*, 1-15.

21. Schmitz, Judith M., Robert Frankel and David J. Frayer (1995), *Best Practice Model for ECR Alliances: Guidelines for the Development, Implementation and Maintenance of Alliances*, a research report prepared for the Best Practices Operating Committee of the Joint Industry Project on Efficient Consumer Response.

22. Yoon, Heon Deok, Edward A. Morash, M. Bixby Cooper and Steven R. Clinton (1995), "Channel Integration and Strategic Alliances for Competitive Advantage in the Pacific Basin," *Proceedings of the Joint Korean Marketing Association and American Marketing Association Conference* (Seoul, Korea), 240-253.

23. Yoon, Heon Deok, Edward A. Morash, M. Bixby Cooper and Steven R. Clinton (1995), "Global Comparisons of Channel Integration Strategies and Strategic Alliances," *Advances in International Marketing*, 6:2, 27-38.

24. Bowersox, Donald J., Roger J. Calantone, David J. Closs, M. Bixby Cooper, Cornelia L. Dröge, Stanley E. Fawcett, Edward A Morash, Lloyd M. Rinehart, Judith M. Schmitz, Steven R. Clinton, James A Eckert, Robert Frankel, David J. Frayer and Thomas J. Goldsby (1994), *Global Logistics Best Practice: An Intermediate Research Report, Michigan State University*.

25. Bowersox, Donald J., David J. Closs, M. Bixby Cooper, Stanley E. Fawcett, Edward A. Morash, Lloyd M. Rinehart, Steven R. Clinton, David J. Frayer, Robert E. Bowles, Hans van der Hoop and Heon Deok Yoon (1994), "Global Logistics Best Practice: An Intermediate Research Perspective," *Proceedings of the Council of Logistics Management*, 1, 27-42.

26. Calantone, Roger J. and David J. Frayer (1994), *Logistical Excellence in Norway: A Research Report Examining Managerial Perceptions of Best Logistics Practices*, prepared for LOGMA (Norway).

27. Closs, David J. and M. Bixby Cooper (1994), "How Leading Logistics Companies Manage Change," *Proceedings of the Council of Logistics Management*, 1, 273-282.

28. Closs, David J. and M. Bixby Cooper (1994), "Logistical Excellence: A Canadian Perspective," *Logistics Canada* (August), Canadian Association of Logistics Management.

29. Closs, David J. and Robb Frankel (1994), "Logistics Excellence: An Australian Perspective," *Proceedings of the Logistics '94 Conference*, Australian Institute of Management, 1-7.

30. Cooper, M. Bixby (1994), *Logistical Excellence: A Japanese Perspective*, a research report prepared for the Japan Institute of Logistics Systems (JILS).

31. Daugherty, Patricia J. (1994), "Strategic Alliances," a chapter in James F. Robeson and William C. Copacino, eds., *The Logistics Handbook* (New York, NY: The Free Press), 757-769.

32. Fawcett, Stanley E. and Judith M. Schmitz (1994), *Logistical Excellence: A Swedish Perspective*, a research report prepared for the Swedish National Association of Purchasing and Logistics (SILF/SMAF).

33. Frankel, Robert, David J. Frayer and Judith M. Schmitz (1994), "Logistics Alliances: Understanding the Process is Key," *Proceedings of the Council of Logistics Management*, 1, 291-300.

34. Frankel, Robert, David J. Frayer and Judith M. Schmitz (1994), "Research on Logistics Alliances: Michigan State University Doctoral Research," *Scope: Periodiek voor Technische Bedrifskunde*, a publication of the Eindhoven Technical University in The Netherlands, 1:2 (February), 34-35.

35. Rinehart, Lloyd M. and Steven R. Clinton (1994), *Logistical Excellence: A French Perspective*, a report prepared for the Institute de Formation aux Techn. d'Implantation et Manuention (AFT-IFTIM).

36. Schmitz, Judith M. (1994), *Design and Evaluation of a General Alliance Model: An Examination of Logistical Alliances Between Manufacturers and Material Suppliers*, an unpublished dissertation, Michigan State University.

37. Schmitz, Judith M., Robert Frankel and David J. Frayer (1994), "Vertical Integration without Ownership: The Alliance Alternative," *Proceedings of the Association of Marketing Theory and Practice* (Spring), 391-396.

38. Van der Hoop, Hans and David J. Frayer (1994), *Logistical Excellence in The Netherlands: A Research Report Examining Managerial Perceptions of Best Logistics Practices*, prepared for Vereniging Logistick Management (The Netherlands).

39. Bowersox, Donald J., David J. Closs, M. Bixby Cooper, Lloyd M. Rinehart and David J. Frayer (1993), "Adapting to the Global Environment," *Proceedings of the Council of Logistics Management*, 1, 357-365.

40. Germain, Richard N. (1993), "The Adoption of Logistics Process Technology in Manufacturers," *Journal of Business Research*, 27:3, 51-63.

41. Bowersox, Donald J. (1992), "Framing Global Logistics Requirements," *Proceedings of the Council of Logistics Management*, 1, 267-277.

42. Bowersox, Donald J. and Patricia J. Daugherty (1992), "Achieving and Maintaining Logistics Leadership: Logistics Organizations of the Future," *Logistics Information Management*, 5:1, 12-17. Originally published in *Proceedings of the Council of Logistics Management*, 1 (1989), 59-72.

43. Daugherty, Patricia J., Robert E. Sabath and Dale S. Rogers (1992), "Competitive Advantage Through Customer Responsiveness," *The Logistics and Transportation Review*, 28:3, 257-271.

44. Dröge, Cornelia L. and Richard N. Germain (1992), "Evaluating Physical Distribution Information Systems," *International Journal of Physical Distribution and Materials Management*, 21:7, 22-27.

45. Germain, Richard N. and Dale S. Rogers (1992), "Organization and Supplier Evaluation in Merchandisers," *Proceedings of the AMA Summer Educators' Conference*, 58, 447-453.

46. Daugherty, Patricia J. and Cornelia L. Dröge (1991), "Organizational Structure in Divisionalized Manufacturers: The Potential for Outsourcing Logistics Services," *International Journal of Physical Distribution and Logistics Management*, 21:3, 22-29.

47. Dröge, Cornelia L., Richard N. Germain and James R. Stock (1991), "Dimensions Underlying Retail Logistics and Their Relationship to Supplier Evaluation Criteria," *The International Journal of Logistics Management*, 2:1, 19-25.

48. Germain, Richard N. (1991), *An Investigation of Performance Measurement: The Impact of Logistics Structure and Strategy*, an unpublished dissertation, Michigan State University.

49. Wardlow, Daniel L. (1991), *Strategic Dimensions of Integrated Services Providers*, an unpublished dissertation, Michigan State University.

50. Bowersox, Donald J., Patricia J. Daugherty and Maurice P. Lundrigan (1990), "Logistics Strategy and Structure: Strategic Linkage," *Proceedings of the Council of Logistics Management*, 1, 53-63.

51. Dröge, Cornelia L. and Richard N. Germain (1990), "Evaluating Physical Distribution Information Systems: The Role of Information Technology, Resource Availability and Firm Characteristics," *Proceedings of the AMA Summer Educators' Conference*, 56, 259.

52. Germain, Richard N. and Cornelia L. Dröge (1990), "The Relationship Among Size, Technology and Structure in Small Versus Large Wholesalers," *Proceedings of the AMA Summer Educators' Conference*, 56, 305.

53. Germain, Richard N. and Cornelia L. Dröge (1990), "Wholesale Operations and Vendor Evaluation," *Journal of Business Research*, 21:2, 119-129.

54. Rogers, Dale S. (1990), *An Investigation of Information Technology: The Impact of Logistics Structure and Strategy*, an unpublished dissertation, Michigan State University.

55. Bowersox, Donald J. and Patricia J. Daugherty (1989), "Making the Leading Edge," *Logistics World*, 2:3, 151-156.

56. Bowersox, Donald J., Patricia J. Daugherty, Cornelia L. Dröge, Dale S. Rogers and Daniel L. Wardlow (1989), "An Examination of North American Leading Edge Logistics," *Proceedings of the Academy of Marketing Science*, XII, 445-449.

57. Bowersox, Donald J. and Cornelia L. Dröge (1989), "Similarities in the Organization and Practice of Logistics Management Among Manufacturers, Wholesalers and Retailers," *Journal of Business Logistics*, 10:2, 61-72.

58. Dröge, Cornelia L. and Richard N. Germain (1989), "The Impact of Centralized Structuring of Logistics Activities on Span of Control, Formalization and Performance," *Journal of the Academy of Marketing Science*, 17:1, 83-89.

59. Dröge, Cornelia L., Richard N. Germain and Patricia J. Daugherty (1989), "Servicing the Exchange Relationship: Organizational Configuration and Its Effects on Intra-Firm and Buyer-Seller Communications," *Proceedings of the Annual Meeting of the Southern Marketing Association*, 153-157.

60. Germain, Richard N. (1989), "The Effect of Output Standardization on Logistical Strategy, Structure and Performance," *International Journal of Physical Distribution and Materials Management*, 19:1, 20-29.

61. Germain, Richard N. and Patricia J. Daugherty (1989), "The Effect of Product Diversification and Size on the Organizational Structure of Demand Servicing Activities," *Proceedings of the AMA Summer Educators'Conference*, 55,126-131.

62. Bowersox, Donald J., Patricia J Daugherty, Cornelia L. Dröge, Dale S. Rogers and Daniel L Wardlow (1988), "Leading Edge Logistics: Competitive Positioning for the 1990's," *Proceedings of the Council of Logistics Management*, 1, 123-132.

63. Daugherty, Patricia J. (1988), *Outsourcing Logistical Services: Firm-Specific Usage Patterns (An Empirical Study)*, an unpublished dissertation, Michigan State University.

64. Germain, Richard N. (1988), "Logistical Systems and Their Relationships with Effective Logistical Product Management," *Proceedings of the AMA Summer Educators' Conference*, 54, 4-8.

65. Bowersox, Donald J. and Patricia J. Daugherty (1987), "Emerging Patterns of Logistics Organization," *Journal of Business Logistics*, 8:1, 46-60.

66. Bowersox Donald J., Patricia J. Daugherty, Dale S. Rogers and Daniel L. Wardlow (1987), "Integrated Logistics: A Competitive Weapon," *Proceedings of the Council of Logistics Management*, 1, 1-14.

67. Bowersox, Donald J. and Patricia J. Daugherty (1986), "Organizational Trends Beyond Stage III," *Proceedings of the Council of Logistics Management*, 2, 49-56.

SIZING GLOBAL LOGISTICS EXPENDITURES

T he logistical cost estimates presented in this appendix were gen-
erated by the Global Logistics Market Sizing, Composition and Trends
Collaboratory at the Eli Broad Graduate School of Management, Michigan
State University.[1] The reported Market Sizing and Composition was mod-
eled by Roger Calantone, Professor of Marketing at Michigan State
University. The following was excerpted from Donald J. Bowersox and
Roger Calantone (1998), "Global Logistics," *Journal of International
Marketing*, Vol. 6, No. 4, pp. 83-93.

Estimating Logistics Methodology Cost On A National Basis

The global use of logistics services is very large yet incredibly robust. As
regions and nations develop, investment in logistics and transportation infrastructures grows faster than GDP. Logistics infrastructure is, in fact, in
investment mode. Roads, rail, and air systems are expanded, modernized, and
sometimes massively imported. These systems can command very high initial prices as the benefits provided to the user sectors in the economy in
terms of competitive advantages to early users, more than outweigh the costs
incurred in their use. The concomitant increases in service efficiency for
users and customers raises the competitive bar(s) and causes a spiral of
demands on ancillary services such as warehouses, freight forwarders, and
communications systems. This causes further developmental spirals provid-

---

[1]In order to maintain compatibility, all Gross Domestic Product (GDP) measures are based on 1997 achievement. The GDP for the United States in 1998 was $8.51 trillion and logistics costs are projected at $894 bil-
lion, which represents 10.5 percent of GDP.

ed that capital of all types (money, people with sufficient expertise, technology, and space) is available with sufficient regulation to insure order and safety but not so much as to stifle enterprise and growth.

Generally, total logistics costs for a national economy can be calculated by a weighted sum of costs in material and goods transportation and storage, administration, and communications. A variety of approaches to capture this data have been proposed, but basically estimation methods derived from samples of economic activity are the norm outside of economies where rigorously collected value-added taxes are the norm. Then census type methods are added in. When one attempts to extend the analysis across a region or even across the developed world, the census of economies is ill matched as measures and databases are generally inequivalent. When extending to developing economies the data series are truly suspect beyond the two top levels of GDP estimation. Thus, surrogates for more micro-levels of activity are sought to act as indicators of latent economic activity that give rise to logistical activities and costs in an economy.

Work in estimating global logistics expenditures was reported by Bowersox.[2] That study reported on an estimation of national level logistics costs mainly in the triad regions of the world based on total GDP, government sector product, industrial sector product, and the total trade ration (i.e., imports & exports/GDP). Subsequent studies by the current team have added a variety of additional measures of latent activity to enable measures of logistics costs over the economic development lifecycle. Thus, size of country, kilometers of roads, percentage of shipments by mode, improvements due to deregulation and infrastructure modernization (such as Electronic Data Interchange) are added to the explanatory variable pool. Further experimentation with costs of packaging, degree of domestic food consumption and a variety of social quality indicators has also yielded positive returns.

Thus a wide variety of economic development and progressive sophistication surrogates are available to help estimate total national logistics costs. Early work in this area used high-level summation techniques.[3] Current computation efficiencies allows the use of neural network based estimation using the explanatory variables of latent economic activity (explained previously) as inputs and total logistics costs as outputs. Artificial Neural Network (ANN) models offer significant advantages of parsimony and flex-

[2]Bowersox, Donald J., "Framing Global Logistics Requirements," *Proceedings of the Council of Logistics Management*, 1992, pp.267-277.

[3]Heskett, J.L., Robert M. Ivie and Nicholas A. Glaskowsky, Jr., Business Logistics (New York: Ronald Press Company, 1964). The basic procedure developed by the authors has been modified.

ibility of form over comparable econometric models when relational forms, degree of polynomials, and feedback structure are generally poorly specified.

The definition of an artificial neural network differs from author to author. This study adopts the following broad definition: An artificial neural network is a grouping of simple processing units connected by weighted, directed paths that are adjusted through a learning process. There are eight aspects common to all neural networks:[4]

- A set of *processing units*.

- A *state of activation* for each unit.

- An *output function* for each unit.

- A *pattern of connectivity* among units.

- A *propagation rule* for propagating patterns of activities through the network connections.

- An *activation function* that combines the signals entering a unit with the current state of that unit to produce a new level of activation for the unit.

- A *learning algorithm* whereby connection weights are modified through experience.

- A *learning paradigm* within which the system operates.

There are three basic decisions that must be made when designing a neural network. The network must adopt a specific: (1) structure; (2) learning paradigm (supervised or unsupervised); and (3) learning algorithm. Taken together, a network that adopts a certain structure, learning paradigm, and learning algorithm has a specific architecture.

The present model utilizes a wide variety of national economic indicators representing three regimes: (1) GDP and components; (2) infrastructure costs and systems; and (3) world trade participation. The two major constructs output by the ANN model are total logistics costs and the proportion

---

[4]Rumelhart, D.E., G.E. Hinton and R.J. Williams, "Learning Internal Representations by Error Propagations," *Parallel Distributed Processing: Explorations in the Microstructure of Cognition*, D.E. Rumelhart, J.L. McClelland and the PDP Research Groups (eds.), Cambridge, MA: MIT Press, Vol. 1: Foundations, pp. 318-362.

of economic *energy devoted* to logistics activities. These models were trained using 10 different multiple feedforward algorithms and the consensus estimates were then validated using a holdout sample. Backcasting work successfully reproduced estimates of previous studies, thus validating the methodology for basic forecasting estimates.

Exhibit A-1 presents estimates of detailed data regarding global logistics expenditures.

EXHIBIT A-1

SIZING LOGISTICS EXPENDITURES 1997 (Dollars U.S. in Billions)				
Region	Country	G.D.P.	Logistics $	Logistics % GDP
North	Canada	658	80	12.1
America	Mexico	695	106	15.3
	United States	8,083	849	10.5
	Total	9,436	1,035	11.0
Europe	Belgium/Lux.	240	27	11.4
	Denmark	123	16	12.9
	France	1,320	158	12.0
	Germany	1,740	228	13.1
	Greece	137	17	12.6
	Ireland	60	8	14.0
	Italy	1,240	149	12.0
	Netherlands	344	41	11.9
	Portugal	150	19	12.9
	Spain	642	94	14.7
	United Kingdom	1,242	125	10.1
	Total	7,238	884	12.2
Pacific-Rim	PRC	4,250	718	16.9
	India	1,534	236	15.4
	Hong Kong	175	24	13.7
	Japan	3,080	351	11.4
	Korea	631	78	12.3
	Singapore	85	12	13.9
	Taiwan	308	40	13.1
	Total	10,063	1,459	14.5
South	Brazil	1,040	156	15.0
America	Venezuela	185	24	12.8
	Argentina	348	45	13.0
	Total	1,573	225	14.3
Remaining Other Countries		9,690	1,492	15.4
TOTAL		38,000	5,095	13.4

CHARLIE CHANGE DIALOG FROM
Logistical Excellence: It's Not Business As Usual

CHAPTER ONE: WHY CHANGE?

Charlie Change has always been the type to get things done or at least that was his reputation throughout the company. It was this reputation that resulted in his being selected to go to Europe three years ago to consolidate the company's marketing efforts on the continent. Soon after top management decided that with "EC 92" coming it was time to get into gear in the European market, Charlie found himself living in France. Charlie successfully completed the European assignment and had recently returned to the general office.

During his first week back, Charlie was called into Randy Good's office. Randy was the CEO. Charlie anticipated being debriefed on the European operations and expected to discuss a more specific assignment than "staff assistant to the CEO." To his surprise, after a few complimentary comments concerning how comprehensive and well-written Charlie's reports were, Randy didn't seem to want to talk about the past. Instead, he began to discuss an entirely new topic – or at least, it appeared entirely new to Charlie! The topic was logistics. Charlie didn't consider himself much of an expert. In fact, during the subsequent conversation, Charlie was not even sure he understood exactly what Randy was talking about. He was happy when Randy told him that the board of directors wanted him to make an appraisal of what should be done to get the company moving in the logistics area.

That night, Charlie made a list of what he perceived logistics to be all about. Basically, Charlie felt logistics focused on "moving and storing products":

transportation: trucks? planes? Somehow material had to be moved into the plants, it had to be moved around inside the plants, and it had to be moved out of the plants. Somehow the final products had to reach the customers.

warehouses: to store supplies? to store finished goods?

inventory: the company sure had a lot of raw materials and finished goods!!

documentation: everything moved or stored had to be documented.

Charlie looked at his list and began to laugh – the list appeared to be ridiculously simple and incomplete. Worse still, the list appeared to have no or at best limited connection to the things that Randy had been talking about. Charlie reviewed his notes listing some of the key phrases that Randy had used over and over:
- integrated logistics
- significant and continuous improvements in efficiency and quality
- enhanced customer service and satisfaction
- JIT and Quick Response capability
- EDI linkages with trading partners
- sustainable competitive advantage
- focused logistics strategy
- interrelated systems
- reduced costs
- flexibility and responsiveness to changing customer requirements
- logistical mission/supply chain management
- asset management

What did any of these have to do with warehouses? What did they have to do with trucks? Charlie could make some connections between his list and the meeting notes, but they seemed trivial. For example, Charlie thought, we could probably get products to customers a lot faster by using a specialized transportation source. But – we would have to pay a premium. Customers would probably be happy with the fast delivery, but could we pass on the additional cost? Everything that Charlie thought of seemed to contain inherent contradictions with something else on the list.

Charlie decided to proceed systematically. The first thing I need is information, he thought to himself, information about the overall picture concerning what is going on in logistics. He also felt he needed to understand the details. Charlie remembered the confidence Randy had expressed in him: "You're the man for the job – you develop the big picture, you find out what has to be done, and you get it done."

CHAPTER TWO: CHANGE IS EVERYWHERE

Within a short time Charlie realized his company was facing a crisis. There was no drastic drop in profitability. No, thought Charlie, this crisis is far more dangerous. The symptoms are subtle and the problems are difficult to pinpoint.

Charlie had come to this preliminary conclusion after talking to numerous people throughout the company. Everyone seemed to acknowledge that their department had problems. They were all quick to point out that they weren't alone – other departments also had problems. Sales complained that competition had intensified significantly during the past few years and as a result it was getting far more difficult to get new customers and hold on to the core of the current business. Manufacturing complained that sales people were making promises to customers that were impossible to keep. Manufacturing and logistics were particularly upset at demands for high levels of service performance on small orders. Sales countered that new customers tested potential suppliers this way. If the supplier didn't perform on the small order task, a big order would never materialize. And so it went – almost everyone Charlie talked to agreed that things were getting tougher.

Charlie remembered one conversation in particular. It would become key to his future actions. Bob was one of the company's top sales managers. Charlie had lunch with Bob at a particularly frustrating time. Like a song that replays uncontrollably in one's mind, so had one of Bob's stories stuck in Charlie's mind... *"You know, Charlie, I've been around a long time, and I know everyone in the business."* Bob proceeded to name key purchasers, key salespeople in competing firms, who had which account, who bought how much from whom, who was after which account, and so on. Bob knew who could deliver what within which time span. Indeed, Bob's grasp of competitive benchmarking was remarkable.

Thinking back, Charlie remembered being impressed, but not surprised – after all, isn't a sales manager supposed to be on top of things? What did surprise Charlie was the name of the competitor Bob was most concerned about...

"Charlie, the numbers tell you that Universal is our main rival. Every guy in the office will tell you that Universal is our main rival. But I'm telling you that they're not. I'm telling you that Special is. They only started two years ago, and in terms of volume they don't compare to Universal – yet. We're much bigger than them – for now. Let me tell you about Special. They'll customize the product down to the last micron... we try to convince the customer that our

standard unit will somehow fit their needs. Special could ship products faster from the moon than we can ship from 150 miles. Special commits to a specific delivery time when the order is received... we're lucky to deliver it in the right year."

Charlie remembered laughing at this obvious exaggeration. However, as the story drifted over and over again through Charlie's mind, Bob's words somehow became less and less amusing. Bob had continued...

"You know Sam, whom I've been selling to for 8 years? Last month he placed an order with Special and requested a 3:00 p.m. Tuesday delivery. Sam told me they had bets going at his place over whether Special would make it. Well, their truck was there and waiting to be unloaded at 3:00 p.m. The order was perfect – nothing missing, nothing broken, nothing defective. Sam says he'll have to give them a whole lot more orders in the future. Sure, Sam still orders much more from us – for now."

Charlie thought of what it would take to accomplish 100 percent fill rate on time with zero defects... surely no company could perform that well all the time. In fact, several people Charlie had talked to had stated that such service was impossible; some had practically laughed at the suggestion; some thought that Japanese firms might try to do it. Everyone had plenty of reasons why it couldn't be done, although there was substantial disagreement over what the exact reasons were. Charlie remembered the rest of Bob's tale...

"It was two weeks ago that Sam tells me another 'little story.' Seems like one of Sam's machines was busted and they couldn't figure out what was wrong with it. So they called Special to delay delivery of some raw material for a couple of days. Special responds by sending a guy over to help them get it running. Then this guy phones Special and reschedules delivery. Sam says to me: they saved us a fortune. Well, I got the real message. Do you know what it is, Charlie? We're slightly cheaper than Special, so Sam's still giving us the big orders. But this one event wiped out weeks of those savings. The last straw came yesterday. Sam tells me that Special's representative came in with this new design that could save them hundreds of thousands of dollars and that Sam's engineers are looking into it. Then he tells me – and this is a real bombshell – that his company is planning to drastically reduce the number of suppliers they have traditionally dealt with. Buzz words like "reorganization," "rationalization," and so on are flying, but again, the real message is simple. They want the right product – not 80 percent of the right product and not the product 80 percent

right. They want it at the right time, at the right place. And they want it all the time, not some of the time, and not most of the time. Finally, they want someone who helps them make money – they want a partner. Special's got a good chance. They're flexible, they're fast, they've got salespeople and plant and everything hooked up computer-wise, they make decisions fast. Around here, it can take days just to find out the status of an order, and every decision is subject to the 10/10 rule: 10 weeks and 10 signatures before anything major is decided!"

Charlie could still envision Bob's intense expression as these last words were spoken. The story stuck because it seemed to incorporate key elements from some major trends impacting American business – trends that Charlie had identified over the past few weeks through observation, study, and reflection. Charlie reviewed these basic trends one at a time, in no particular order...

TREND #1: The focus is on customer satisfaction
      Delighting the customer leads to loyalty.

TREND #2: Globalization and international competition
      The world is shrinking.

TREND #3: Market concentration in the United States
      The middle is squeezed.

TREND #4: The computer revolution's effects are everywhere
      The mechanization or management?

TREND #5: Many organizations are flatter than before:
      Tasks and functions are also being reorganized.
      Doings things right.

TREND #6: Supplier-customer strategic alliances are being formed: Are
      corporations becoming hollow?
      Recognizing common interests.

TREND #7: The knowledge era and the value of innovativeness
      Knowledge and newness pay off.

TREND #8: Strategy in the competitive environment:
      Implementation has strategic value
      Doing the right things right.

Charlie knew that whatever specific change scenario developed in his firm, success could not be assured if major forces in the environment were ignored.

CHAPTER THREE: LOGISTICS 1990'S STYLE

Charlie knew he had to quickly get up to speed on what was going on in logistics – he wanted the details, the particulars. It is one thing to sense the overall picture. It's quite another to have an appreciation of what the leaders in the field are doing. Charlie decided that the quickest way to get up to speed was to attend an intensive weeklong logistics seminar at a major Midwestern university. At the very least, such a seminar would give him a good overview of what it takes to get things done in logistics. Thought Charlie – *"such a seminar should give me an idea of what should be done!"*

Charlie was skeptical about how well the program would integrate the macrotrends he had identified. Charlie knew that his mission was not to reorganize the trucking routes!!! He had to have broad-based information and knowledge that would enable him to implement major changes in basic practices of management. He had to convince others that drastic revamping was essential.

When Charlie arrived at the university seminar, he was surprised at the number of executives from other firms attending. In fact, the exchange of "war stories" alone almost made the trip worthwhile!! For the first time, Charlie felt that he was not the only person that was pursuing this particular road. All of the people at the seminar seemed to be seeking the right way to improve overall logistics performance. His original expectations of what he'd get from the seminar were more than fulfilled. Three key concepts emerged as essential ingredients to launching a logistical orientation: formalization, technology adoption, and continuous performance measurement. At the end of the week, Charlie was anxious to get started on improved performance measurement. By measuring and evaluating his firm's performance, Charlie could potentially gain the ammunition necessary to institute real change. The reason was simple: the "right" performance measurements and the "right" benchmarking would enable Charlie to demonstrate not only that change was necessary, but also *what* change was necessary.

While at the seminar, Charlie heard about the upcoming meeting of the Council of Logistics Management. He decided to attend the professional meeting in order to learn more and to hear different perspectives. Charlie was one of 4000 business executives and academics in attendance. It was during the meeting that Charlie became totally committed to the potential of logistics. After he arrived back home, Charlie felt he had a good grasp of how all the things he had been reading about and learning about fit together. Charlie remembered the intense conversations with Bob – and with others. It all fit now. Charlie looked in his desk and found his original list of "what logistics was all about":

transportation: trucks? planes? Somehow materials had to be moved into the plants, it had to be moved around inside the plants, and it had to be moved out of the plants. Somehow the final product had to reach the customers.

warehouses: to store supplies? to store finished goods?

inventory: the company sure had a lot of raw materials and finished goods!!

documentation: everything moved or stored had to be documented.

He remembered having laughed at the list because it seemed pathetically incomplete. Now he laughed at his own list because it seemed incredibly naive, even incorrect!!

CHAPTER FOUR: FACT OR FICTION - AN ASSESSMENT

Charlie felt he had progressed sufficiently along the learning curve to start making some real changes. However, before moving forward he had to know three things:

Where are we now?

Where are we headed?

What opportunities exist for strategic redirection?

In fact, Charlie felt that he had a pretty good grasp on the *answers* to these questions. He constantly had to temper his enthusiasm for immediate action by the knowledge that he couldn't do it without the substantial support from the entire organization – top management as well as key personnel throughout middle and lower levels. Charlie knew he had to have a comprehensive and credible assessment of costs, benefits and risks. He realized it was necessary to develop a believable rationale for change supported by a systematic implementation plan. He knew that he not only had to convince others that things could not continue the way they were, but that he also had to propose and defend a particular course of change. He was aware that there would be substantial obstacles and resistance. He knew it was essential to provide leadership. Charlie set out to build his case.

First off, Charlie assembled as much information as possible. He wanted to look at historical trends – What did the sales pattern for the last five years look like? How volatile is any particular product line – how frequently are new products added or old products dropped? How does the company's business pattern compare relative to the industry norm – is the company an industry leader or is it relegated to being a "follower" that is constantly trying to catch up? Charlie also knew he needed to be able to evaluate the company's efficiency and productivity – are costs within an acceptable range as compared to the competition or should this be a top priority?

Once he had developed a comprehensive overview of past and current operations, Charlie began to look to the future. Where does the company want to be five years from now? A review of the strategic plan and discussions with key personnel provided Charlie with a vision of the company's long-term objectives and goals. Briefly, management's vision was to move out of the second tier of competitors and become an industry leader. Talk about a challenge!

Now Charlie knew what had to be accomplished, but not how to do it. What opportunities are there for improving overall competitive positioning? He began to make another list – what are the company's strengths? weaknesses? After spending considerable time on the list, he turned his attention to the marketplace and the industry. What do the customers really want in terms of customer service? What are the most likely changes anticipated in the future? How could he use logistics strategically to provide better service than the competitors? Charlie had become convinced that service was the key issue – he needed to outline a plan for gaining a competitive edge by offering superior logistical service.

CHAPTER FIVE: MOVING THE MOUNTAIN

Charlie was convinced something had to be done – and he had a pretty good idea of what it was. Charlie thought back to what Bob had said: "*...the numbers tell you that Universal is our main rival. Every guy in the office will tell you Universal is our main rival. But I'm telling you that they're not.*" Charlie recalled that when he had spoken with "every guy in the office," it had indeed been the case that everyone had named Universal. In fact, only one other person had even alluded to Special. If we can't even agree as to what is going on, thought Charlie, how are we going to agree as to what to do about it? Charlie grimaced as the thought occurred to him that the various departments in his own company probably spent more time competing among one another than they did competing with either Universal or Special!

Charlie knew that a few largely cosmetic changes would not suffice. It was going to take major change to position the company for the future. A truly revolutionary and fundamental change was going to be necessary. Charlie thought of the feedback he had received so far to what he felt were modest ideas and suggestions. He reflected on the "red flag" words he had spoken unwittingly, and on the reactions he had encountered.

"we have to be faster...we have to be more flexible...we have to get it right the first time"

When this comment was floated, everyone agreed! In fact, many were positively enthusiastic! However, the more Charlie thought about it, the more he realized that people were merely agreeing to a "motherhood and apple pie" kind of statement. Every time Charlie had tried to put some number, some measurement parameter on the statement, the conversation quickly disintegrated.

Different departments had substantially different criteria to determine what was "fast," "flexible," and "right." Furthermore, being "fast" in one department could automatically create an enormous bottleneck in another department! Charlie worried about what each of these key words *meant* to the people involved. Nowhere did "fast" mean *today*, "flexible" mean *no problem* and "right" mean *100 percent*. Indeed, on-time perfectionism seemed to be frightening and irritating to many – or, at least, what it took to be an on-time perfectionist seemed to be perceived as irritatingly aggressive nitpicking.

Charlie recalled the stories he heard about this production manager that had been brought in a while back. "He was never satisfied" was the comment Charlie heard the most and that comment was always said in a derisive fashion. Apparently, he had pushed other managers for changes – pushed too hard. He was never in his office, and once showed up at a meeting with grease on his hands. Apparently, he was unsuccessful at getting things done. *"Can you imagine? That aggressive SOB tried to tell me what to do. I told him to get his own place fixed up first. When he can fix his own numbers, then he'll have proved that he has something to tell me."* So went a common story. No one liked him, except, Charlie recalled, some of the guys who actually worked on the floor. Even they didn't so much seem to like him as one would like a buddy, but rather they seemed to talk with a great deal of pride about *themselves* when they talked about *him*. No one knew whether the guy had left or whether he had been told to leave. Bob seemed to be the only one who knew where the guy was now – in charge of production at Special. The guy was one of the five guys who ran that company.

"we have to delight our customers... satisfying them is not enough"

This comment also led to an echo of widespread agreement and enthusiasm! The only trouble was that most managers seemed to think that customers were satisfied. Indeed stories about "delighted" customers were frequently offered for consideration. Bob's comments were extremely pessimistic in comparison, yet Charlie knew that Bob was not a pessimist. And Bob was the top account manager! Also, Charlie recalled, there seemed to be quite a proportion of "unreasonable" customers who were always on the phone complaining. *"These guys are always on the phone: where's their order, how come this and that was missing, this carton arrived damaged, and so on and so on..."* was what Charlie remembered hearing.

Charlie began to wonder why no one was tracking complaints. The sales representatives were expected to handle some of the complaints, but complainers were also calling shipping, production, accounting, in fact, virtually all departments. What was their total number, and what were the complaints about? No one seemed to know exactly. Charlie did know how many reached the CEO's office because it was a secretary's job to answer letters with one of six form letter replies and then pass the complaint on to the "correct" department. This secretary had actually kept a record of the people to whom letters had been sent, but had no compilation of what the complaints were about or what was done to correct them. Charlie began to wonder if "unreasonable" customers were simply going elsewhere with their business.

Another problem was that different people seemed to believe that different actions were required to satisfy customers. Production thought keeping the price low through long runs was the most important aspect of servicing customers. Sales, on the other hand, never gave a thought to production runs and according to production seemed to think that inventory would appear from nowhere. Sales complained that production just didn't understand customers: *"They're not the ones who have to talk to these guys."* Logistics often found themselves in the middle.

"change the way we're organized"

This one really got people's goat. "Not again" was a common reaction, followed by long horror stories about what happened "last time." Charlie heard endless stories about what "my department" had gained or lost. Invariably, what was gained was now being handled much better than before and what was lost was being handled much worse than before by others. However, Charlie got the impression that what happened "last time," or, as many had specified, "the last six times," was only part of the story. The rest of the story, which was never spoken, concerned individual power and careers.

People were afraid of losing power! Managers had their little fiefdoms, and the bigger they became, the more power they had. And the more they got paid. Charlie thought hard if anyone had ever been promoted to a position where he or she had fewer people or fewer functions to "manage." Moving up the ladder – what did it really mean? A bigger office? An office with a corner window? An office that was furthest removed from the actual value-added activities performed by the company? A private secretary? A better parking space?

People were also concerned about their careers. Some seemed afraid of losing their jobs. Rumors about what had happened at other companies spread throughout the firm. How can you move up if you've lost your job and are now competing with hundreds of others who have also lost theirs? Even if you keep your job, how can you move up, when the "up" has been reduced by 50 percent?

And it was not only the way people were organized that caused an uproar! Suggestions as to hooking up computers caused some problems, too. It seemed that each department's computer requirements were so unique that others couldn't possibly "understand." In fact, according to several departments, even MIS didn't "understand." In any event, it appeared that MIS worked only for accounting, or so other departments complained: *"They're real good at payroll and billing... well, most of the billing gets out in a reasonable time."* Meanwhile, accounting wasn't too happy with MIS either. And MIS complained that it was grossly under-staffed, and couldn't possibly keep up with the numerous "special" requests. Such special requests represented about a two-year backlog of work.

Departments didn't understand why MIS had all the data, and yet couldn't produce the information that they wanted. Certainly, MIS had records of every transaction – why couldn't they produce a list of all customers of a certain type in Atlanta? The net result was that departments created their own information. Indeed, some individuals had created software that they didn't even want to share with others in the same department! Charlie began to really understand what the old saying "information is power" meant in the computer age. Charlie tried to get a handle on what the obstacles really were.

CHAPTER SIX: BRINGING HOME THE BACON

As Charlie thought about the obstacles that confronted him, he sometimes got discouraged. He knew that he was perceived as power hungry by some, and just plain misguided or idealistic by others. The battle lines had been drawn, and Charlie found himself a target of everybody's rifle scope. Of course, everybody had a different reason for targeting him, but that alone was not very reassuring. Charlie seriously contemplated looking for another position. He didn't know how much longer he could take this level of frustration.

Suddenly things began to move. First, Randy Good started to throw his weight behind Charlie. This helped enormously because the levels of conflict and outright hostility were immediately reduced. Charlie began to feel that others were giving him a fair hearing and they were not actively trying to sabotage him. Glimmers of cooperation began to surface. Second, Super, their largest customer, wanted to jointly evaluate the potential of an operating alliance. They were talking about modifying how the two firms do business together in an effort to both benefit from a closer working relationship. This seemed nothing short of a miracle – what timing!!

Within days, a logistics steering committee was set up, and their mandate from Randy was to "get the show on the road." The composition of the committee sent a clear message to everyone in the firm. Top managers from key departments were chosen, and Randy made it clear that he expected both a blueprint for change and a timetable for its implementation within each and every department. *"Right now, we have to think in terms of departments, because that's what we've inherited,"* said Randy, *"But, when the dust settles, I want everyone thinking in terms of customers, in terms of what we can do to create value for customers. When we do things right, our customers don't think 'Wow, Joe Smith in manufacturing really did his job' and when things go wrong, our customers don't think 'Joe Smith really messed up.' Everything any of us does reflects on our company as a whole – our reputation – and in this dog eat dog environment, our reputation is all we really have. In manufacturing we **do** manufacture products and in accounting **we do** process orders and so on, but no one should ever lose sight of what it is we **really do**. Every second of every day, we either enhance our reputation by creating satisfied customers or we don't. We either deliver value to customers (**not** warehouses) or we don't."*

Charlie's group started with a logistics mission statement and plan that were congruent with the company's overall business strategy. They specified a technology evaluation plan and installed a new logistics performance measurement program. In fact, once their mission was specified and the committee was empowered by Randy, Charlie found that it was not as difficult as he had thought to get a commitment to action. One breakthrough came when everyone agreed that value-adding processes had to be accomplished faster and with more accuracy. Then someone had said *"Hey, our trucks can only go as fast as the speed limit, and there's a limit to how fast our machines and personnel can work!"* Trucks, thought Charlie, we're back to my original list with those damn trucks! As it turned out, those "damn trucks" made everyone realize that they couldn't just do the same things the same way, but faster and more accurately, without hitting inherent "speed limits." Suddenly, everyone was forced to abandon the "faster and better" *platitude*, and deal with the fact that "faster and better" really meant a whole new way of accomplishing the core value-adding activities of the firm. For example, interrelatedness implied the necessity for integration in the timing of flows, in information systems, in performance assessment, etc. Most importantly, the final plan incorporated a way of institutionalizing logistics as a key business process – a way of ensuring that a logistics management mindset was permanently implanted in "our way of doing our business." This way of looking at logistics as a business process, Charlie realized, was far more important than any particular change that could be made in organization structure. If successful, it would begin what could amount to permanent change in the way "we do business."

Charlie reviewed the steps required to stimulate real change: CEO support, the composition of the change committee, the focus on customers and value-added processes, clear mission, a specific plan and programs, and so on. Charlie had obtained a commitment to action from the top managers from key departments, but he did not stop there. He realized that to sustain the difficult follow-through, *everyone* from the top down had to be thoroughly convinced that the correct and necessary steps were being taken. *"The burden of proof is up to me and the committee,"* thought Charlie, *"and I must dot every 'i' and cross every 't' in this endeavor. No matter how tedious, no one will ever be able to say that I didn't cover all the bases! I have to document every step in great detail."* Charlie's goal was to convince even hard core skeptics and jaded survivors of previous attempts at change.

CHAPTER SEVEN: DEVELOPING STRATEGIC ALLIANCES

At this point, Charlie felt he had learned a great deal about the relationship of key activities within his firm's operations. However, he realized that to build a truly successful alliance with Super, their number one customer, he needed to find out more about Super's business.

Charlie contacted Super's senior logistics person, Dan. During that conversation, Charlie detailed how he thought they should proceed. Charlie proposed that he spend some time – a minimum of two weeks, but more if possible – on the premises learning how Super operated. Charlie emphasized that it would be necessary to get exposure to a variety of areas – Sales, Marketing, Logistics, Store Operations. He wanted to be sure to come away with a comprehensive picture of what would be needed based on an appreciation for the interactions and relationships within the company. Charlie knew he had to be in a position to realistically assess whether his firm and Dan's were good candidates for an alliance arrangement. Alliance partners must work closely together – not unlike a marriage – and he knew that it was critical that their two operations be "compatible." He also wanted to develop a greater appreciation for what Dan's people expected from a strategic partnering arrangement.

Dan was at first surprised that Charlie would be interested in such a wide variety of areas – after all, what was being proposed was a *logistics* alliance. However, he was impressed that Charlie was willing to make such a significant investment in terms of time and effort. He liked that "spirit of commitment." But before proceeding further, Dan said he needed to have at least some indication of how the proposed alliance would work and a good idea of "what's in it for us." They scheduled a meeting for the next week. Charlie's charge was to come in and "sell" Dan and his colleagues on the idea.

As Charlie prepared for the meeting, he knew there were some basic and important points he needed to get across if his plan was to have any chance for success. He didn't want to be perceived as self-serving. Sure, his company hoped for potentially significant improvement ... but so did Dan's. The venture must be two-way. He had to make the point that each side would bring different, but complementary-even synergistic-capabilities to the party. By proper leveraging, the idea was to gain a competitive advantage for both sides.

Charlie was faced with a dilemma. To really convince Dan and the others to proceed, he needed to come up with concrete reasons and benefits that would materialize from an alliance. However, in order to be able to clearly define alliance-associated benefits, he needed to know more about Super's business.

Charlie had decided it would be necessary to compromise. He would need to do a "generic" selling job on the advisability of developing an alliance and ask for conditional approval to proceed. If he could sell Dan and his colleagues on the potential of an alliance, then he would ask if he could do an "internship" within their operations and use the information gained to tailor a long-term working arrangement.

During the meeting Charlie focused on the advantages to be gained by working cooperatively. This would allow each firm to specialize in select areas and result in subsequently more efficient overall operations. He high-lighted the benefits of working together to increase flexibility and respon-siveness. He tried to realistically assess the strengths of both firms and define expectations.

At the meeting, Charlie presented a strong case for further exploring the potential benefits of a strategic alliance. Dan and his colleagues became enthused about the possibilities. They were especially interested in Charlie's projections about the time that could be cut from their typical order cycle. They all agreed to go ahead. Arrangements were made for Charlie to spend time at the retailer's facilities. They formed a joint task force to work out definitive operating guidelines for the new alliance. The task force was eager to get to work.

What transpired was truly astonishing. Working together Charlie's group and the retailer's people worked out a way to share information and revamp delivery times so that inventory turns in the channel went from seven to over forty times per year. The result was a substantial reduction in inven-tory for both firms. Even more important, Charlie could clearly see that business gains were going to far surpass those projected to support the new arrangement. It was clearly a WIN-WIN situation.

CHAPTER EIGHT: THE DAY AFTER SUCCESS

When the results started to become apparent, Charlie scheduled a meet-ing with key personnel to recap how the successful alliance with Super was established. He reported that Super's management was truly impressed with the alliance, and Dan's people were truly committed to expanding the scope of the arrangement. Charlie emphasized it was critical that their people develop an equivalent level of commitment. He restated the responsibilities and the potential for sharing of benefits – "we're all in this together."

In order to bring home his point, he spent a great deal of time elaborat-ing on "what's in it for us." He not only mentioned improvements in busi-ness efficiency, he also brought it down to the personal level – job security. Logistics capabilities had to be developed, implemented, and continuously improved in order to maintain a competitive edge. The new cooperative venture would allow each of the alliance partners to focus on what they were capable of doing best thus realizing via improvements reduced costs and improved service. It would also give each of the partners new perspectives thus introducing the possibility of developing new innovative solutions to business problems.

Charlie concluded by saying, *"That's history. Our ideas were good enough and the potential for improvement great enough to convince the retailer to work with* *us **now**. But what's ahead? How do we ensure that this alliance continues to grow and succeed? And how do we develop other key customer or supplier alliance arrangements?"*

People really got involved; ideas were introduced one after another and intense discussion followed. Many of the key ideas focused on remaining *aware*. Too often in the past, things got bogged down because people became too involved in day-to-day "fire fighting" to concentrate on the bigger picture. Although Charlie's team had a pretty good idea of "where the company has been" and "where we are now," they recognized the importance of developing a future orientation. A future orientation involves monitoring the external environment, really establishing a dialogue with customers, investigating new technologies, etc. These things could not be left to chance. It was decided that formal guidelines and the designation of specific responsibilities were necessary to ensure continued development and progression of the firm's logistical excellence.

Just as Charlie and the others were trying to specify and formalize the initiative, Charlie got a call from Randy Good's office. The CEO wanted to see Charlie in fifteen minutes. Leaving the others to develop future-oriented management guidelines, Charlie headed for Randy's office.

Charlie assumed the CEO wanted to hear more about the strategic alliance with Super. However, as he entered Randy's office, he sensed that Super was not the topic at all.

Charlie was briefed that the firm had finalized a merger with a major competitor. Charlie was surprised, but he was also pleased. The combined operations would clearly be an industry leader. They've been doing a lot of things right ... but not everything. Charlie started to think about how the two firms could be blended together to form one "new and improved" operation. What synergies were possible? Undoubtedly, a merger would require a significant rationalization to eliminate duplication. His mind quickly reviewed which areas would offer the best opportunities for "collapsing" and the elimination of personnel, equipment, etc. Charlie could envision an exciting opportunity for significant synergism. As he began to think about what might be, he heard Randy say: *"You're the man for the job – you develop the big picture, you find out what has to be done and you get it done."*

RESEARCH RESULTS BY INDUSTRY

This appendix presents detailed results by individual question of the 1999 Michigan State University Supply Chain 2000 research survey. Data regarding top logistics executives' professional opinions were collected in three specific areas: 1) logistical processes; 2) logistics strategy; and 3) performance measurement.

The 306 total responses were segmented into ten distinct industry groups, including the following:
- Appliances, Furniture, and Hardware
- Motor and Transportation
- Building and Lumber, Mining, Metals
- Chemicals and Petroleum
- Office Equipment and Supplies (Computers to Paper)
- Food Processing and Distribution
- Mass Merchandising and Retail
- HBA and Pharmaceutical
- Clothing and Textile
- All Other

Exhibit C-1 shows specific results for each individual industry group. Data show the arithmetic mean of responses to statements designed to obtain executives' professional opinion regarding logistics processes and performance measurement. Data presented for logistics strategy shows the frequency of firms in each industry that responded to each strategy category.

The results are also contained in a Microsoft Excel 6.0 file in the compact disk.

EXHIBIT C-1

SURVEY RESULTS BY INDUSTRY

Columns of data correspond with the following industries:

1. Appliances, Furniture, and Hardware
2. Motor and Transportation
3. Building and Lumber, Mining, Metals
4. Chemicals and Petroleum
5. Office Equipment and Supplies (Computers to Paper)
6. Food Processing and Distribution
7. Mass Merchandising and Retail
8. HBA and Pharmaceutical
9. Clothing and Textile
10. Other

PART ONE: LOGISTICAL PROCESSES

Data shows the arithmetic mean of responses to statements designed to obtain executives' professional opinion concerning logistics practices (1=Strongly Disagree, 2=Disagree, 3=Neither Agree nor Disagree, 4=Agree, 5=Strongly Agree).

		1	2	3	4	5	6	7	8	9	10
1	My firm uses logistical requirements as a basis of customer segmentation.	3.07	3.08	2.81	3.11	2.86	3.22	2.68	3.21	3.02	3.14
2	My firm is pursuing a plan to establish partnerships/alliances.	3.93	4.03	4.04	3.89	4.05	3.95	3.77	4.00	4.25	3.95
3	Using 25% as the mid-point (3), my firm has increased inventory turns by more or less during the past three years.	3.79	3.10	3.07	2.40	3.25	3.15	3.09	3.26	3.68	3.02
4	My firm extensively utilizes cross-functional work teams for managing day-to-day operations.	3.43	3.75	3.26	3.61	3.14	3.33	3.18	3.47	3.75	3.27
5	My firm clearly defines roles and responsibilities with our supply chain partners.	3.50	3.25	2.93	2.89	3.24	3.42	3.50	3.59	3.25	2.88
6	Logistics information systems in my firm are being extended to include more integrated applications.	3.79	3.75	3.26	3.22	3.59	3.67	4.09	3.84	3.75	3.36
7	My firm effectively shares operational information externally with selected suppliers and/or customers.	3.57	3.38	3.19	2.67	3.46	3.33	3.45	3.16	3.42	3.57

#	Statement										
8	My firm has adequate ability to share both standardized and customized information externally with suppliers and/or customers.	3.29	3.23	3.08	2.83	3.14	3.11	3.00	3.42	3.08	3.23
9	My firm actively encourages best practice implementation.	3.43	3.70	3.56	3.39	3.65	3.69	3.64	3.76	3.75	3.86
10	My firm has extensively redesigned work routines and processes over the past three years.	4.07	4.08	3.67	3.67	3.78	2.97	4.05	3.79	3.75	3.64
11	My firm's compensation, incentive and reward systems encourage adherence to stated policies and procedures.	3.71	2.95	3.19	2.89	3.11	2.84	3.14	3.47	2.92	3.33
12	My firm's logistical operations are focused on facilitating our key customers' success.	3.79	3.80	3.41	3.39	4.11	3.71	2.82	3.84	3.75	3.85
13	My firm is able to accommodate a wide range of unique customer requests by implementing preplanned solutions.	3.14	3.13	3.04	2.72	3.27	2.97	3.14	3.35	3.00	3.10
14	My firm obtains information directly from customers to facilitate operational plans and reduce reliance on forecasting.	3.21	3.10	2.93	2.67	3.08	2.84	2.82	3.00	3.00	3.00
15	The quality of data available for performance measurement in my firm is better today than three years ago.	4.00	4.00	3.63	3.33	3.76	3.71	4.14	3.92	3.75	4.18
16	My firm has developed performance measures that extend across supply chain relationships.	3.21	3.23	2.59	3.00	2.92	3.20	3.27	3.34	3.00	3.37
17	Managers in my firm understand how our overall logistical performance compares to major competitors.	2.57	2.42	2.52	2.44	2.68	2.74	3.14	2.87	2.25	2.91
18	My firm has different, unique logistics service strategies for different customers.	3.00	3.28	3.19	3.44	3.70	3.22	3.08	3.42	3.17	3.27
19	My firm experiences improved performance by integrating operations with supply chain partners.	3.36	3.40	3.35	3.06	3.30	3.26	3.64	3.34	3.33	3.27
20	My firm successfully utilizes time-based logistics solutions like continuous replenishment, quick response and Just-in-Time with customers and/or suppliers.	3.57	3.41	3.19	2.72	3.35	3.23	2.95	3.16	3.25	3.27
21	My firm has reduced formal organizational structure to more fully integrate operations.	3.29	2.90	3.15	3.61	2.86	3.13	3.18	3.26	3.33	3.18
22	My firm has supply chain arrangements with suppliers and customers that operate under principles of shared rewards and risks.	2.93	2.63	2.88	2.78	2.76	2.94	2.59	2.82	2.75	2.63

SURVEY RESULTS BY INDUSTRY

Columns of data correspond with the following industries:

1. Appliances, Furniture, and Hardware
2. Motor and Transportation
3. Building and Lumber, Mining, Metals
4. Chemicals and Petroleum
5. Office Equipment and Supplies (Computers to Paper)
6. Food Processing and Distribution
7. Mass Merchandising and Retail
8. HBA and Pharmaceutical
9. Clothing and Textile
10. Other

		1	2	3	4	5	6	7	8	9	10
23	My firm rejects logistics service suppliers who lack environmental awareness.	3.07	3.15	3.23	4.11	3.25	2.89	2.91	3.35	3.25	3.06
24	Logistics operating and planning data bases are integrated across applications within my firm.	2.64	2.60	2.48	2.22	2.72	2.74	2.55	3.03	3.00	2.82
25	My firm maintains an integrated database and access method to facilitate information sharing.	2.64	2.75	3.00	2.56	2.94	2.93	2.91	3.21	3.00	3.05
26	My firm places employees at a business facility of suppliers and/or customers to facilitate coordination.	1.57	2.45	2.26	2.17	2.41	2.29	2.29	2.63	2.28	2.18
27	Logistical operations throughout my firm are performed in a standard manner.	3.43	3.00	2.78	3.00	3.11	3.07	3.14	3.26	3.09	3.19
28	My firm has substantially reduced facility and operational complexity over the past three years.	3.36	3.13	3.22	2.94	3.22	2.68	3.00	3.47	3.00	3.41
29	My firm has redesigned our logistic system for greater environmental efficiency.	2.86	2.98	2.81	3.06	2.97	3.76	2.73	2.97	3.08	3.27
30	The consistency of my firm's delivery has increased over the last three years.	4.14	4.00	3.56	3.56	3.73	3.69	4.18	3.97	3.83	3.86
31	My firm has substantially reduced marketing complexity related to products and promotions over the past three years.	2.33	2.83	2.98	2.67	2.51	2.27	2.45	2.80	2.60	2.25
32	My firm actively pursues business relationships and programs designed to achieve customer involvement over and above individual sales transactions.	3.32	3.65	3.57	3.28	3.46	3.40	3.73	3.49	2.79	3.45

#	Statement										
33	My firm has assigned customers to primary and secondary stockpoints to automatically accommodate stockouts.	2.55	2.61	2.91	2.92	2.58	2.28	2.53	2.61	2.09	2.48
34	My firm has increased operational flexibility through supply chain collaboration.	3.14	3.03	3.11	3.06	3.12	3.15	3.28	3.05	2.92	3.45
35	My firm recycles materials whenever possible.	4.07	3.68	3.93	3.83	3.92	3.71	4.09	3.87	3.75	3.76
36	My firm has developed programs to facilitate postponement of final product manufacturing, packaging, labeling, or assembly until customer preferences become more certain.	3.28	2.92	2.92	2.94	3.24	2.74	2.58	2.65	2.92	2.99
37	The number of internal performance measures regularly used by my firm has increased over the past three years.	4.14	3.85	3.66	3.61	3.84	3.69	4.14	3.74	3.58	3.62
38	Managers in my firm make decisions using total cost measurement.	2.86	2.90	2.85	2.94	3.00	2.95	3.05	2.97	2.67	2.82
39	My firm benchmarks best practices/processes and shares results with suppliers.	3.00	2.65	2.70	3.06	3.03	2.71	2.86	2.89	2.67	2.91
40	The orientation of my firm has shifted from managing functions to managing processes.	3.86	3.53	3.37	3.39	3.41	3.31	3.32	3.58	3.33	3.52
41	My firm clearly defines specific roles and responsibilities jointly with our supply chain partners.	3.36	2.83	2.85	2.94	3.27	3.17	3.19	3.13	3.00	2.91
42	Using 25% as the mid-point (3), my firm has reduced customer order-to-delivery cycle time by more or less during the past three years.	4.00	3.49	3.61	3.00	3.61	3.35	3.23	3.62	3.37	3.43
43	Middle managers in my firm are empowered to use their own discretion within broad guidelines to make decisions.	3.71	3.58	3.56	3.89	3.70	3.53	3.59	3.63	3.75	3.73
44	My firm successfully integrates operations with customers and/or suppliers by developing interlocking programs and activities.	3.08	3.13	2.93	3.00	3.30	2.89	3.05	3.00	3.00	3.27
45	My firm rejects materials suppliers who lack environmental awareness.	3.00	2.98	3.19	3.89	3.16	2.82	2.91	3.24	2.92	2.91
46	The information available in my firm is accurate, timely and formatted to facilitate.	2.93	3.08	2.78	2.67	2.81	2.89	3.05	2.97	2.92	2.77
47	My firm effectively shares operational information between departments.	2.79	3.15	3.11	3.00	3.14	3.31	3.36	3.21	3.17	3.23
48	My firm has adequate ability to share both standardized and customized information internally.	2.93	3.18	3.15	2.72	3.08	3.13	3.05	3.26	3.17	3.23

Columns of data correspond with the following industries:

1. Appliances, Furniture, and Hardware
2. Motor and Transportation
3. Building and Lumber, Mining, Metals
4. Chemicals and Petroleum
5. Office Equipment and Supplies (Computers to Paper)
6. Food Processing and Distribution
7. Mass Merchandising and Retail
8. HBA and Pharmaceutical
9. Clothing and Textile
10. Other

	1	2	3	4	5	6	7	8	9	10
49 My firm has common, agreed to policies and procedures to standardize logistics operations.	3.38	3.18	2.89	3.11	3.30	3.24	3.50	3.39	3.42	3.11
50 My firm has active programs to enforce standardized logistical performance.	3.50	3.08	2.89	3.00	3.27	2.95	3.36	3.27	2.92	3.28
51 My firm has a flexible program of special services that can be matched to changing customer requirements.	3.14	3.18	3.19	3.11	3.27	3.16	3.39	3.26	3.17	3.41
52 My firm has a established a program to authorize and perform special requests made by selected customers.	3.21	3.50	3.44	3.06	3.62	3.27	3.19	3.24	3.28	3.68
53 In comparison to three years ago, my firm's logistical capability is significantly more responsive (pull) as compared to predetermined (push).	4.21	3.44	3.45	3.44	3.68	3.25	3.91	3.53	3.58	3.55
54 Performance measurement data is available on a more timely basis today than it was three years ago.	4.21	3.80	3.70	3.72	3.68	3.45	4.05	3.71	3.33	3.86
55 My firm utilizes a formal program to measure customer satisfaction in addition to internal customer service statistics.	3.50	3.53	3.30	3.28	3.49	2.97	3.36	3.21	2.92	3.59
56 My firm benchmarks outside our primary industry.	3.07	2.86	2.62	2.78	2.97	2.62	2.73	3.03	2.42	3.05
57 My firm benchmarks performance metrics.	3.36	3.18	3.04	3.11	3.22	2.84	2.96	3.24	2.67	3.05
58 My firm is committed to achieving zero defect logistical performance.	3.57	3.48	3.44	3.44	3.30	2.95	3.23	3.47	2.75	3.41
59 My firm believes that the strategic direction, role and performance of our supply chain partners are critical to achieving our success.	4.00	3.75	3.52	3.72	3.46	3.44	4.32	3.82	3.58	3.68

#	Statement										
60	My firm's logistics network employs a combination of distribution facilities, cross-docks, and specialty delivery operations to accommodate unique customer requirements.	4.14	3.64	3.33	3.36	3.41	3.36	3.93	3.26	3.17	3.45
61	My firm has active programs to capture the experience and expertise of individuals and transfer this knowledge throughout the organization.	2.50	2.80	3.00	3.00	2.65	2.69	3.09	3.03	2.50	3.07
62	My firm has guidelines for developing, maintaining and monitoring supply chain relationships.	3.21	3.98	2.59	2.94	2.89	2.87	3.05	3.00	2.50	3.09
63	My firm's logistics information systems capture and maintain real time data.	3.00	3.05	2.81	2.61	3.11	2.78	3.23	3.03	2.67	3.18
64	My firm is willing to share strategic information with selected suppliers and/or customers.	3.93	3.55	3.74	3.39	3.49	3.47	3.77	3.50	3.58	3.48
65	My firm actively utilizes industry standards for data exchange.	3.29	3.40	3.29	3.02	3.46	3.50	2.93	3.61	3.17	3.14
66	My firm has substantially reduced channel complexity over the past three years.	3.00	2.80	3.07	3.00	3.05	2.75	2.82	3.32	3.25	3.00
67	My firm regularly achieves stated logistical performance goals.	3.93	3.29	3.74	3.28	3.58	3.55	3.68	3.50	3.25	3.64
68	My firm regularly reviews specific customer service offerings for potential expansion or dissolution.	3.07	3.43	3.48	2.91	3.39	3.19	3.16	3.29	3.00	3.51
69	My firm's logistical operations can be synchronized to integrate with customer and supplier operations.	3.71	3.13	3.16	3.11	3.33	3.13	3.25	3.16	3.69	3.10
70	My firm extensively measures logistics performance in terms of cost, productivity, customer service, asset management and quality.	3.79	3.51	3.02	2.94	3.38	3.40	3.73	3.61	3.25	3.50
71	My firm has established a well-defined set of environmental policies and procedures.	2.93	3.46	3.52	4.11	3.22	3.19	2.92	3.53	3.08	3.15
72	My firm uses activity-based costing in logistics.	2.50	2.70	2.33	2.67	2.32	2.84	2.55	2.92	2.58	2.26
73	My firm has invested in technology designed to facilitate cross-organizational data exchange.	3.21	3.53	3.26	2.89	3.27	3.60	3.14	3.42	3.33	3.45
74	My firm jointly develops strategic plans in collaboration with key customers.	2.93	3.28	3.11	3.06	3.38	3.15	3.02	3.30	3.00	3.36
75	My firm has a track record of allowing suppliers to participate in strategic decisions.	2.71	2.69	2.58	2.72	2.86	2.78	2.64	2.76	2.58	2.82

Columns of data correspond with the following industries:

1. Appliances, Furniture, and Hardware
2. Motor and Transportation
3. Building and Lumber, Mining, Metals
4. Chemicals and Petroleum
5. Office Equipment and Supplies (Computers to Paper)
6. Food Processing and Distribution
7. Mass Merchandising and Retail
8. HBA and Pharmaceutical
9. Clothing and Textile
10. Other

	1	2	3	4	5	6	7	8	9	10
76 My firm provides objective feedback to employees regarding integrated logistics performance.	3.14	3.03	2.86	3.17	3.35	3.09	3.27	3.13	3.08	3.09
77 Logistical performance in my firm is presented in terms of return on investments or assets.	3.29	2.78	2.44	2.83	2.73	2.60	2.59	2.87	2.83	3.12
78 My firm has established a program to integrate and facilitate individual customer requirements across our strategic business units.	3.00	3.25	2.89	2.72	3.19	3.13	3.06	2.97	2.92	3.09
79 My firm has developed a range of acceptable practices for supplier/customer cooperation in situations wherein we are not the dominant participant.	2.86	2.90	2.92	2.67	3.11	2.96	2.72	2.89	2.83	3.18
80 My firm employs a formal logistics visioning process to identify future customer and consumer logistics requirements.	2.64	2.77	2.81	2.60	2.73	2.78	2.77	2.95	2.75	3.05
81 My firm has developed performance incentives based on process achievement.	3.07	2.73	3.00	2.83	3.14	3.15	3.00	3.03	3.00	2.82
82 Environmental initiatives within my firm are primarily driven by regulatory requirements.	3.57	3.40	3.36	3.22	3.42	3.35	3.79	3.51	2.92	3.25
83 My firm is willing to share the results of supplier performance with cooperating material suppliers.	3.71	3.37	3.54	3.22	3.17	3.32	3.23	3.22	3.36	3.32
84 My firm is willing to assist service suppliers finance capital equipment.	2.43	2.22	2.53	2.94	2.63	2.50	2.27	2.43	2.29	2.40
85 My firm is willing to help suppliers finance capital equipment.	2.50	2.22	2.49	2.83	2.47	2.51	2.23	2.31	2.12	2.31

#	Statement										
86	Information systems in my firm are being expanded to reflect more enterprise wide integrated processes (ERP).	3.50	3.82	3.67	3.94	3.85	3.65	3.91	3.75	3.75	3.45
87	My firm's logistics information systems facilitate electronic commerce using internet capability.	2.79	3.23	2.81	2.89	3.38	2.73	3.00	3.11	2.92	3.09
88	My firm has guidelines for terminating partnerships and alliances.	3.07	2.95	2.74	2.94	2.95	2.74	3.09	2.86	3.08	2.86
89	My firm collaborates in forecasting and planning with suppliers and/or customers.	3.57	3.35	3.42	3.33	3.32	3.22	3.38	3.26	3.67	3.39
90	Logistical performance in my firm is related to Economic-Value-Added (EVA).	3.21	2.70	2.56	2.77	2.83	2.72	2.95	2.94	3.08	3.13
91	My firm strives to achieve best-in-class environmental performance.	2.79	3.28	3.23	3.83	3.14	3.04	2.95	3.22	2.92	2.92
92	My firm has active programs to positively impact our supplier's suppliers.	2.29	2.39	2.48	2.22	2.62	2.49	2.00	2.70	2.50	2.73
93	My firm shares technical resources with key suppliers to facilitate operations.	3.36	3.34	3.17	3.11	3.24	3.23	3.00	3.30	3.27	3.18
94	My firm employs initiatives to identify end-consumer value-added that is contributed to logistics.	2.79	2.90	2.81	2.50	2.94	2.80	2.89	2.97	2.91	2.86
95	My firm is willing to consider investment in supply material or process.	3.43	3.69	3.50	3.72	3.61	3.46	3.80	3.54	3.58	3.34
96	My firm is willing to share the results of superior performance with cooperating service suppliers.	4.07	3.44	3.63	3.50	3.35	3.54	3.82	3.41	3.46	3.30
97	My firm is willing to share the results of superior performance with cooperating customers.	4.00	3.68	3.73	3.72	3.57	3.68	3.88	3.64	3.67	3.53
98	My firm has simplified our product and promotional offering to reduce ordering and invoice complexity.	2.48	2.51	2.98	2.87	2.34	2.59	2.67	3.01	2.56	2.45
99	My firm has substantially reduced operating complexity by developing separate operations focused on individual channels over the past three years.	2.77	2.84	2.84	3.22	3.08	2.52	2.30	3.00	3.08	2.67
100	My firm conducts formal environmental audits on a regular basis.	3.00	3.25	3.61	4.22	2.96	3.44	2.73	3.20	2.92	2.83
101	My firm's compensation, incentive, and reward systems encourage integration.	2.71	2.52	2.85	3.11	2.81	2.92	3.09	2.95	2.92	2.77
102	Logistical performance in my firm is reported on a total cost basis that includes an accepted cost of capital deployed.	3.15	3.03	2.89	2.61	3.14	3.13	2.95	3.19	2.75	3.23
103	Management in my firm understands that supply chain involvement requires substantial empowerment.	3.21	3.28	3.07	3.28	2.86	3.33	3.45	3.32	3.42	3.23

SURVEY RESULTS BY INDUSTRY

Columns of data correspond with the following industries:

1. Appliances, Furniture, and Hardware
2. Motor and Transportation
3. Building and Lumber, Mining, Metals
4. Chemicals and Petroleum
5. Office Equipment and Supplies (Computers to Paper)
6. Food Processing and Distribution
7. Mass Merchandising and Retail
8. HBA and Pharmaceutical
9. Clothing and Textile
10. Other

	1	2	3	4	5	6	7	8	9	10
104 My firm has developed information linkages with customers that permit substantial last-minute accommodation without loss of planned efficiencies.	2.50	2.77	2.70	2.50	2.81	2.67	2.80	2.68	2.67	2.94
105 Managers in my firm are able to determine order and cost profitability.	2.57	3.05	3.00	2.89	2.86	2.60	2.81	2.97	2.92	3.05
106 My firm has clearly defined a legal framework to guide involvement in supply chain collaboration.	2.36	2.81	2.85	2.94	2.67	2.68	2.49	2.96	2.83	2.65
107 My firm uses logistical capabilities as a basis for supplier selection.	3.07	2.83	3.11	3.39	3.08	3.07	2.91	3.05	2.75	2.73
108 My firm shares research and development costs and results with primary suppliers.	2.81	2.54	2.88	2.83	2.46	2.69	2.39	2.56	2.80	2.77
109 My firm is committed to sharing responsibility with suppliers in new product/service development and commercialization.	3.22	3.03	3.23	3.06	2.82	3.12	3.14	3.01	3.35	3.18
110 My firm acknowledges the importance of functional excellence but focuses on process achievement.	3.50	3.33	3.33	3.44	3.31	3.46	3.32	3.39	3.03	3.36
111 My firm has developed performance incentives based on process improvement.	3.00	2.95	3.07	3.33	3.00	3.17	2.77	2.97	2.84	3.27
112 My firm has significantly reduced the number of suppliers to improve operational integration.	3.57	3.29	3.53	3.50	3.36	3.33	2.86	3.52	3.17	3.23
113 In leadership situations, my firm has clearly specified ranges of acceptable behavior in a partnership or alliance.	3.21	3.23	3.16	3.28	3.31	3.05	3.32	3.51	3.33	3.19

	1	2	3	4	5	6	7	8	9	10
114 My firm has increased the use of integrated inventory, transportation, and warehousing planning systems over the past three years.	3.64	3.26	3.23	3.00	3.14	3.34	3.33	3.42	3.42	3.45
115 My firm has facilitated a strong supply network fostering cooperation with the entire chain of primary and secondary suppliers.	2.86	2.97	2.70	2.78	2.83	3.00	2.81	3.02	2.83	3.04
116 My firm is willing to enter into long-term agreements with suppliers.	4.07	3.84	3.85	4.06	3.68	3.80	3.73	3.65	3.81	3.30
117 Logistical performance in my firm is presented in terms of impact on business profit statement.	3.14	3.43	3.35	3.28	3.42	3.62	3.36	3.42	3.17	3.38
118 My firm has increased use of industry EDI standards during the past three years.	3.79	3.83	3.67	3.17	4.14	3.67	3.58	4.13	3.75	3.55
119 My firm is actively involved in initiatives to standardize supply chain practices and operations.	3.21	3.61	3.33	3.44	3.27	3.23	3.55	3.53	3.33	3.41
120 My firm actively pursues and shares a common set of expectations with supply chain partners.	3.57	3.32	3.00	3.00	3.22	3.31	3.32	3.45	3.33	3.27

PART TWO: LOGISTICS STRATEGY

Data presented shows the frequency of firms in each industry that responded to each logistics strategy category.

	1	2	3	4	5	6	7	8	9	10
1a Process A process-based strategy is concerned with managing a broad group of a firm's internal logistics activities and related service suppliers as a value-added chain. Emphasis is on achieving efficiency from managing purchasing, manufacturing, scheduling, and physical distribution as an integrated system.	35.7%	40.0%	64.0%	52.9%	50.0%	5307%	52.4%	44.7%	50.0%	42.9%
1b Market A market-based strategy is concerned with managing a limited group of logistics activities for a multidivisional single business or across multiple business units. The logistics organization seeks to make joint product	21.4%	27.5%	16.0%	11.8%	36.1%	35.2%	14.3%	21.1%	33.3%	28.6%

SURVEY RESULTS BY INDUSTRY

Columns of data correspond with the following industries:

1. Appliances, Furniture, and Hardware
2. Motor and Transportation
3. Building and Lumber, Mining, Metals
4. Chemicals and Petroleum
5. Office Equipment and Supplies (Computers to Paper)
6. Food Processing and Distribution
7. Mass Merchandising and Retail
8. HBA and Pharmaceutical
9. Clothing and Textile
10. Other

	1	2	3	4	5	6	7	8	9	10
1c	shipments to common customers for different product groups and seeks to facilitate sales and logistical coordination by a single order-invoice. Often the senior sales and logistics executives report to the same manager. Channel Channel-based strategy (also known as a supply chain strategy) is concerned with managing logistics activities performed jointly with dealers, distributors and customers. The strategic orientation places a great deal of attention on external control. Significant amounts of finished inventories are typically maintained forward or downstream in the distribution channel.									
	42.9%	30.0%	12.0%	17.6%	8.3%	7.4%	9.5%	23.7%	0.0%	14.3%
1d	Other									
	0.0%	2.5%	8.0%	17.6%	5.6%	3.7%	23.8%	10.5%	16.7%	14.3%
2	Using the following scale, what is the primary emphasis of your logistics strategy (1=lowest total cost, 5=highest customer service)?									
	3.43	3.35	3.30	2.81	3.35	3.39	3.57	3.42	3.25	3.10
3	An executive title using the words "Supply Chain" is employed by my firm. (Data shows percent saying "yes")									
	14.3%	12.5%	3.7%	33.3%	5.4%	21.8%	28.6%	39.5%	0.0%	27.3%
4	During the past two years my firm has increased its organizational commitment to a more comprehensively integrated supply chain.									
	3.79	3.60	3.48	3.72	3.32	3.49	3.95	3.63	3.67	3.32
5	My firm's logistics strategy includes a priority to reduce the number of facilities.									
	3.15	3.00	2.92	3.11	3.57	3.35	3.50	3.29	3.08	3.29

	1	2	3	4	5	6	7	8	9	10
6 My firm's logistics strategy includes a priority to reduce the number of product/material suppliers.	3.71	3.32	3.78	3.72	3.57	3.35	3.30	3.42	3.42	3.68
7 My firm's logistics strategy includes a priority to reduce the number of logistics service suppliers.	3.50	3.32	3.54	3.56	3.59	3.49	3.86	3.42	3.42	3.43
8 My firm's logistics strategy includes a priority to reduce the number of marginal customers (retailers need not answer this question).	2.62	2.95	2.75	3.11	3.03	2.76	2.56	3.03	3.10	3.83
9 My firm's logistics strategy includes a priority to reduce the number of products or UPCs.	2.79	2.41	2.76	2.89	2.86	2.89	2.24	2.82	2.58	3.29
10 My firm's logistics strategy includes a priority to reduce the overall complexity of logistics operations.	3.64	3.35	3.62	3.56	3.51	3.36	3.81	3.55	3.58	3.14

PART THREE: PERFORMANCE MEASUREMENT

1 Please indicate if you formally benchmark each of the following performance areas relative to competitors. (Data shows percent answering "yes").

	1	2	3	4	5	6	7	8	9	10
a. Asset Management	46%	32%	16%	50%	41%	24%	23%	31%	17%	50%
b. Logistics Cost	54%	46%	38%	39%	58%	55%	64%	51%	42%	75%
c. Productivity	54%	54%	38%	61%	41%	42%	45%	42%	25%	33%
d. Customer Service	50%	57%	54%	67%	63%	56%	64%	65%	42%	83%
e. Logistics Quality	33%	57%	44%	22%	29%	25%	27%	49%	17%	92%

2 Please specify the performance of your firm in relation to its major competitors for the past year (1997) for each indicated measure (1=Worst than Competitors, 3=Comparable with Competitors, 5=Better than Competitors)

SURVEY RESULTS BY INDUSTRY

Columns of data correspond with the following industries:

1. Appliances, Furniture, and Hardware
2. Motor and Transportation
3. Building and Lumber, Mining, Metals
4. Chemicals and Petroleum
5. Office Equipment and Supplies (Computers to Paper)
6. Food Processing and Distribution
7. Mass Merchandising and Retail
8. HBA and Pharmaceutical
9. Clothing and Textile
10. Other

	1	2	3	4	5	6	7	8	9	10
a. Return on Assets (ROA): The ratio of income before interest expense divided by average total assets.	3.78	3.34	3.45	3.47	3.37	3.26	3.61	3.19	2.50	3.91
b. Product Flexibility (Customization): The ability to handle difficult, nonstandard orders to meet special customer specifications and to manufacture products characterized by numerous features, options, size and/or colors.	3.90	3.52	3.78	3.41	3.66	3.57	3.72	3.09	3.33	4.09
c. Low Logistics Cost: The ability to achieve the lowest total cost of logistics through efficient operations, technology and/or scale economies.	3.58	3.58	3.61	3.19	3.38	3.49	3.67	3.36	3.40	3.58
d. Delivery Speed: The ability to reduce the time between order receipt and customer delivery to as close to zero as possible.	4.00	3.59	3.39	2.88	3.71	3.39	3.38	3.62	3.90	3.64
e. Delivery Dependability: The ability to meet quoted or anticipated delivery dates and quantities on a consistent basis.	4.08	3.70	3.91	3.41	3.77	3.53	3.71	3.71	3.80	3.92
f. Responsiveness to Key Customers: The ability to respond to the needs and wants of key customers.	4.00	3.84	3.91	3.71	4.35	3.89	3.72	3.85	3.80	4.09
g. Order Fill Capacity: The ability to provide desired quantities on a consistent basis.	4.33	3.53	3.70	3.53	3.74	3.67	3.67	3.65	3.44	3.64

h.	Order Flexibility: The ability to modify order size, volume or composition during logistics operation.	3.55	3.37	3.70	3.35	3.60	3.46	3.20	3.53	3.30	3.82
i.	Delivery Time Flexibility: The ability to accommodate delivery times for specific customers.	3.58	3.66	3.74	3.47	3.93	3.59	3.33	3.85	3.70	3.64
j.	Advanced Shipment Notification: The ability to notify customers in advance of delivery when products will arrive.	3.67	3.65	3.48	3.24	3.39	2.93	3.11	3.26	3.40	3.00
k.	Inventory Turns: The ratio of cost of goods sold divided by the average investment in inventory during a time period.	3.83	3.50	3.27	2.75	3.09	3.30	3.33	3.00	3.22	3.18
l.	Customer Satisfaction: The global judgement regarding the extent to which perceived logistics performance matches customer expectations.	3.50	3.59	3.86	3.47	3.75	3.60	3.52	3.68	3.20	3.64
m.	Information Systems Support: The ability of information systems to provide operational managers with sufficient and timely information to manage logistical activities.	3.08	3.00	2.86	2.65	2.97	2.88	2.81	2.94	3.00	3.88

COMPARING LOGISTICS 95 AND LOGISTICS 99

The Logistics 95 assessment and diagnostic have been widely used since 1995, but a number of managers have suggested that the benchmarks for high achieving firms may have changed in the past five years. Specifically, updated world class or high achiever logistics benchmarks are necessary. The research conducted in support of this book provides that update. The results indicate the extent to which perceived firm competency and capability levels have changed in recent years.

Exhibit D-1 reports the 1995 and 1999 means for each logistics competency and capability. A comparison of the data suggests four conclusions. Bold values indicate that the reported performance has increased over the past four years. Starred values indicate the differences between the two reported means are statistically significant.

EXHIBIT D-1

RESULTS OF WORLD CLASS COMPETENCY ASSESSMENT, 1995 AND 1999		
Competency / Capability	1995 Mean	1999 Mean
Positioning	51.69	54.01
Strategy	12.71	13.26*
Supply chain	13.86	14.19
Network	12.33	13.45*
Organization	12.79	13.11
Integration	92.17	89.35
Supply chain unification	13.64	12.14*
Information technology	13.29	12.32*
Information sharing	13.88	13.10*
Connectivity	12.04	12.13
Standardization	13.48	13.35
Simplification	11.48	12.55*
Discipline	14.03	13.74
Agility	39.06	38.83
Relevancy	13.79	13.84
Accommodation	12.29	12.38
Flexibility	13.53	12.61*
Measurement	40.37	38.37*
Functional assessment	14.66	14.84
Process assessment	13.36	12.06*
Benchmarking	12.35	11.47*
OVERALL LOGISTICS	223.39	220.56

* Note: Bold values indicate that reported performance has increased over the past four years. The starred values indicate a statistically significant difference.

First, in terms of an overall average, firm achievement did not change substantially between 1995 and 1999. Specifically, the 1999 mean score of 220.49 reflects a drop of 3.3 points since 1995. This may reflect sample differences or an actual lack of improvement in their perceived capabilities. There is not enough evidence to determine the reason.

Second, while overall firm achievement has declined slightly, there has been improvement in a number of the seventeen capabilities. Firms report increases in ten capabilities and statistically significant increases in three of these. Statistically significant improvements are reported for the strategy, network and simplification capabilities.

Third, firms have improved their positioning competency. This is particularly apparent in the network capability that reflects efforts to rationalize distribution centers and plant networks. It appears that firms are starting to focus their supply chain, physical resources and organizational resources on the needs of key customers. All this suggests a growing emphasis on high level service ("perfect orders") to key customers.

Fourth, the assessments reveal a significant decrease in several areas: supply chain unification, information technology, information sharing, flexibility, process assessment and benchmarking. The differences could be due to sampling, but it is possible that several years ago firms believed they were willing, for example, to share information with supply chain partners but subsequent experience has proved otherwise. Significant declines in these capabilities suggests that logistics managers are not as satisfied as they were before with their firm's abilities in these areas. Updated high achiever benchmarks resulting from the new data are reported in Exhibit D-2.

EXHIBIT D-2

UPDATED HIGH ACHIEVER BENCHMARKS	
Competency / Capability	1999 High Achiever Benchmarks
Positioning	63.19
Strategy	16.11
Supply chain	17.00
Network	16.18
Organization	15.91
Integration	105.70
Supply chain unification	15.10
Information technology	15.59
Information sharing	16.04
Connectivity	15.15
Standardization	16.03
Simplification	15.31
Discipline	16.39
Agility	45.59
Relevancy	16.54
Accommodation	14.88
Flexibility	15.22
Measurement	46.34
Functional assessment	17.66
Process assessment	15.05
Benchmarking	14.99
OVERALL LOGISTICS	257.57

In summary, it appears that North American firms are improving logistics competency with respect to positioning. In other words, strategy and resources are being focused on using operational excellence to benefit key customers and enhance competitiveness. However, declines in a number of areas suggest the need for a better understanding of what firms are doing to achieve supply chain strategic and operational integration. The updated survey indicates that although firms may want to reach high achiever logistics standards, they are having difficulty with competency in integration and measurement. Therefore, the capabilities that facilitate internal and external integration are the focus of this research. *21ˢᵗ Century Logistics* refines the earlier framework and extends it to a broader supply chain management context.

STRATEGIC PROFIT MODEL

While profitability is an important measure of financial performance, the most critical measure of strategic success is in terms of *return on investment* (ROI). There are two ways of viewing ROI. The first is *return on net worth* (RONW), which measures the profitability of the funds that the owners of the firm have invested. The second is *return on assets* (ROA), which measures the profitability of the assets that the firm uses in its operations. While owners and investors are most likely interested in RONW, ROA is a better measure of how well management had utilized the assets of the company to earn profits.

Exhibit E-1 presents the *strategic profit model* (SPM), which is an analytic tool frequently used to determine ROI in a business firm. Actually, the SPM is a tool that incorporates both income and balance sheet data and demonstrates how these data relate to each other to result in RONW and ROA.

One of the primary benefits of the SPM is that it shows very clearly that the strategic objective of a firm is ROI. Too often, managers focus on more limited objectives. For example, sales management may focus on sales as the primary objective of the business and therefore, will base their analysis on sales volume. Other managers may focus on cost minimization as the primary objective. Still others may focus on turnover and feel that decisions must be based on increasing the firm's efficient utilization of assets. All three of these approaches neglect the fact that the company must earn an adequate rate of return. Otherwise, investments may be withdrawn from the company and placed where higher returns can be earned.

EXHIBIT E-1

STRATEGIC PROFITABILITY MODEL

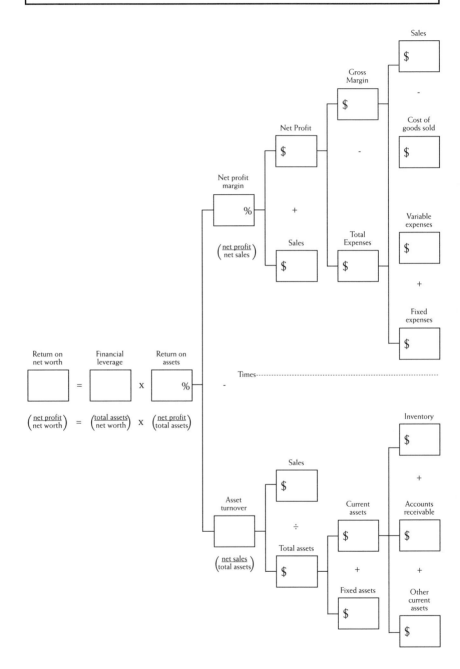

Another advantage of the SPM is that it demonstrates that there are three ways in which a firm can increase return on net worth. The three prime components of RONW are leverage, asset turnover, and net profit margin. Exhibit E-2 presents the SPM ratios for two fictitious retail firms. It is important to note that the RONW for these firms is considerably higher than the RONW for an average retail store. What is particularly interesting about this data is that although all the firms have achieved a high RONW, their performance with respect to the various components of the SPM varies considerably. Even firms that operate in the same industry elect strategies that emphasize different aspects of the SPM. For example, consider the difference in the variables for Company A and Company B. Exhibit E-2 shows the differences between Company A's strategy (which relies on low profit margins with higher asset turnover and high leverage) and Company B's strategy (which relies on higher profit margins, lower turnover, and little usage of leverage). The conclusion to be drawn from these data is that there are different paths that may be followed by a particular firm attempting to achieve a high overall RONW. While no company can totally ignore one of the basic components of return, different firms choose strategies that emphasize different components of the return model.

EXHIBIT E-2

SPM RATIOS FOR TWO FICTITIOUS RETAILERS					
	Return on net worth	Leverage	Return on assets	Asset turnover	Net profit margin
Company A	26.1	5.55	5.5	2.20	2.9
Company B	24.6	2.73	10.5	1.99	6.2

USING THE DIAGNOSTIC

The combined Logistics 99 and Supply Chain 2000 diagnostic are contained on a compact disk (CD) formatted for IBM-compatible personal computers in a windows-based environment using Microsoft Excel 97. The following sections briefly describe the commands for diagnostic use.

Beginner Tips

After Microsoft Excel is opened, a blank spreadsheet will appear on the screen. At the extreme top of the spreadsheet a menu toolbar is displayed that is used to enter spreadsheet commands. This is the only command menu that should be used in conducting the assessment exercise. The mouse pointer arrow is used to facilitate selection of items.

File Retrieval

The diagnostic spreadsheet is retrieved as follows:

• Insert diagnostic disk into CD drive.

• On the menu toolbar, located at the top of the spreadsheet, use the mouse pointer to select the FILE option.

• A secondary menu appears that lists a variety of options. The OPEN command should be selected with the mouse.

- This command displays a window that allows the user to select the CD drive that contains the diagnostic disk. The appropriate drive is selected in the indicated box followed by "clicking" the box labeled OK (or Open).

- The CD contains three files. This can be seen under FILENAME (or Name) on the left hand side of the OPEN menu. To open the diagnostic tool, highlight the file name "Supply Chain 2000.xls" and then "click" OK (or Open).

Using The Arrow Keys

The diagnostic contains eight worksheets or tabs. Each worksheet or tab is accessed using the mouse to select the desired sheet. To begin the exercise, select the first worksheet, the "questionnaire."

Printing A Worksheet

To produce a printed copy of the questionnaire or the other worksheets, the menu bar is used. The program is formatted to utilize a Hewlett-Packard LaserJet Series Printer although other equipment may be used. A worksheet is printed as follows:

- Select the FILE option from the menu bar.

- Select the PRINT option from the secondary menu.

- A window appears that asks whether the selected sheet or the entire workbook is to be printed. Highlight the SELECTED SHEET (or Active Sheet) option (if not already done) and "click" OK.

- The questionnaire is then be printed

Saving The File

It is necessary to save the diagnostic whenever exiting the file, particularly if there have been changes made to any of the worksheets you wish to retain. The file can be saved at any point the user feels necessary. In order to maintain a clean diagnostic file, we recommend saving each iteration or session under a different filename. However, each worksheet need not be saved separately. Individual worksheets are saved when the entire file is saved. To save the file, complete the following:

- Select the FILE option from the menu bar.

- Select the SAVE option from the secondary menu.

- The file will save any previously made changes.

- To exit the file, select FILE from the menu bar and then select CLOSE from the secondary menu.

To save under a new filename, complete the following:

- Select the FILE option from the menu bar.

- Select the SAVE AS option from the secondary menu.

- Under DRIVES (or Save In), select the appropriate disk drive.

- Under FILENAME type in a name with a file extension of .XLS (for example, the filename ROUND1.XLS could be used).

- The file will be saved under the new name.

- To exit the file, select FILE from the menu bar and then select CLOSE from the secondary menu.

Using The Worksheets

The diagnostic file contains eight separate worksheets or tabs. The worksheet names are displayed at the bottom of the spreadsheet between the arrow keys. They are:

(1) Questionnaire; (2) Response Sheet; (3) Diagnostic Results SCM 2000; (4) SCM 2000 Summary; (5) SCM 2000 GAP; (6) Diagnostic Results LOG 99; (7) LOG 99 Summary; (8) LOG 99 GAP.

Worksheet One - Questionnaire

Once the "questionnaire" worksheet has been selected, the top of the document will appear. If not, the right side arrow keys can be used to move to the top of the document (or by simultaneously pressing the CTRL and

HOME keys). This worksheet contains the randomly ordered questions to be answered by participating managers in the exercise. The only step that needs to be taken in this worksheet is to produce a printed copy for use by managers (see *Printing a Worksheet*).

Worksheet Two – Response Sheet

Once managers participating in a self-assessment have separately answered the diagnostic questionnaire, the administrator should input responses into Worksheet Two. Following the file retrieval procedures (see *File Retrieval*), the second worksheet is selected using the lower left arrow keys.

When Worksheet Two is displayed, the user should position at the top of the worksheet using the right side arrow keys (or by simultaneously pressing the CTRL and HOME keys). Each participant should be designated a specific column into which their responses will be entered. The administrator should only input questionnaire responses ranging from 1 to 5. Responses should be input beginning in the column and row of the first question, which is cell C5. Cells are referenced by their column and row positions. If a cell does not allow a response to be input, that cell's contents are protected in the worksheet. This protection is to eliminate deletion of program information or incorrect placement of responses in the spreadsheet. Once a response is entered, the enter key or arrow keys on the keyboard arrow keys or the mouse can be used to move to any part of the worksheet. Following entry of all participant responses, the third worksheet is retrieved to complete the self-assessment. It is recommended that the file be saved (See *Saving the File*), before proceeding to the final worksheet.

Worksheets Three And Six – Diagnostic Results

Once all individual responses of an assessment group are input, the final results are obtained from Worksheet Three and Six labeled "Diagnostic Results SCM 2000" and "Diagnostic Results LOG 99." These worksheets are selected by "clicking" the appropriate name on the bottom worksheet menu.

The final results appear without any additional commands from the administrator. The worksheet is formatted to automatically compute the means and ranges of participants' responses to be used for comparison among group members before comparison is made to the benchmarks. The questions randomly ordered in the questionnaire are now automatically sequenced according to capability and competency, and corresponding scores are computed and displayed for each facet of the Supply Chain 2000 and Logistics 99.

This worksheet also displays the high achiever benchmark scores. These scores appear in a column immediately to the right of the firm mean for each question, capability and competency.

Worksheets Four And Seven – Summary

The summary worksheets, "SCM 2000 Summary" and "LOG 99 Summary," provide only the firm's low, high, mean and benchmark values. This allows for an easy printing of the summary results.

Worksheets Five And Eight – Gap

The gap worksheets, "SCM 2000 GAP" and "LOG 99 GAP," include two sections each which provide the capability and competencies and the gap between the firm mean and the benchmark scores. To facilitate analysis, click on the sort button to re-order the capabilities and competencies in descending order. This will allow management to focus on the areas with the largest differences from the firm mean as compared to the research benchmarks.

Finally results for any of the worksheets may be printed (see *Printing a Worksheet*) for group discussion. Once again, before exiting the program, it is highly recommended to save the file using the instructions provided. The research scores offer a basis for comparison against company scores as part of the benchmarking exercise described earlier.

REFERENCE MATERIALS

This appendix provides a listing of general reference materials in four categories: 1) logistics book/texts; and 2) related research publications. These lists are not intended to be exhaustive, but rather highlight a variety of available resources.

Logistics Books/Texts

The following are a selection of logistics books and texts published in the 1990's.

1. Ackerman, Kenneth B. (1994), *Warehousing Profitably – A Manager's Guide* (Columbus, OH: Ackerman Publications).

2. Ballou, Ronald H. (1998), *Business Logistics Management: Planning Organizing, and Controlling the Supply Chain* (Upper Saddle River, NJ: Prentice Hall College Div.).

3. Banfield, Emiko (1999), *Harnessing Value in the Supply Chain: Strategic Sourcing in Action* (John Wiley & Sons).

4. Bowersox, Donald J. and David J. Closs (1996), *Logistical Management: The Integrated Supply Chain Process*, 4th edition (New York, NY: McGraw-Hill, Inc.) [currently in revision].

5. Bowersox, Donald J. and M. Bixby Cooper (1992), *Strategic Marketing Channel Management* (New York, NY: McGraw-Hill, Inc.)

6. Boyson, Sandor (1999), *Logistics and the Extended Enterprise: Benchmarks and Best Practices for the Manufacturing Professional* (New York, NY: John Wiley & Sons).

7. Christopher, Martin (1999), *Logistics and Supply Chain Management: Strategies for Reducing Costs and Improving Service* (Burr Ridge, IL: Financial Times Management).

8. Copacino, William C. (1997), *Supply Chain Management: The Basics and Beyond* (Boca Raton, FL: St. Lucie Press).

9. Coyle, John J., Edward J. Bardi and C. John Langley Jr. (1996), *The Management of Business Logistics*, 6th edition (St. Paul, MN: West Publishing).

10. Glaskowsky, Nicholas A., Jr., Donald R. Hudson and Robert M. Ivie (1992), *Business Logistics*, 3rd edition (Orlando, FL: The Dryden Press).

11. Goldratt, Eliyahu M. and Jeff Cox (1984), *The Goal: A Process of Ongoing Improvement* (Great Barrington, MA: North River Press).

12. Handfield, Robert B. and Ernest L. Nichols (1998), *Introduction to Supply Chain Management* (Upper Saddle River, NJ: Prentice Hall College Division).

13. Johnson, James C. and Donald F. Wood (1993), *Contemporary Logistics*, 5th edition (New York, NY: MacMillan College Division).

14. Lambert, Douglas M., James R. Stock, and Lisa M. Ellram (1997), *Fundamentals of Logistics Management* (McGraw Hill College Division).

15. Lambert, Douglas M. and James R. Stock (1993), *Strategic Logistics Management*, 3rd edition (Homewood, IL: Irwin).

16. Langford, John W. (1994), *Logistics and Supply Chain Management: Strategies for Reducing Costs and Improving Service* (McGraw Hill).

17. Pagonis, Lt. General William G. and Jeffrey L. Cruikshank (1994), *Moving Mountains: Lessons in Leadership and Logistics from the Gulf War*

(Boston, Mass: Harvard Business School Press).

18. Poirier, Charles C. (1999), *Advanced Supply Chain Management: How to Build a Sustained Competitive Advantage* (San Francisco, CA: Publishers' Group West).

19. Poirier, Charles C. (1996), *Supply Chain Optimization: Building the Strongest Total Business* (San Fransisco, CA: Berrett-Koehler Publishers).

20. Pollack, Daniel (1997), *Precipice* (Oak Brook, IL: Council of Logistics Management).

21. Robeson, James F. and William C. Copacino eds. With R. Edwin Howe, associate ed. (1994), *The Logistics Handbook* (New York, NY: The Free Press).

22. Ross, David Frederick (1997), *Competing Through Supply Chain Management* (New York, NY: Chapman & Hall).

23. Tompkins, James A. (1997), *Goose Chase: Capturing the Energy of Change in Logistics* (Tompkins Press).

24. Tompkins, James A. and Dale Harmelink, eds. (1994), *The Distribution Management Handbook* (New York, NY: McGraw-Hill, Inc.).

25. Tyndall, Gene R., Christopher Gopal, Wolfgang Partech, and John Kamauff (1998), *Supercharging Supply Chains* (John Wiley & Sons).

26. Wood, Donald F., James C. Johnson, Paul Murphy and Daniel L. Wardlow (1998), *International Logistics*, 7th edition (New York, NY: Chapman & Hall).

Related Research Publications

This section contains research publications related to the subject matter of 21ˢᵗ Century Logistics.

1. *Achieving Customer Satisfaction Leadership in Europe*, a 1992 study report on behalf of the European Logistics Association by A.T. Kearney.

2. *Benchmarking Study on Logistics Management and Technology*, a 1994 study by KPMG Peat Marwick.

3. *Creating Logistics Value: Themes for the Future* (Oak Brook, IL: Council of Logistics Management), a 1995 book by Robert A. Novack, C. John Langley, Jr. and Lloyd M. Rhinehart.

4. *European Logistics Strategies After 1992: Infrastructure Changes*, a 1992 report by Coopers and Lybrand Europe.

5. *The Growth and Development of Logistics Personnel*, a 1999 study sponsored by the Council of Logistics Management.

6. *Logistics Excellence in Europe*, a 1993 study report on behalf of the European Logistics Association by A.T. Kearney.

7. *Logistics Futures in Europe*, a 1993 study by Cranfield Centre for Logistics and Transportation.

8. *Measuring Logistics Activities in the Supply Chain*, a 1999 study sponsored by the Council of Logistics Management.

9. *A North American Common Market?*, a 1992 survey on North American Free Trade by Cleveland Consulting Associates.

10. *Reconfiguring European Logistics Systems* (Oak Brook, IL: Council of Logistics Management), a 1993 book by Anderson Consulting and Cranfield School of Management.

11. *Third-Party Logistics*, a 1991 study by Robert C. Lieb (Northeastern University). Follow-up research completed in 1994 by Robert C. Lieb and Hugh Randall (Mercer Management Consulting, Inc.).

12. *Top Performing Companies* (Japan), a 1991 study by A.T. Kearney. World-Class Logistics Performance: How North American, Western European and Japanese Companies Use Logistics to Compete, a 1993 report by A. T. Kearney.

13. *White Paper: Development and Implementation of Reverse Logistics Programs*, a 1998 study conducted by James R. Stock for the Council of Logistics Management.